Ownership Structure, Related-Party Transactions, and Firm Valuation

The book examines the effect of ownership structure and disclosure of related-party transactions (RPTs) on firm valuation of group-affiliated firms in India. Value-relevance models examine the effect of ownership rights on market value of equity (MVE) and valuation effect of related-party (RP) trading, asset transfer, investment, and loan transactions.

It contributes to the extant literature by recording distinct valuation of RPTs involving group-member firms from similar transactions involving subsidiary/ holding firms and providing evidence on the role of pyramid structures in understanding the valuation of RPTs. The findings provide evidence that RPTs between group-member firms are valued differently from RPTs involving subsidiary and holding firms. The tunneling incentives of controlling shareholders, measured by indirect ownership rights, influence the valuation of RPTs related to group-member firms, whereas the nature of transactions affects the valuation of RPTs between subsidiary and holding firms.

Amrinder Khosa is Lecturer at the Monash Business School, Monash University. His research interests are accounting education, corporate governance in group-affiliated firms, and related-party transactions.

Kamran Ahmed is Professor of Accounting at the La Trobe Business School at La Trobe University. His research interests are corporate disclosure, corporate accounting policy choice, earnings management, international accounting harmonization, accounting and reporting practices in South Asia, and microfinance reporting.

Darren Henry is Associate Professor of Finance and Head of the Department of Economics and Finance at the La Trobe Business School at La Trobe University. His research interests include all aspects of mergers and acquisitions, corporate governance and wider ownership and control issues, corporate restructuring and cross-listing activities, and empirical corporate finance issues such as capital structure decision-making, dividend policy, and capital raising activities.

Ownership Structure, Related-Party Transactions, and Firm Valuation

Evidence from Indian Business Groups

Amrinder Khosa

Kamran Ahmed

and

Darren Henry

CAMBRIDGE
UNIVERSITY PRESS

University Printing House, Cambridge CB2 8BS, United Kingdom

One Liberty Plaza, 20th Floor, New York, NY 10006, USA

477 Williamstown Road, Port Melbourne, vic 3207, Australia

314 to 321, 3rd Floor, Plot No.3, Splendor Forum, Jasola District Centre, New Delhi 110025, India

79 Anson Road, #06–04/06, Singapore 079906

Cambridge University Press is part of the University of Cambridge.

It furthers the University's mission by disseminating knowledge in the pursuit of education, learning and research at the highest international levels of excellence.

www.cambridge.org
Information on this title: www.cambridge.org/9781108492195

First published 2019

Printed in India by Shree Maitrey Printech Pvt. Ltd., Noida

A catalogue record for this publication is available from the British Library

ISBN 978-1-108-49219-5 Hardback

Contents

Contents

Tables

Chapter 1

Introduction

Expropriation by controlling shareholders is an important issue in emerging economies. Concentrated ownership and family dominance in Indian business groups make outside investors vulnerable to expropriation. Furthermore, weak investor protection makes the Indian setting more conducive for the expropriation of minority shareholders. This book investigates whether inside-concentrated ownership provides opportunities for expropriation of minority shareholders and results in value loss. To provide evidence, we examine the market valuation of ownership rights and related-party transactions (RPTs) of group-affiliated firms in India.

This chapter begins by highlighting the group structure and its inherent problems. The second section describes the underlying motivation of the book, followed by a section that outlines the main research objectives. The fourth section highlights the contribution of the book, and the final section outlines how the book is organized.

Statement of the problem

The business group structure has a significant impact not only on emerging economies but also on developed nations such as the US and Japan.[1] Although business groups have contributed significantly to the wealth of emerging economies, our understanding of the operations of these groups remains insufficient (Yiu et al., 2005). This study expands our understanding of the

---

[1] The business groups are found in several developed and emerging economies; including the US, Japan, India, South Korea, Russia, and China. Davis, Diekmann, and Tinsley (1994) and Dewenter, Novaes, and Pettway (2001) highlight the role of diversified business groups in the economies of developed nations and other studies like Bhattacharya and Ravikumar (2001), Perotti and Gelfer (2001), and Yiu, Bruton, and Yuan (2005), in emerging economies.

concentrated ownership, and RPT phenomenon within business groups in India, which is one of the fastest emerging economies in the world. Khanna and Yafeh (2005) identify that the role of business groups in India is poorly understood. As the existence of concentrated ownership is the primary feature of business groups, business-group membership can affect firm value in one of two competing ways: the entrenchment effect and the alignment effect. The entrenchment effect presents incentives for controlling shareholders to expropriate the wealth of minority shareholders (Fama and Jensen, 1983b). The alignment effect presents the competing view that concentrated ownership creates greater monitoring by controlling shareholders and, thus, higher firm value (Demsetz and Lehn, 1985). This study disentangles the incentive and entrenchment effects of controlling shareholders of Indian group firms. Specifically, the effect of the controlling shareholders' direct and indirect ownership rights on firm value is examined to seek evidence on the alignment or entrenchment effects. This study also examines whether differences in ownership structure at the firm level can explain the variation in the value relevance of RPTs. In particular, this study examines whether the use of RPTs is viewed as efficient and valued positively, or entrenchment and valued negatively.

A business group is a collection of firms which are separate legal entities, but are bound by economic (equity and debt) and social (family and kinship) ties. Groups might be vertically controlled through a pyramid structure, or horizontally linked through cross holdings. Khanna and Rivkin (2001, 47) define a business group as 'a set of firms which, though legally independent, are bound together by a constellation of formal and informal ties and are accustomed to taking coordinated action.' This implies that each firm is a separate legal entity under the Indian Companies Act, 1956 but are associated with each other in terms of ownership and management. As each firm is a distinct legal entity, annual reports are prepared and issued at the firm level and each firm has its own board of directors. However, the business decisions are often taken by considering the group as a whole and personal interests at firm level are ignored (Gopalan, Nanda, and Seru, 2007). This may impose costs on minority shareholders and consequently lead to an agency conflict between controlling and minority shareholders.[2]

The existing literature suggests that these groups have a significant effect on emerging economies. For instance, in India, group-affiliated firms

---

[2] This issue is discussed later in the chapter.

accounted for 89 per cent of total sales and assets of the private sector in 1993 (Ghemawat and Khanna, 1998). Group firms account for 60 per cent of the 500 largest Indian companies and 65 per cent of total capitalization of the largest 500 companies (Chakrabarti, Megginson, and Yadav, 2008). Of the total industrial production of China, 60 per cent is contributed by business groups (SSB, 2000). In South Korea, 40 per cent of total output is contributed by the top 30 business groups (Chang and Hong, 2000). Despite the significant contribution of business groups to the Indian economy, studies examining these groups have been limited to the evolution and transformation of business groups (Kedia, Mukherjee, and Lahiri, 2006), group performance (Khanna and Palepu, 2000b), the tunneling behaviour (Bertrand, Mehta, and Mullainathan, 2002; Kali and Sarkar, 2011) and the investment behaviour (Lensink, van der Molen, and Gangopadhyay, 2003) of these business groups. However, there is no empirical evidence on valuation of RPTs amongst group-affiliated firms.

Family members often control these group firms by boarding memberships, recruiting top management, coordinating actions among member firms, and lobbying the government (Khanna and Palepu, 2000b). It is important to note that affiliation can be associated with a conflict of interest between controlling and minority shareholders. Family members can enforce their controlling power to benefit other firms in the group which might not be in the best interests of public shareholders. The controlling shareholders have even greater incentives to expropriate the wealth of minority shareholders when they have lower cash-flow rights. Bertrand et al. (2002) provide evidence of tunnelling among Indian business groups.

Studies such as those of Khanna and Yafeh (2005) and Hoshi, Kashyap, and Scharfstein (1991) highlight the risk-sharing phenomenon among member firms. Ghemawat and Khanna (1998) suggest that business groups operate an internal capital market when the external market is inefficient because of informational problems. Similarly, Gopalan et al. (2007) suggest significant operational and financial inter-linkages between member firms in the group. There could be several motives for the transfer of resources across member firms, including:

- Investments: resources can be transferred from one firm to the other to finance profitable new investment opportunities. Stein (2003) suggests that an internal capital market structure can economize the cost of financing. A similar situation may be that of a group cross-subsidizing a firm in the group involved in a price war to obtain market share, such as an airline in fare discounting.

- Support: another motive behind the transfer of resources can be to support firms in financial distress. Group firms might be concerned about their reputation because a default by any firm in the group may send a negative signal to the market about group performance.
- Tunnelling: controlling shareholders may have incentives to transfer resources from a firm with low cash-holding rights to firms with higher cash-holding rights. Bertrand et al. (2002) find evidence supporting a significant amount of tunnelling among Indian business groups.

Gopalan et al. (2007) also examine the functioning of internal capital markets and report that a significant amount of loans have been provided across group firms. A firm in a better financial position tends to provide loans to weak firms. They further examine the subsequent performance of firms that receive loans, and found that receiving firms significantly underperform in the subsequent two years, which is inconsistent with the notion that loans are used to finance profitable investment opportunities. Furthermore, the results suggest marginally greater support in the form of loans to higher insider holdings firms in a group. The support provided by group loans is found to be an important factor in avoiding the bankruptcy of weak firms. Group loans are also typically provided at an interest rate that is significantly lower than the market borrowing rate, by almost 10 per cent.

The findings mentioned above suggest that group loans are often provided on favourable terms and for non-profit investments, which reveals the cost for the firm which provides the loans. In other words, these group loans involve costs for the firms providing the loans, and this might be a way to expropriate the wealth of minority shareholders by transferring funds from firms with lower cash-flow rights to firms with higher cash-flow rights. The bankruptcy of any group firm signals negative information about the group and it leads to a reduction in the total external financing (debt and equity) by other healthy firms in the group. It appears that group firms support weak member firms to reduce bankruptcy probability as the bankruptcy event within the group is followed by a fall in the investments of healthy firms in the group. This also suggests that personal interests of individual firms are ignored to save the image of the group as a whole.

Motivation for the study

The literature on agency theory reveals two types of agency problems. The first type arises from the separation of ownership and management, which is the case in non-family firms. The second type arises due to conflicts between controlling and minority shareholders, which is a characteristic of family firms (Demsetz and Lehn, 1985). Family firms face less severe Type 1 agency problems because they are likely to be actively involved in management. Controlling shareholders hold significant stock ownership, which gives them incentive and power to monitor any opportunistic behaviour. Moreover, family members have better knowledge of their business activities, which enables them to detect any irregularities. However, family firms face the second type of agency problem. The boards of family firms tend to be less independent and more dominated by family members and, consequently, there is a risk of expropriation of minority shareholders by controlling shareholders. As a result, family firms face more severe Type 2 agency problems. Consequently, the overall effect on firm value cannot be predicted and it becomes an empirical question. The motivation of this book is to expand our knowledge on the agency problems of family-controlled group firms.

Research objectives

We address two broad questions regarding the underlying benefits and costs involved in family ownership. The first objective of this study is to disentangle the incentive and entrenchment effects of controlling shareholders of Indian group firms. The second objective is to examine the valuation of RPTs and if these transactions are opportunistic or efficient. Within the framework of the research objectives, we will address the following questions:

1. Which of the two opposing forces (convergence-of-interest or entrenchment effect) dominates at different levels of ownership rights of controlling shareholders.
2. Whether the market values RPTs based on the nature of the transaction, the relationship with the party involved in RPTs, and the personal incentives of controlling shareholders.

Contribution

Firms with high ownership concentration suffer from unique agency problems arising from principal–principal conflict. The conflict between controlling and minority shareholders has been examined mainly in the context of East Asia and South Korea and, to lesser extent, in the context of India (Claessens et al., 2002; Joh, 2003; and Bertrand et al., 2002). Family dominance in

India, together with inadequate regulation and weak enforcement, generates an environment best suited for extraction of firm resources. The aim of this study is to employ the framework of two competing forces (that is, alignment effect and entrenchment effect) to demonstrate accountability issues in firms with concentrated ownership.

Several studies investigate the expropriation of outsiders by controlling shareholders. Claessens et al. (2002), Joh (2003), Lemmon and Lins (2003), and Lins (2003) provide evidence on the extraction of firm resources by controlling shareholders from Asian and other emerging markets, whereas Bertrand et al. (2002) and Kali and Sarkar (2011) provide evidence of tunnelling in Indian business groups. We contribute significantly to this body of literature in a number of ways which have not been examined in previous studies. We adopt the view that useful insights into the extent of resolution of the principal–principal conflict are obtained by examining the multiple control mechanisms. We note that a key aspect of much of the prior research is that the ownership rights of the controlling group are assumed to operate to alleviate or aggravate agency costs in isolation, and the role of other blockholders such as institutional investors is often ignored. We suggest that important linkages should not only exist among the shareholdings of different groups but also among other governance mechanisms such as board members and CEOs. Furthermore, prior studies on the expropriation of minority shareholders of Indian business groups provide indirect evidence only. For example, Bertrand et al. (2002) and Kali and Sarkar (2011) provide evidence of tunnelling through shock sensitivity. There are very limited studies which examined RPTs to seek evidence of expropriation of minority shareholders in the Indian context.

Prior studies on the valuation of RPTs do not identify the relationship of parties involved in the transaction. However, we examine whether RPTs involving subsidiary and holding firms are valued differently from RPTs involving member firms in the groups. Moreover, we also examine if the indirect ownership (obtained through cross holding) of controlling shareholders influences the valuation of RPTs. Earlier studies have not examined these issues on the valuation of RPTs. This work will add significantly to the extant literature on RPTs.

We extend Bertrand et al. (2002) and Kali and Sarkar (2011) in several ways. Firstly, our proxy to measure cash-flow rights is more appropriate than what was used in these studies. Bertrand et al. (2002) use director ownership to capture direct cash-flow rights of controlling shareholders, which tends to overstate direct rights if directors are not family members. In contrast, we obtain direct and indirect cash-flow rights of controlling families from disclosure information about shareholders. Second, we control for large blockholders (other than the founding family) which appear to challenge controlling families, which Bertrand et al. (2002) ignored completely. Third, we seek evidence of whether the expropriation of outsiders occurs through RPTs, which is a direct measure, while Bertrand et al. (2002) and Kali and Sarkar (2011) use an indirect measure via industry shocks to determine the extent of tunnelling.

This study has implications for various groups such as investors, forecasters, and policy-makers. The results are important from the standpoint of outside investors. Not only do group-affiliated firms impose costs on outside investors in the form of entrenchment but outside investors can also be benefitted by the efficient use of RPTs. Khanna and Palepu (2000b) argue that group-affiliated firms overcome the imperfections of external markets with the help of internal institutions. Kohlbeck and Mayhew (2010) also argue that RPTs can fulfil the underlying needs of the firm.

As regulation affects shareholder wealth, our study has implications for policy-makers. The evidence of tunnelling requires stringent rules and regulations to restrict entrenchment effects by controlling shareholders. The message for policy-makers from this evidence of entrenchment consequences is quite clear: strong investor protection encourages not only domestic investors but also foreign direct investment (FDI). The findings of our study will bevery useful to policy-makers in India where corporate reporting practices are weak and in a very nascent stage. The standard-setting bodies are currently formulating adequate accounting regulations so that they are consistent with international practices. Regulators need to account for the potential conflicting interests between shareholders in the policy-setting process. However, the rent-seeking literature highlights that policy-makers may also exploit the competition between different interest groups for their own benefit. McChesney (1997) identifies that political officeholders exploit their incumbency to demand payments from economic groups. Payments can take the form of election campaign contribution or political support. The evidence of this rent-seeking behaviour can be found in the literature. For example, Bittlingmayer and Hazlett (2000) report that the antitrust scrutiny of Microsoft was partly a result of Microsoft's lack of 'Washington presence'. Microsoft contributed little to political campaigns in comparison with other large firms. Similarly, Sheila Dikshit's government in Delhi was accused of giving unfair advantage to Reliance Group, and the newly formed government of the Aam Aadmi Party (AAP) ordered an audit by the Comptroller and

Auditor General of India (CAG) of the private power distribution companies owned by Reliance Group (*TOI*, 2014).

In this framework, policy-makers might have incentives not to enforce legislation which protects outside investors if they receive payments from big business groups. This study raises questions about such a political environment and highlights the importance of a more transparent system to ensure investor protection. In particular, we highlight the nature of the transactions conducive for expropriation of minority shareholders and inadequate regulations pertaining to RPTs.

As we are using the Indian setting, the book will also help in understanding one of the most important emerging markets in the world which is relatively unexplored.[3] An enhanced understanding of Indian business groups will prove useful for other counterpart firms (local and foreign) that aim to compete against or establish links with these business groups (Kim, Kandemir, and Cavusgil, 2004).

There are several benefits of using India as a setting. First, India provides a large sample of firms for analysis because there are several thousand companies listed on the Bombay Stock Exchange (BSE) and the National Stock Exchange (NSE). Second, unlike Japanese *keiretsu*, groups are easily identifiable in India. Furthermore, firms are a member of only one group and, generally, there is no movement of firms across the groups because of strong family ties. Finally, despite the group affiliations, accounting standards require each firm to disclose financial information. As each firm is a separate legal entity, the ownership and financial information is available at the firm level for examination. Significant variation would be lost if the information is required to be analysed at the group level.

Structure of the book

The book is divided into nine chapters. These are as follows:

Following this introductory chapter, the next chapter provides some understanding of the Indian setting. It discusses the evolution and transformation of Indian business groups. A qualitative assessment of business groups in an international context is provided. Furthermore, the history and

---

[3] Claessens, Djankov, and Lang (2000), Ball, Robin, and Wu (2003), Lins (2003), Lemmon and Lins (2003), and Claessens, Fan, and Lang (2006) investigate the expropriation of minority shareholders and firm valuation in the Asian context but they exclude India.

present state of the Indian economy is provided in the chapter. It also discusses the Indian accounting standard-setting process, the weak enforcement system in India, and rules pertaining to RPTs.

Chapter 3 provides the theoretical framework on Type 2 agency costs, entrenchment effects, and alignment effects. Furthermore, the chapter reviews empirical studies conducted on business groups around the world. These include examination of the firm performance and market valuation of diversified business groups. The evidence on the effect of ownership on firm value is provided. This chapter also examines studies on the investment and tunnelling behaviour of family business groups and valuation of RPTs.

Chapter 4 develops hypotheses to empirically examine the effect of direct and indirect ownership rights on firm value. The effect of minority ownership on firm value is also predicted. Moreover, the hypotheses are developed to examine the valuation of various RPTs. The hypotheses are based on agency theory, with specific reference to the Type 2 agency problem as a result of conflict between controlling and minority shareholders. The entrenchment effect of controlling shareholders also provides support for the hypothesis development.

Chapter 5 outlines the methodology employed in this study. First, the sample selection procedure is illustrated. The description of the sample is provided in the next section. The proxies used to measure the key variables and the empirical models to be estimated are described in the last section.

Following the discussion of methodology, descriptive statistics and univariate analysis results are provided in Chapter 6. This chapter also provides a correlation matrix to identify any potential harmful levels of multicollinearity.

Chapter 7 presents the empirical results of the ordinary least squares (OLS) regressions used to test the developed hypotheses. First, the results for the effect of direct and indirect ownership rights of controlling shareholders on firm value are presented. The next section presents results on the association between minority ownership and firm value. Finally, results on the earnings-market valuation of various RPTs are presented.

Chapter 8 provides additional tests to support the main findings. First, the results of panel-based fixed-effect models are presented. The next section presents results for analysis of only RPT firms, followed by the results for the valuation of individual RPTs. Some governance variables are further explored to assess the robustness of the main findings.

Last, Chapter 9 summarizes the empirical findings and draws conclusions. This section also acknowledges the limitations of the study and recommendations for future research are provided.

Chapter 2

The Evolution of Business Groups, Institutional Framework in India, and Related-Party Transactions

Introduction

This chapter provides the background on the evolution of business groups and the institutional framework in India. It begins by discussing family control of business groups, followed by the facts on the evolution and transformation of these business groups. The next section looks at the Indian economy, while the fourth section provides information on the accounting standard setting process in India. The fifth section draws attention to the weak enforcement system in India, which is followed by a discussion on the rules pertaining to RPTs. The last section summarizes the main themes outlined in the chapter.

Family control

Chua, Chrisman, and Sharma (1999, 25) define a family business as 'a business governed or/and managed on a sustainable, potentially cross-generational, basis to shape and perhaps pursue the formal or implicit vision of the business held by members of the same family or a small number of families.'

Most Indian business groups started as family businesses. They moved aggressively after Independence in 1947 and their operations became well diversified. For instance, the Birla group was established by Seth Shiv Narayan Birla in 1870 as a small cotton and jute trading business. Over the years, the group has diversified its operations into petrochemicals, textiles, telecommunications, cement, automobiles, and financial services, and the group now consists of more than 40 companies. Although each firm within the group is a separate legal entity, control still resides with the promoter families. In the case of the Birla group, Kumar Mangalam Birla, the only son of Aditya Birla, is the current chairman. Considering the nature of these business groups (family controlled), the literature on family firms would be relevant to examine the attributes of Indian business groups. The terms 'business groups' and 'family firms' will be used interchangeably in this study. Khanna and Yafeh (2007) identify that groups are generally family firms and their behaviour can be understood better from this perspective.

The literature on property rights suggests that the legal system shapes the structure of property rights. Fan and Wong (2002) view share ownership rights as property rights, with shareholders being entitled to certain rights. First, the shareholder has control rights. Second, the shareholder has cash-flow rights, and finally, the right to transfer the shares. The value of the shares depends on the enforcement of such rights. The enforcement is undertaken by the owner and the state (Fan and Wong, 2002). The individual owners play a vital role in enforcing property rights in economies with less effective property rights. This view suggests that controlling shareholders have the power and incentives to enforce corporate contracts. In contrast, minority shareholders lack the power and incentives to enforce such contracts. As a consequence, the benefits of concentrated ownership are greater in countries with less developed legal systems to enforce property rights (Shleifer and Vishny, 1997). Consistent with La Porta, Lopez-de-Silanes, and Shleifer (1999) and given that in India the legal enforcement mechanism is weak, it is reasonable to expect concentrated ownership to be generally in the hands of the family.

Evolution and transformation of business groups since Independence (1947)

It is evident from the studies presented in the previous chapter that groups tend to overcome the imperfections of capital, product, and labour markets (Ghemawat and Khanna, 1998; Khanna and Palepu, 1999, 2000b; Khanna and Rivkin, 2001). Financial intermediaries such as investment bankers, financial analysts, and efficient stock exchanges were missing in underdeveloped India in the period immediately following Independence. In such an environment, business groups generated capital and managerial talent from internal markets (Kali and Sarkar, 2005).

In the absence of well-functioning business markets, these business groups could use their political connections for their private interest (Ghemawat and Khanna, 1998). For instance, the Tata Group benefitted from the Nehru (Congress) government after Independence by getting involved in several projects as part of nation building, in return for supporting the Congress in the freedom movement (Kedia et al., 2006). Business groups that are viewed as government supported, continued to enjoy favourable terms in the transition phase of the Indian economy. There is evidence of groups exercising their power to oppose institutional changes. The formation of the Bombay Club is an example of industrialists' attempt to lobby for restricting the entry of multinationals in the Indian market (Tripathi, 2004). However, the ties between business groups and the government do not seem to be smooth. The business groups were also harmed by certain restrictions imposed on them by the government. For example, anti-big business group legislation, such as the Monopolies and Restrictive Trade Practices (MRTP) Act, came into being (Khanna and Yafeh, 2007). It appears that the relationship between business groups and the government changed over time, as the economic environment changed for the country as well as for the business groups.

Business groups have been encouraged by the governments in emerging economies to stimulate economic growth. For example, the Indian government's policy of entry barriers for foreign firms and a high level of government intervention in the private sector helped the growth of diversified business groups in the pre-reform era (Kedia et al., 2006). Guillen (1997) highlights the role of the government's industrial policy and export-led strategy for the growth of Korean *chaebols*. Peng (2001) highlights the role of the Chinese government in the formation of business groups. Existing literature suggests that government involvement has been very important in the formation of business groups in emerging economies: Latin America (Strachan, 1976), Indonesia (Schwartz, 1992), China (Keister, 1998), Pakistan (White, 1974), and South Korea (Chang and Choi, 1988; Guillen, 1997).

The business reforms in the early 1990s changed the market conditions in India and, therefore, we will analyse the transformation of business groups in two parts; the pre- and post-reform eras.

Pre-reform era

The pre-reform era was strictly regulated, and the government intervened extensively in the business sector. Many regulatory mechanisms, such as the Industrial Policy Resolution (1956), the MRTP Act (1969), and the Industrial Licensing Policy Inquiry Committee (1969), were put in place to monitor the private sector and restrict the entry of foreign investors (Majumdar, 2004). For instance, the entry of private businesses was restricted to certain areas under the industrial policy resolutions issued in 1948 and 1956. Furthermore, business firms faced the problem of weak contract enforcement as a result of inadequate rules and regulations (Khanna and Palepu, 1997). The problems discussed above challenged the survival of business firms. Li, Ramaswamy, and Pecherot Petitt (2006) report that diversified business groups could add more value compared to individual firms in such situations. The business groups diversified into wide areas to overcome market deficiencies and imperfections (Khanna and Palepu, 1997). For instance, the financial resources of one firm can be used by another, which substitutes for the funding role of the external capital market, and labour can similarly be mobilized between firms (Li et al., 2006). Irrespective of their unrelated business activities, business groups manage to add value. The value addition of business groups might be a result of increased institutional relatedness (IR). Imports were discouraged with very high duties and complicated quota and licensing requirements (Mohan, 1992). The restrictions were imposed on foreign investment under the MRTP Act, 1969 (Dandekar, 1992; Vachani, 1997). The favoured licensing policies and lack of competition facilitated these business groups' profits (Mohan, 1992).

Post-reform era

The market conditions changed significantly in the early 1990s as a result of liberalization and deregulation reforms. In 1991, the then finance minister, Manmohan Singh, initiated several changes. The abolition of regulation and licensing gave a boost to the Indian economy (Kedia et al., 2006). For example, it resulted in the reduction of excise and import duty from 100 per cent in 1991 to about 30 per cent in 2000, and the MRTP Act was abolished. Private business firms were allowed to enter into new areas which were earlier reserved for the public sector. Furthermore, foreign investment was encouraged. Tariffs to imports were reduced and restrictions on direct foreign investment (DFI) were also relaxed (Joshi and Little, 1996). The deregulation and increased globalization changed business practices in India. If business reforms in the 1990s opened new industries for business groups which were earlier reserved for the government sector, it also exposed business groups to local and foreign competition. Licenses secured by the groups became valueless (Manikutty, 2000), as new firms were allowed to enter the market without any license. The changed regulation forced business groups to compete not only with local firms but also with foreign firms, since the restrictions on foreign investment were relaxed. Financial resources became less critical with the inflow of FDI and deregulation of markets, and business groups were less advantaged by their internal capital markets.

The changed approach, which led to business restructuring, was a response to the deregulated and liberalized market. For instance, the Tata group went through a significant restructuring around 1998 and reduced its business segments to almost half (Kedia et al., 2006). This is consistent with the resource-based view which suggests that firms tend to diversify into related products (MacDonald, 1985; Montgomery and Hariharan, 1991). In contrast, the Thapar group tried to maintain a much more diversified business and consequently failed to perform well. Kedia et al. (2006) ranked the Thapar group amongst the low value-added groups in the post-reform era. The Mahindra group decided to concentrate on automobiles and related products and carried out the divestment of its elevator and graphics businesses (Manikutty, 2000). The restructuring of the business portfolios was done to build strength in their core sectors and it proved successful. For example, Tata Steel spent Indian Rupees (INR) 23 billion (US$377 million) to increase its production capacity from 2.7 million to 3.5 million tonnes of steel per annum (Manikutty, 2000). Tata Engineering and Locomotive Company (TELCO) established a design facility to develop a small car named Indica. The design was developed in 31 months at a cost of INR 1.7 billion (Manikutty, 2000). Ranbaxy increased its Research and Development (R&D) expenditure from 3 per cent in 1993 to 7.5 per cent in 1999 (Ghemawat and Kothavala, 1998) to move away from generic drugs to new molecular and branded formulations. Today, Ranbaxy is known for being an integrated and research-based international pharmaceutical group.

In a highly competitive environment, these family groups made efforts to obtain better synergies between the group resources. The Tata Group established Tata Administrative Services with the objective of serving group firms with highly professional managers (Khanna, Palepu, and Wu, 1998). Furthermore, the Tata group recruited top managers in a concerted fashion and rotated them where needed (Khanna and Palepu, 1997). Similarly, the Birla group transformed Birla Management Centre into a corporate centre for deriving synergies from the member firms. The Mahindra and Reliance groups also established strategic units for the group as a whole (*Business Today*, August 22, 1999). The Tata group also established a venture capital fund for member firms with a funding of INR 1.26 billion (Khanna and Palepu, 1997).

Another change in these family groups is in employing professionals at the top level. The second generation of these families is more educated than the founders of these groups. Manikutty (2000) reports that K. M. Birla, head of Birla group, is a qualified chartered accountant (CA) and he also obtained an MBA from London Business School. Both Ambani brothers, Mukesh and

Anil, have MBA degrees from Stanford University and the Wharton School of the University of Pennsylvania, respectively. Moreover, the approach of these groups seems to be changing from being family-centred to business-centred (Singer and Doronho, 1992). The culture of these groups was earlier seen as autocratic, and personal loyalty was emphasized rather than professionalism. These family groups have realized the value of professional managers, and have started employing them in higher positions. For example, the Birla group hired a former director from Levers and a former CEO of Blow Blast Limited in 1997 (*Business Today*, 7 October 1999). These professionals are not only recruited into top positions but also empowered with more freedom and authority to make business decisions (Barker, 1992) which were earlier restricted in the hands of the family.

Indian economy

The Indian economy, which is considered to be the world's 11th largest economy today in terms of nominal gross domestic product (GDP), has evolved gradually but steadily over decades. It is now one of the world's fastest growing economies. To understand how the Indian economy reached where it is today, we need to examine its history.

Pre-colonial age

Before India became a colony of the British, agriculture was the main source of economic activity and income for the people. As one of the world's oldest civilizations, India was blessed with all the important factors required for a productive agricultural system, from fertile land to abundant water bodies to a favourable climate. A planned economic system had existed even in the oldest of Indian civilizations like Indus Valley Civilization, the Aryan Civilization, the Mauryan Empire, the Gupta Empire, and most other dynasties. Although coins were also issued in some dynasties, the barter system formed the main form of trading in those times. The economic rule required all the farmers and villagers to provide the kings or the landlords with a part of their crops.

Even during Muslim rule, the Indian economy largely depended on agricultural produce. The Mughal Empire established some trade relations with the British, French, and Portuguese merchants during the latter part of the Mughal period. Finally, the British East India Company came into existence, following the Battle of Plassey, giving rise to colonial rule in India.

While reading the history of the Indian economy, one will find that the colonial era formed an integral part of the Indian economy. During this phase, a notable change was witnessed in the process of taxation in the form of revenue taxes and property taxes that led to large-scale economic breakdown. Terrible losses were suffered by many industries, including the Indian handicrafts industry.

During this period, the financial and banking system as well as free trade was created, a single currency system with exchange rates was established, standardization of weights and measures took place, and also a capital market was formed. Apart from these institutional attributes, infrastructure and new telegraph lines were established. Transportation also improved as railway lines and roads were constructed. Foreign investment in India also increased before Independence; however, the role of foreign capital diminished after 1947 as a result of the sale of British interests to Indian entrepreneurs. For instance, the number of business groups controlled by the British fell from 61 in 1938 to 25 in 1962 (Chhibber and Majumdar, 1999).

Post–Independence to the 1990s

In the post-Independence era, great attention was paid to bolstering the economic system of India. This era saw great development in sectors like agriculture, village industries, mining, and defence. There was an overall improvement in the standard of living of people in rural areas as new roads, dams, and bridges were built, and access to electricity increased.

Furthermore, the government formulated five-year plans, under which it implemented several economic reforms and policies. To make the economy both diverse and self-sufficient, the government also acted to increase the quantity and quality of the export items and minimize the volume of imports.

Business regulations, central planning, and nationalization of the industries in mining, electricity, and infrastructure was also given due attention by political leaders during this period.

The 1960s witnessed yet another significant economic reform, which helped the country to become self-sufficient in food grain production. The Green revolution movement came into being, which aimed at dealing with issues such as afforestation, increased irrigational projects, improved seed usage, better farming techniques, and the use of fertilizers.

Rajiv Gandhi, the then prime minister, took the first step in the 1980s to liberalize the market. He passed tenure under which restrictions on a number of sectors were eased, pricing regulations were abolished, and efforts were made to improve the GDP of the country.

From the 1990s to the present time

With the dissolution of the Soviet Union, which was India's main trading partner, the so-called golden sparrow, India, had to deal with a huge balance of payment problems. The situation worsened since government loans were increasing and the IMF was demanding a bailout loan. Before the 1990s, strict regulations and high tariffs existed in the Indian private sector and imports were restricted. In the 1980s, India's share of worldwide trade fell below 0.5 per cent because of its anti-trade policies.

The economic conditions changed significantly with the election of the new government of Narasimha Rao in 1991. The newly elected finance minister, Manmohan Singh, reversed policies that had complex regulations and licensing requirements. Furthermore, lower tariff rates protected domestic industries. For example, the tariff rate for the manufacturing sector was reduced from 71 per cent to 36 per cent. Undoubtedly, this proved to be a great boon to the Indian economy, since FDI was welcomed, public monopolies were reduced significantly, and banking, service, and tertiary sectors were developed.

India has always been a capital-scarce economy for a number of reasons. First, India lacks natural resources like oil and other minerals. Overpopulation further makes the resources insufficient to sustain economic growth. Second, India failed to attract high foreign investment. In the last 25 years, the magnitude of foreign investment in India amounts to less than 25 per cent of foreign investment in China. Foreign investment was restricted before the 1990s and it was only after the reforms in the early 1990s that the market was deregulated, and steps were taken to attract foreign capital. Now, liberalized India has become one of the most attractive destinations for foreign investment. Ernst and Young's 2010 European Attractiveness Survey ranks India as number 2 following China in attracting FDI in the coming three years. The Indian government continues to relax regulations on foreign investment. For example, the government has empowered the Foreign Investment Promotion Board (FIPB) to approve FDI proposals up to US$258.3 million. Earlier, any proposal above US$129.2 million was subject to the approval from Cabinet Committee of Economic Affairs (CCEA). Third, India failed to concentrate on export-oriented business, which resulted in low foreign currency growth. Unlike China, India could not capitalize on low-cost economic activities.

Indian accounting standard setting process

Having been a British colony for over 100 years, accounting standards in India are modelled on the British standards. The main professional body in India is the Institute of Chartered Accountants in India (ICAI) which was established in July 1949 under the Chartered Accountants Act, 1949. It is the world's second largest accounting body after the American Institute of Certified Public Accountants (AICPA) in terms of membership, with 220,000 members as of 29 June 2013.

To regulate public companies, the Company Act, 1913 was introduced in India based on the English Companies Act, 1908. This statute, however, had gone through several amendments. The Companies Act, 1956 allows ICAI to develop accounting standards and every entity is required to comply with these accounting standards. Section 211 (3A) of the Companies Act, 1956 requires every profit and loss statement and balance sheet to comply with the accounting standards. Furthermore, Section 211 (3C) clarifies that 'accounting standards' means the standards issued by the ICAI.

The Indian accounting standard setting process is subject to direct or indirect oversight by several regulatory bodies, such as the Securities and Exchange Board of India (SEBI), National Advisory Committee on Accounting Standards (NACAS), Insurance Regulatory and Development Authority (IRDA), and the Reserve Bank of India (RBI) (Khatri and Master, 2009). The Companies Act, 1956 provides guidance on financial accounting matters, and the provisions of the company law will prevail in case of any inconsistency between particular accounting standards and the company legislation. Furthermore, Indian courts have the power to endorse particular accounting treatments.

The ICAI established the Accounting Standards Board (ASB) in 1977 to formulate accounting standards and integrate them, to the extent possible, with International Financial Reporting Standards (IFRS). The board of the ASB is represented by members from all interest groups, including industry, financial institutions, professional bodies, academia, government, and other regulatory bodies. The Associated Chambers of Commerce and Industry (ASSOCHAM), the Confederation of Indian Securities (CII), and the Federation of Indian Chambers of Commerce and Industry (FICCI) represent the industry group. Academics from the Indian Institute of Management (IIM), Institute of Company Secretaries of India, Institute of Cost and Works Accountants of India, and other universities are also present on the ASB. The RBI, the CAG, the Central Board of Excise and Customs, and the Ministry of Company Affairs represent the government.

Indian accounting continues to be driven by the legal form of the transaction, and not by the substance of transactions. For instance, the upfront fee charged by telecom service firms is recognized as income under Indian GAAP because it is non-refundable by contract. On the contrary, the income would be deferred over the estimated period of the service contract under IFRS. The reason is that customers pay the activation fee not for any services received but in anticipation of future services. Furthermore, the group firms are required to prepare consolidated financial statements under the IFRS to present a true and fair view. The Indian GAAP only mandates the preparation of consolidated financial statements for listed firms, and only annual statements and not interim financial statements.

Indian Accounting Standard (AS) 24 requires the disclosure of RP relationships, type of transactions, and amount. The Indian GAAP requires disclosure of RPT amounts, whereas IFRS are more focused on qualitative information and requires firms to disclose the terms of RPTs. There is more discussion on rules pertaining to RPTs in one of the sections of this chapter below. The Indian GAAP allows long-term deposits and advances to be disclosed under current assets and, thus, fails to provide information on current and non-current portions, and consequently, the liquidity position of the firm.

In many accounting standards, such as valuation of inventories (AS 2), depreciation accounting (AS 6), intangible assets (AS 26), impairment of assets (AS 28), and provisions, contingent liabilities, and contingent assets (AS 29), flexibility is involved and professional judgment is exercised to a certain extent. The fixed assets can be revalued under Indian GAAP and this provision highlights the inherent subjectivity involved with the revaluation process. The fair value is currently limited to impairment of assets, mark-to-market treatment for derivatives, and measurement of retirement benefits. Therefore, property, plant, and equipment (PPE), intangible assets, investment properties, and other financial assets can be measured at fair value. The discretion provided by the standards specified above can be used differently by family-controlled group firms to achieve their reporting objectives.

It is not only the discretion provided by accounting standards but also the weak enforcement of the regulation which might facilitate personal reporting objectives. La Porta et al. (1998) measure legal enforcement in terms of rule of law, corruption, and risk of expropriation. They also estimate the quality of national accounting standards. With reference to corruption, the Indian score is 4.58, whereas countries like Canada and New Zealand score 10. The risk of expropriation is higher in India with a score of 7.75, whereas the UK, USA, and Canada attain scores of 9.71, 9.98, and 9.67 respectively. The

Indian score is 4.17 for rule of law, whereas countries like the USA and UK score 10. For interpretation purposes, it is important to note that a lower score depicts lower efficiency for the respective measures. Indian accounting standards obtain a score of 57, whereas the UK, Singapore, and Australia score 78, 78, and 75 respectively for the quality of their accounting standards. It is reasonable to expect that accounting information might be influenced by reporting incentives in India, especially when accounting standards are poor and the legal enforcement system is weak.

The Satyam scandal, which analysts have called India's own Enron scandal, represents the perfect case of false account details. On 10 January 2009, the shares of the company plunged to INR 11.50, which was their lowest level since March 1998 compared to a high of INR 544 in 2008. Similarly, in 2008, the shares of the company on the New York Stock Exchange traded at US$29.10 whereas, in March 2009, they were trading at nearly US$1.80.

In the period of one week, some $2 billion of cash that belonged to 3 lakh shareholders disappeared. The company was filed against in multi-million-dollar lawsuits, its founder (Raju) was jailed, and shareholders' net worth plummeted from a positive INR 8,529 crore to a negative INR 278 crore.

Before the scandal came to be in the public eye, Raju had been boosting the valuation of the company so that he could borrow more money against his shareholding and keep the company in the top league of IT service providers. However, when the company's share prices plunged in January 2009, Raju failed to pay up and, thus, lenders began to sell shares. As a result, the promoters' (Raju's) holding fell to 3.6 per cent in comparison to 26 per cent in 2001.

The accounting information was found to have been manipulated. Satyam had been inflating profits for many years by inflating cash and bank balances of INR 5,040 crore. Court questioning also revealed that the accrued interest of INR 376 crore was not present, and that the debtors' position of INR 490 crore was exaggerated. Raju also had understated liabilities by INR 1,230 crore on account of funds.

The auditors, PricewaterhouseCoopers, in an attempt to distance themselves from the issue, declared that false information provided by Satyam management may have rendered their audit report inaccurate.

Weak enforcement system

Chakrabarti et al. (2008) report that the Indian judicial system is extremely slow, and the country's courts are overburdened. Despite the fact that India has 10,000 courts, excluding tribunals and special courts, it lacks the required number of judicial officers. India has just over 10 judges per million citizens, whereas the US has a comparative figure of 107 judges and Canada over 75 judges per million people. Moreover, the same courts deal with civil and criminal matters and criminal matters receive priority. This results in further delays in economic disputes. For example, Hazra and Micevska (2004) reveal that 3.2 million cases are pending in the High Courts and 23 million in the lower courts of India.

Another important aspect of investor protection is securities market regulation. The SEBI has significant problems in enforcing compliance with the law. Bose (2005) shows that SEBI took action in only 481 cases between 1999 and 2004. In contrast, the US Securities and Exchange Commission (SEC) initiated 2,789 cases during the same period. Furthermore, the decisions in 30 to 50 per cent of appeals before higher authorities, such as the Securities Appellate Tribunal or the Finance Ministry, go against the SEBI.

Slow debt recovery makes contract enforcement ineffective for creditors. The introduction of the Securitisation and Reconstruction of Financial Assets and Enforcement of Security Interest (SARFAESI) Act, 2002 and Debt Recovery Tribunals are aimed to accelerate the judicial process. The enactment of SARFAESI allows debt holders to seize the assets of a defaulting borrower. However, the borrower has the right to approach Debt Recovery Tribunals, the Debt Recovery Appellate Tribunal or High Court, which can delay the process for 3 to 4 years. In India, it takes 10 years, on an average, to go through the bankruptcy process and recovery rates are very low (Kang and Nayar, 2004).

In the absence of a strong enforcement system, businesses operate with informal mechanisms based on reciprocity and reputation (Khanna and Palepu, 2000b). The rights of minority shareholders can be compromised by controlling shareholders in private deals. This environment, with weak legal enforcement and widespread corruption, is highly conducive to the expropriation of minority shareholders.

Rules pertaining to RPTs

RPTs comprises transactions between a firm and an RP, where the related party would have the power to influence corporate decision making and may secure better terms than in the case of arm's-length transactions. As per the OECD Principles of Corporate Governance (2004), related parties can include firms that control or are under common control of the firm, significant shareholders including their family members, and key management personnel. Transactions between two firms controlled or owned by the same shareholder, often regarded as group-affiliated firms, are very common in India and present a potential conflict of interest. These transactions can result in situations where they are used as a means to channel funds from one firm to another and business opportunities can be lost to an RP at the cost of minority shareholders (OECD, 2014). However, not all RPTs are detrimental to the interests of the firm or minority shareholders. Some transactions can facilitate business purposes.

RPTs can be further decomposed into several categories, which include loans and guarantees, asset transfers, sale and purchase of goods and services, and bailouts (OECD, 2014). Some RPTs are more prone to abuse than others. For example, Berkman , Cole, and Fu (2009) suggest that the issuance of a loan guarantee is unambiguously a tunnelling practice. Lo, Wong, and Firth (2010) focus on RP sales to examine financial statement distortions. They report that firms with a higher percentage of parent directors are more likely to manipulate transfer prices. Srinivasan (2013) reports loans and deposits as a major RPT using a small sample of Indian firms listed on the BSE. Khanna and Yafeh (2005) and Jian and Wong (2010) use RP sales to investigate propping as RP sales are one of the most frequently made RPTs in their sample.

The fact that RPTs can impose costs on the firm or its minority shareholders gives rise to the question of how legal systems can prevent the abusive use of RPTs. One way of addressing the abusive use of RPTs is the prohibition of these transactions. Prohibition of RPTs has two main drawbacks. First, it would rule out value-creating RPTs with a view to reducing transaction costs and second, it may not be effective unless the prohibition of other forms of tunnelling is in place (Enriques, 2015). In the case of prohibition of RPTs, controlling shareholders can use equivalent substitutes to extract private benefits.

The other way to address tunnelling via RPTs is by establishing procedural safeguards to minimize the risk without stifling value-enhancing transactions. Most countries provide rules on how to enter into RPTs and related disclosure requirements. For example, countries like Hong Kong and the UK require shareholder approval for different types of RPTs. Furthermore, Belgium and Singapore require that the companies make an independent evaluator's opinion available to shareholders to supplement the disclosure on RPTs or help them in their vote on the RPTs. Voluntary use of independent lawyers or investment banks in the negotiation process is a common practice and such advice usually includes a fairness opinion (Enriques, 2015). In some countries, the fairness opinion is required by law to be disclosed. For example, if a fairness opinion is released, it has to be disclosed in Italy. However, the value of such fairness opinions may be limited. Outside experts, be they lawyers or investment banks, may be less independent than they appear, as they rely more on other advisory and investment banking roles than providing fairness opinions (Davidoff, 2005). While the effectiveness of fairness valuations is doubtful, the information on which the fairness opinions are based, like the management's projection of future cash flows and assumptions, can be particularly helpful (Enriques, 2015). Delaware in the US is the only main jurisdiction that has developed a wide body of case on law on this issue. Most other countries appear to be less detailed in their requirements relating to fairness disclosure.

Considering the potential to abuse RPTs, OECD (2012) emphasizes three mechanisms which represent good practices in the presence of controlling shareholders: first, minority-shareholder approval for different types of RPTs to protect the rights of minority shareholders; second, the power of minority shareholders in selecting board members of their choice; and third, the fiduciary duty of the controlling shareholder towards minority shareholders and the firm.

In India, shareholder approval is not required for RPTs, except for the issuance of shares, other than rights or bonus issues. In other countries, such as Australia, not only is the majority of minority approval required but also the regulator's comment on the proposed resolution. Shareholder approval is required under the Listing Rules of the Stock Exchange of Hong Kong (SEHK) and there is a similar requirement in Singapore under Chapter 9 of the Listing Rules of Singapore Stock Exchange for shareholder approval. In Canada, a formal valuation from a qualified and independent evaluator and majority approval by minority shareholders are necessary to approve RPTs. There is a similar requirement in the UK for approval of RPTs. It is evident that the minority shareholders in India do not have the benefit of a shareholder approval requirement. Nevertheless, RPTs require board approval. All non-equity RPTs are required to be reviewed by an audit committee. Clause 49 of the Listing Requirements issued by the SEBI states that audit committees should comprise at least three members and be at least two-thirds independent. Clause 49 does not only give directions on the composition of audit committees but also outlines that all members should be financially literate and at least one should have accounting and financial management experience.

It is critical to understand the role of independent directors when they are given the duty to stop abusive use of RPTs. The mere title 'independent' is not enough to fulfil the assigned duty, when they could be under enormous pressure from controlling shareholders. First, these independent directors are appointed by controlling shareholders and this may compromise their independence. Khanna and Mathew (2010) report that, in their small sample, independent directors viewed their role as strategic advisors to controlling shareholders, not as monitoring management and controlling shareholders. Second, the non-executive independent directors acknowledge their reliance on promoter families because of their directorships in other group-affiliate firms. Sarkar and Sarkar (2009) note that independent directors hold 67 per cent of their directorships in group affiliates and about 43 per cent of their directorships are concentrated in the same business group.

Chakrabarti, Subramanian, and Tung (2010) analyze the resignations of independent directors in the wake of the Satyam scandal. In this event study, resignations of independent directors led to lower returns; however, such an impact was insignificant for family-held firms. This suggests that independent directors are not regarded as effective in the presence of promoter families, mainly because of the reasons listed above.

In terms of directors' duties, the Companies Act of India, 1956 does not outline the duties of directors in great detail. It does not explicitly deal with RPTs except for self-dealing. As directors are in a position of trust, they should not exercise their powers for personal advantage. Section 300 of the Companies Act restricts directors from voting or participating in any board discussions regarding matters they are directly or indirectly related with. The company law does not make reference to the problems arising from acting on group strategies at the cost of the company. Nonetheless, the minority shareholders can apply to the Company Law Board against any oppression and mismanagement.

It is not just that the Indian market lacks mechanisms such as shareholder approval, directors' independence, clear role of directors; legal enforcement has been problematic too. OECD (2012) reports that 20 million cases are pending in the lower courts and 3.2 million cases are pending in the high courts. As both civil and criminal matters are tried in the same courts, economic disputes suffer greater delays. Furthermore, litigants might have to bear the cost of the action but the rewards are often paid to the firm, if the judgment is in favour of the litigant. The SEBI has greater responsibility when enforcement is weak through overburdened courts.

The jurisdiction of SEBI is limited to cases pertaining to issuance and transfer of securities. Matters of oppression and mismanagement by the majority fall under the powers of the Company Law Board/Ministry of Corporate Affairs. MCA/CLB had 60,000 pending cases at the beginning of year 2009–2010 (OECD, 2012). Widespread corruption in government departments does not make it any easier for minority shareholders.[4]

---

[4] Dutta (1997), La Porta et al. (1998), and OECD (2012) emphasize the problem of corruption in India.

New requirements under the Companies Act, 2013 and SEBI guidelines

There have been some recent regulatory changes in relation to RPTs and corporate governance. Under Clause 49 of the Listing Requirements of SEBI, all material RPTs require shareholder approval through special resolution. Any transaction with an RP that exceeds 5 per cent of the annual turnover or 20 per cent of the net worth of the company as per last audited financial statements, whichever is higher, will be considered material. Furthermore, Clause 35B of the Listing requirements has been changed to provide for an e-voting facility for all shareholder resolutions, which allows minority shareholders to express their views.

There have been more changes under the Listing Requirements and Companies Act, 2013 on independent directors. An independent director can only serve two consecutive terms of five year each. There is also a restriction on the maximum number of boards a person can serve on as an independent member. The maximum number of directorships one person can take is seven, and three in the case of individuals serving as a full-time director in any listed firm. However, the listed firms were required to abide by the above-mentioned changes from October 2014 and companies were subject to the old regulations for the sample period of this study (2008–2012).

Section 188 of the Companies Act, 2013 contains a provision requiring approval of disinterested shareholders and prohibits interested shareholders from voting on transactions with related parties. However, experience in countries like Israel has shown that classifying shareholders as disinterested may pose practical difficulties (OECD, 2014). Each shareholder who votes in an AGM will be required to notify the company about his or her personal interest in the transaction prior to the vote, which will help the company to classify the shareholder as interested or disinterested. Further, minority shareholders often own a small fraction of the shares and lack incentive to challenge the controlling shareholders. The Russian experience in the 1990s may imply that dysfunctional enforcement institutions can also deprive the majority of minority clause of its 'self-enforcing' appeal (Enriques, 2015). Despite the introduction of new laws under the Companies Act, 2013, we believe that minority shareholders are still at the risk of expropriation through RPTs due to practical difficulties and lack of incentive. Therefore, we firmly believe that the results will not materially change despite this provision, and the findings are still relevant in the current context.

The Companies Act, 2013 requires companies to obtain shareholder approval only for transactions above the 5 per cent threshold. Transactions below this threshold only require disclosure, which does not have to go further than the nature of the RP relationship, the amount of the transaction, the name of the RP, and other related information to assess the transaction.

Summary

This chapter presented the institutional framework in India. It highlighted family dominance in Indian business groups and the transformation of groups from family businesses to well-diversified groups that consist of many listed firms. Furthermore, the weak enforcement system makes the Indian setting more conducive for the expropriation of minority shareholders. The analysis of regulations pertaining to RPTs also highlights the potential abuse of such transactions. The rights of minority shareholders are not protected by shareholder approval requirements for different types of RPTs. However, all RPTs are required to be reviewed by an audit committee. Therefore, non-executive independent directors are assigned the key responsibility of stopping the abusive use of RPTs; however, the influence of controlling shareholders might impair the independence of non-executive directors in monitoring management and controlling shareholders. Overall, the weak enforcement system, inadequate protection of minority shareholders, and the excessive influence of controlling families on non-executive directors make the Indian setting conducive for the expropriation of minority shareholders. A major aim of this study is to determine whether such expropriation occurs, and its consequences.

Chapter 3

Theory and Literature Review

The previous chapter presented the background and institutional framework in India. This chapter presents the theoretical framework of the study and reviews relevant literature. This starts with the discussion of agency theory. In particular, Type 2 agency costs are discussed in detail—form that prevails in family firms. The proposed framework establishes the research foundation of this study.

Agency theory

Agency theory has been extensively used by researchers in finance (Fama, 1980), economics (Spence and Zeckhauser, 1971), accounting (Fan and Wong, 2002), management (Douma, George, and Kabir, 2006; Peng and Jiang, 2010), and organizational (Schulze, Lubatkin, Dino, and Buchholtz, 2001) studies. Agency theory advanced the risk-sharing literature[5] to account for the problem that occurs when cooperating parties have different goals (Eisenhardt, 1989). The divergence of interest between a principal and agent imposes a cost on the firm, which is commonly known as a Type 1 agency cost. Jensen and Meckling (1976) argue that agency costs are likely to decrease with the level of insider ownership and, thus, corporate performance improves with the level of insider ownership in the firm. However, Demsetz (1983) argues that an increased level of inside ownership presents a principal–principal conflict. This is called a Type 2 agency cost, which arises from the conflict between two groups of shareholders.

Entrenchment effect and convergence-of-interest arguments also suggest similar view about underlying agency costs.

---

[5] During the 1960s and early 1970s, economists described the risk-sharing problem as one that arises when cooperating parties have different attitudes towards risk (Arrow, 1971).

Entrenchment effect: The entrenchment effect is consistent with the traditional view that family firms tend to be less efficient because concentrated ownership encourages controlling shareholders to expropriate the wealth of minority shareholders.[6] Family members generally occupy important positions in family firms, which provide them with the power to expropriate outsiders. The family-dominated board may lack independent oversight and, thus, result in ineffective monitoring by the board. The indirect ownership obtained through cross-holdings makes the situation even worse. The controlling shareholders have greater incentives to expropriate the wealth of shareholders when they have lower cash-flow rights.[7] Bertrand et al. (2002) provide evidence of expropriation of outsiders by controlling owners of business groups in India. Douma et al. (2006) also provide evidence of unique agency problems arising from principal–principal goal incongruence in group-affiliated firms in India. Another potential cause of expropriation is the existence of (or greater degrees of) information asymmetry between controlling shareholders and outsiders.[8] Francis, Schipper, and Vincent (2005) associate information asymmetry with lower transparency of accounting information. Furthermore, Fan and Wong (2002) present that concentrated ownership adversely affects the accounting information flow to outsiders. A higher level of family ownership will result in lower levels of public equity and, thus, lesser need to disclose financial information publically and vice versa.

Alignment effect: The competing argument is that concentrated ownership creates greater monitoring by controlling shareholders (Shleifer and Vishny, 1997) because of their long-term approach. The interests of the controlling shareholders are well aligned with the interests of the firms and they have increased incentive to manage the firm effectively because this increases their wealth too. This effect suggests higher relative value for firms with concentrated ownership. Controlling owners provide high-quality accounting information to preserve the family name and long-term firm performance. On the contrary,

---

[6] Starting with Fama and Jensen (1983a), it has been argued that controlling managers are more likely to pursue actions that deviate from the interests of residual claimants. Morck, Shleifer, and Vishny (1988) and Shleifer and Vishny (1997) present similar arguments.

[7] Jensen and Meckling (1976) show that controlling shareholders bear only a fraction of the cost of their controlling decisions.

[8] The entrenchment effect and the information effect have been considered complementary by Fan and Wong (2002), as both exaggerate the agency problem. Wang (2006) includes information asymmetry in the entrenchment effect.

managers of firms with diffused ownership may have a short-term focus and they may act in their own interest, rather than in those of the firm. Khanna and Palepu (2000b) provide evidence of superior performance of group-affiliated firms in relation non-group firms in India.

Agency cost Type 2

While concentrated ownership results in stronger incentives to manage the firm effectively, it offers opportunities to expropriate minority shareholders. The existing literature provides support for the entrenchment hypothesis, in that concentrated ownership results in value loss (McConnell and Servaes, 1990; Morck et al., 1988). The notion of self-interest implies that the natural tendency of the controlling group is to allocate firm resources in their own interest, which creates conflict with outside shareholders. The existence of divergence between cash-flow and control rights provides opportunities and the means for expropriation of minority shareholders (Claessens et al., 2000). Furthermore, the institutional setting makes the enforcement of agency contracts more problematic and costly in emerging economies (Wright et al. 2005). Insider ownership combined with ineffective external control mechanisms results in more frequent conflicts between controlling and minority shareholders (Morck, Wolfenzon, and Yeung, 2004). Therefore, the principal–principal conflict has become a common trait in emerging economies. For example, Bertrand et al. (2002) explore this issue in India; Claessens et al. (1999) explore this issue in East Asian countries including Thailand, Indonesia, Taiwan, Singapore, and Japan; and Cheung et al., (2009) provide evidence of conflicts in China between the two group of shareholders (controlling and minority).

Group-affiliated firms in India are likely to be subject to higher agency cost Type 2 for the following reasons. Indirect ownership is very common amongst group-affiliated firms in India and corporate control is maintained by founding families either through direct or indirect ownership or both. Indirect rights, by their very nature, are smaller than direct rights because they are diminished as they pass through the chain of ownership (Bertrand et al., 2002). The higher the proportion of indirect rights, the higher the separation between cash flow and control rights. The higher the separation between cash flow and control rights, the greater the incentives for controlling shareholders to extract firm resources and vice versa. Douma et al. (2006) report that the positive influence attributed to corporate ownership (indirect ownership) is reduced in the case of group-affiliated firms, which provides evidence consistent with the use of indirect ownership as a vehicle by controlling families to extract private benefits.

Furthermore, regulation pertaining to minority shareholder protection in India is inadequate and ineffective. La Porta et al. (1998) report that the risk of expropriation is significantly higher in India in relation to developed countries (that is, the UK, USA, and Canada). They also rank India lower in accounting standards. Dutta (1997) and OECD (2012) also highlight that the regulation in India presents weak protection to minority shareholders and that the legal system is prone to corruption. As a consequence, controlling shareholders are more likely to pursue their personal goals and considerable shareholder value is lost as a result of value-reducing activities.

Family firms characterized by concentrated ownership suffer from two major problems: (*a*) self-control and (*b*) ineffective external control mechanisms, which adversely impact on business performance. The next section explains how family dynamics, and specifically altruism, exacerbate agency problems in family-controlled firms.

Self-control

The problem associated with economists' notion of altruism is profound in family firms. This trait positively links the welfare of an individual with others (Becker, 1981; Bergstrom, 1995). Parents' generosity, for example, is not only a result of their love but also an act of protecting their own welfare (Becker, 1981). Altruism lends family firms history, loyalty, and commitment to the firms' long-term prosperity (Gersick, 1997; Ward, 2011). However, altruism can cause parents to threaten their children with moral hazard (Buchanan, 1997). For example, because of a parent's desire to enhance their own welfare, their increased generosity may cause their children or family members to free-ride. The existing literature provides evidence of benefits provided to family members in the form of secure employment and other perquisites and privileges, which they might not be entitled to receive otherwise (Gersick, 1997; Kets de Vries, 1996). Therefore, family members will have incentives to free-ride and parents (founder-managers) will have difficulty monitoring and disciplining their actions, which involves costs to the firm and outside shareholders.

Effectiveness of external control mechanism

The self-control problem existing in family firms also undermines the effectiveness of outside non-executive directors. In spite of the obvious advantages of outside directors in the form of expertise, monitoring skills, and diversity, family firms are less likely to use them for the following reasons (Schulze et al., 2001). First, they pose a challenge to family owners in terms of perceived loss of control. Second, while the independent status of these directors enhances their ability to provide advice on some matters, they have little influence on matters involving family members (Nelson and Frishkoff, 1991). Third, 'handpicking' independent directors for reasons other than effective supervision of the management can undermine their value (Rubenson and Gupta, 1996). For example, the tendency of controlling families to appoint outside members to their company board who are friends or have a fiduciary relationship with them (their accountant or board member from another firm of the family group) compromises true independence. Third, outsiders rarely attain the status of blockholder in family firms, which they sometimes do in widely held firms (Alderfer, 1988). Therefore, they are likely to be less motivated than family members. The arguments presented above suggest that family firms are less likely to use formal monitoring and control mechanisms than their widely held counterparts.

Family firms face an increased threat of adverse selection caused by the influence of concentrated ownership on the efficiency of their labour markets (Schulze et al., 2001). The terms of the employment contract systematically attract individuals who best match the requirements (Besanko, Dranove, and Shanley, 1996). For instance, higher-salary jobs attract more competent workers, while performance-based compensation plans attract risk-taking individuals. Family firms cannot offer prospective employees similar terms of employment as non-family firms. For instance, while widely held firms may offer stock options to managers to align their interests, controlling shareholders of family-held firms are less likely to dilute their control of the firm by issuing such options (Lew and Kolodzeii, 1993; Morck, 1996).

These inefficiencies have the following important implications for the cost of governing family-controlled firms. Widely held public firms promise talented employees promotional opportunities because key management positions are allocated on the basis of willingness to bear risk- and decision-making skills (Fama and Jensen, 1983a). On the contrary, these key positions are often held by controlling shareholders in family firms (La Porta et al., 1999), which discourages high-quality managers from accepting positions in family firms. Furthermore, the appointment of capable employees may not necessarily result in better outcomes due to the constant influence of controlling shareholders on the management. This poses the risk that these firms will inadvertently recruit poorer-quality managers because of the limited quality and size of the labour pool which serves them. Second, whereas widely held public firms offer stock options to talented employees to assure them that the firm will not take advantage of them (Rajan and Zingales, 1998), the reluctance of family firms to dilute ownership limits their ability to post equally effective bonds. Third, concentrated ownership increases monitoring cost. Limited opportunities for promotion and ineffective bonding arrangements reduce these agents' incentive to monitor each other's behaviour and to compete against each other (Besanko et al., 1996; Fama and Jensen, 1983a).

Literature review

This section reviews the relevant literature on business groups. The existing literature in economics and finance on business groups focuses on two issues: the first body of literature investigates the performance of business groups and the second body of literature examines the conflict of interest between controlling and minority shareholders, which is the focus of our study. In the first section, we review literature on the performance, market valuation, and investment behaviour of business groups. Since most of the business groups in India are family controlled, we review literature on family firms in the second section. In the third section, we review literature on the effect of the separation between cash flow and control rights on firm value. This is followed by a literature review on RPTs.

Business groups

This section is divided into three sub-sections. First, we review literature on firm performance of group-affiliated firms. As groups are often diversified, we analyse the market valuation of diversification in the next section. Finally, we review literature on the investment behaviour of group-affiliated firms and highlight the potential for tunnelling and propping among group firms mainly through RPTs.

Business groups and firm performance

The existing literature perceives business groups as a response to transaction costs (Caves, 1989; Khanna and Palepu, 1997) and market imperfections (Hoshi et al., 1991; Khanna and Palepu, 2000b; Lincoln, Gerlach, and Ahmadjian, 1996). In emerging markets, the business transaction which is economically beneficial to both buyer and seller fails to be consummated because the indirect costs outweigh the benefits of the business transaction (Williamson, 1975). Khanna and Palepu (1997) suggest that emerging markets have weak institutions for trade, weak contract enforcement, and weak disclosure requirements, which result in costly transactions. A group can overcome such problems with the help of internal transactions, that is, transferring capital within the group (Khanna and Rivkin, 2001). The group structure not only overcome capital market failure but also labour, product, and technology imperfections. For example, the Tata group recruits top managers in a concerted fashion and rotates them where needed (Khanna and Palepu, 1997). Amsden and Hikino (1994) highlight the role of business groups in assimilating foreign technology in emerging economies.

Group firms also benefit from political connections in weak economies. Prior studies have provided evidence of the superior performance of group-affiliated firms. For example, Khanna and Rivkin (2001) investigate the effect of business groups on the performance of affiliated firms. They collect data from 14 emerging economies: Argentina, Brazil, Chile, India, Indonesia, Israel, Mexico, Peru, Philippines, South Africa, South Korea, Taiwan, Thailand, and Turkey. Group membership generates benefits in terms of easy access to labour, capital, and product markets, but it also imposes costs in the forms of an obligation to bailout weak firms and inefficient trade between sibling firms. Therefore, it is an empirical question whether the benefits outweigh the costs. They report that group firms perform better than non-group firms in six countries, including India, and worse in three countries, and that there is no significant difference between group-firm and non-group firm performance in the remaining five countries. They further examine if the performance of member firms is consistent with each other, and the results support this hypothesis in 12 out of 14 countries. This suggests that the knowledge of group affiliation is more valuable than industry affiliation as performance matches more closely across member firms than with firms across their industry.

Another study which compares the performance of group-affiliated firms with stand-alone firms in India is Khanna and Palepu (2000b). Using Tobin's Q and Return on Assets (ROA), Khanna and Palepu (2000b) initially find no significant difference between the performance of group-affiliated and unaffiliated firms; however, performance is found to differ between group and non-group firms when they divide groups into diversification categories. The moderately diversified business groups have lower profitability than stand-alone firms, but the most diversified groups are significantly more profitable than stand-alone firms. This suggests that the performance of business groups initially decreases with diversification but then, after a certain threshold, subsequent increases in diversification result in higher profitability. Khanna and Palepu (2000b) further reveal potential sources of costs and benefits associated with group affiliation in India. Affiliated firms issue more global depositary receipts (GDR), and financial analysts following is also higher for affiliated firms in comparison to unaffiliated firms.

In terms of ownership structure, foreign institutional ownership is positively, and domestic institutional ownership is negatively associated with firm performance. Moreover, insider ownership is positively associated with firm performance and this is valid for both affiliated and unaffiliated firms. They find no difference in investment cash-flow sensitivities across affiliated and unaffiliated firms, which rules out the possibility of internal capital market motives for business-group creation. Khanna and Palepu (2000b) examine firm performance for the year 1993 only and, therefore, caution is required in generalizing their findings. The proxies used to measure firm performance are also questioned in the literature. For instance, ROA suffers from business cycle effects (Benston, 1985) and Tobin's Q makes the problematic assumption that stock prices correctly reflect the benefits and costs associated with diversification. This assumption appears to be questionable considering inefficient capital markets and a weak enforcement system in India.

The group affiliation structure might prove beneficial because of several reasons. Like any other emerging market, the Indian market is characterized by inadequate disclosures, weak corporate governance, problematic enforcement of securities legislation, and less involvement by intermediaries such as financial analysts, mutual funds, and investment bankers. The imperfections mentioned above make it costly for business firms to acquire capital, labour, and other required inputs. Diversified business groups tend to overcome these market imperfections and, thus, business firms might benefit from being part of business groups that act as an intermediary between business firms and imperfect markets. Yet group affiliation may also impose costs on the firm. The conflict of interest between controlling and minority shareholders often results in expropriation of minority shareholders, and the firm interests are ignored in deference to group interests. These business groups, which are normally managed by family members, can also make suboptimal decisions because of their family ties. Perez-Gonzalez (2006) emphasizes that it might be hard for a family CEO to break pre-existing implicit contracts with related stakeholders such as local associations or employees. Conversely, a professional

CEO will not have the pressure to follow an existing approach or tradition of honouring implicit contracts. This suggests that the impact of group affiliation on firm performance is an empirical question.

A significant amount of the literature documents the fact that diversified conglomerates underperform compared with non-diversified counterparts in the US because of inappropriate decision rights, inefficient allocation of capital, and poor internal corporate governance (Hoskisson and Hitt, 1990; Ramanujam and Varadarajan, 1989; Shin and Stulz, 1998). Berger and Ofek (1995) report a 13 to 15 per cent value loss as a result of diversification during the period from 1986 to 1991. They also examine the possible causes of value loss of diversified firms and they find that over investment and cross-subsidization lead to value losses.

Indian business groups, which are generally characterized by family businesses, are quite different from the US conglomerates and Japanese *keiretsu*. Japanese groups are bank-focused, which is not the case with Indian groups. The findings which associate diversification with underperformance in the US may not be appropriate for Indian group companies because of the different institutional environment in which they operate. Khanna and Palepu (2000b) assert that the largest groups in India are more diversified than the largest groups in the US.

Diversification and market valuation

Corporate diversification, especially into unrelated activities, is seen as destruction of shareholder wealth and, therefore, is valued at a discount by the market. However, a diversified business structure may overcome the imperfections of emerging markets, and the potential benefits of diversified business groups were outlined in the last section. Fauver, Houston, and Naranjo (2003) report that the diversification discount is a feature of developed countries and there is no market discount in low-income countries. Similarly, Claessens et al. (2003) find a diversification discount in richer countries and the existence of a diversification premium in relatively poor countries of East Asia. The excess value of groups tends to decline with the degree of development of the market. Khanna and Palepu (2000a) report a decline in the group premium of Chilean firms over a decade associated with economic reforms. Similarly, Lee, Peng, and Lee (2008) shows a diversification premium until the early 1990s for firms affiliated with Korean *chaebols*, which turned into a discount later in the decade. This phenomenon also appears to be valid in the US context. De

Long (1991) observes that firms affiliated with the J. P. Morgan group traded at a premium in the early decades of the twentieth century, whereas recent studies like Berger and Ofek (1995) associate diversification with value loss.

Lins and Servaes (2002) examine the cost and benefits associated with diversification in emerging markets. Corporate diversification is found to be value enhancing in emerging markets, where the operation of internal markets overcomes the imperfections of external markets.[9] In emerging markets, information asymmetry increases the cost of external capital relative to internal capital, which makes internal funds more attractive. Diversification allows firms or divisions with high cash flows, but poor investment opportunities, to transfer funds to firms or divisions with low cash flows, but good investment opportunities. However, the empirical evidence in the US context suggests that funds may flow in the opposite direction.[10] The misallocation of resources is also reported in emerging nations. La Porta et al. (2003) report that funds are misallocated in diversified business groups, as younger and fast-growing firms do not benefit from internal capital market operation. This phenomenon is considered to be tunnelling and expropriation of minority shareholders (Claessens et al., 2006 and Gopalan et al., 2007).

Lins and Servaes (2002) examine if the cost associated with diversification outweigh the benefits for firms from Hong Kong, India, Indonesia, Malaysia, Singapore, South Korea, and Thailand. They find that diversified firms trade at a significant discount to single-segment firms. They also examine the reasons for the valuation discount for diversified firms. First, diversified firms are found to be less profitable than single-segment firms. Second, the diversification discount is more substantial for group firms, which suggests that business group structure allows controlling shareholders to expropriate minority shareholders. Third, the diversification discount is severe when insiders have substantial control and when their control rights exceed their cash-flow rights. Overall, the results suggest that the diversification discount is related to the ability of controlling shareholders to expropriate the wealth of minority shareholders.

Kali and Sarkar (2011) argue that a diversified corporate structure facilitates expropriation of minority shareholders. They conduct two sets of analyses

---

[9] Khanna and Palepu (2000b) and Khanna and Palepu (1997) provide evidence on the benefits of diversification.

[10] Rajan, Servaes, and Zingales (2000) and Shin and Stulz (1998) report that divisions with excellent investment opportunities transfer funds to divisions with poor investment opportunities.

to test this empirical question. First, they link group diversification with incentives to tunnel. The separation between ownership and control rights and ownership opacity are the two proxies used to measure tunnelling incentives. Consistent with the hypothesis, they find that firms with a lower wedge between cash flow and control rights than the core firm, as the one with the largest asset base in a group, are more likely to operate in unrelated activities, so the funds can be transferred away from the core business. Second, they test the existence of tunnelling with the help of the sensitivity model proposed by Bertrand et al. (2002). They examine the sensitivity of a firm to its own industry shocks and shocks affecting other member firms in the group. The results confirm that firms with a lower wedge between cash flow and control rights are more sensitive to its own industry shocks, suggesting inflow of tunnelled resources in addition to the effect of industry shocks. Affiliated firms are found to be more sensitive to shocks affecting firms with a higher wedge than lower-wedge firms.

Investment behaviour

Another body of literature compares the investment behaviour of group-affiliated firms with individual firms and examine if group-affiliated firms are less capital constrained than stand-alone firms. Using RP loans and investments provides access to internal funds. Furthermore, group-affiliated firms may have better access to external funds for the following reasons:

- Business groups develop an internal capital market to overcome information asymmetries (Kali and Sarkar, 2005) and group firms obtain funding from other member firms within the same group (Lensink et al., 2003). The funding by other member firms may provide a positive signal about the firm's prospects and, thus, banks and other financial institutions might also invest.
- Group-affiliated firms get involved in cross-holdings of equity, inter-firm loans, and debt-guarantees. These relationships between group-affiliated firms might prove effective in risk sharing and mitigating moral hazard problems (Berglöf and Perotti, 1994) and, consequently, banks might be more willing to lend to group firms.
- Group firms might enjoy a better reputation in the market because of their long-term operating and investment focus. Most Indian business groups are family businesses and reputation might be of great importance to them. Group firms are less likely to indulge in

any irregularities so as to maintain their reputation, and consequently would be advantaged in accessing external funds.

- When corruption is widespread in government-owned financial institutions (Dutta, 1997), business groups are in a better position to take advantage of external funding from government-owned financial institutions because of their strong political connections and better access to bureaucracy.

Lensink et al. (2003) examine the effect of group affiliation on corporate investment behaviour in the Indian context. They report that member firms hold a significant share of group affiliates' equity, which suggests that group affiliation plays an important role in funding each other's projects. Lensink et al. (2003) find that group affiliates have lower cash-flow sensitivities than stand-alone firms and the results remain unchanged after testing several models. As cash-flow sensitivity is a measure of financing constraints, lower cash-flow sensitivity suggests that group-affiliated firms have better access to external funds than their stand-alone counterparts. However, they did not attempt to find the cause of the difference.

The question of whether group firms' better access to external funds is caused by the superior access to financial institutions or the existence of an internal capital market remains unaddressed. The better access of group firms to external funds might also be a result of their strong political connections and access to the bureaucracy of the government-owned banks. Dutta (1997) reports that corruption is widespread in government-owned Indian banks and other financial institutions, and apparently large business groups are in a better position to take advantage of it. Business groups have been closely associated with the government over a long period of time. The evidence suggests that political connections played an important role in the rise of business groups. For instance, Hindalco and Telco collaborated with the government to develop the aviation sector in India. Khanna and Rivkin (2001) suggest that Indian business groups had industrial embassies in Delhi to coordinate lobbying activities.

Eastwood and Kohli (1999) examine if small-scale firms face different financing constraints from large firms. They report that small firms are more financially constrained than large firms. Furthermore, they study the impact of government policies introduced to increase bank credit to small firms. These policies relaxed the financing constraints faced by small firms. Another study which examined if financing constraints are different for large firms compared to small firms is Athey and Laumas (1994). They use data for the period from 1978 to 1986 and find that internal funds are a comparatively more important determinant of investment spending for large firms. They show that small firms are less financially constrained, which is inconsistent with Eastwood and Kohli (1999). The different findings could be a result of the different timeframe used in both studies.

Athey and Reeser (2000) divided their sample firms into small firms, large firms with limited access to capital markets, and large firms with easy access to capital markets. Large firms with easy access to capital markets include firms belonging to the top three business groups (Tata, Birla, and Mafatlal). They find that internal funds form an insignificant portion of total funds borrowed for small and large firms with easy access to capital markets, which proves that small and large firms with easy access to capital markets face less financial constraints. It is important to note that firms belonging to the top three business groups face lower or fewer finance constraints in general.

A number of studies on developed nations concentrated on the investment sensitivity of business groups. The most prominent study on Japanese groups is Hoshi et al. (1991), who reported that *keiretsu* firms are less sensitive to fluctuations in their internal funds in comparison withstand-alone firms. Fewer financing constraints for group firms are expected to be a result of their strong relationships with a major bank. Perotti and Gelfer (2001) report consistent results for Russian industrial groups, thus suggesting the existence of an internal capital market. Shin and Park (1999) examine the investment decisions of Korean *chaebols*. They report that group firms' investments are independent of internal funds availability, whereas stand-alone firms are sensitive to internal funds. They find evidence of internal capital markets in group firms, which makes their investment decisions independent of internal funds.

La Porta et al. (2003) investigate the incentives for insiders to divert cash for their personal benefits through related lending. Consistent with the entrenchment effect, the borrowing terms offered to related parties were significantly better than those for unrelated parties. The interest rates on related loans are found to be considerably lower than loans to unrelated parties. Furthermore, related loans are found to be less likely to be backed by collateral and, as a result, related loans had lower recovery rates and higher default rates than unrelated loans. The worst-performing loans are found to be made to entities more closely associated with controlling shareholders. These findings suggest that controlling shareholders use their control to extract firm resources and benefit at the cost of minority shareholders.

Claessens et al. (2006) examine the benefits and costs associated with internal capital markets among group-affiliated firms of East Asia. Prior literature highlights the role of internal markets in reducing transaction costs, especially in underdeveloped markets. In particular, the existence of an internal capital market overcomes the imperfections of the external financial market and provides capital to financially constrained firms (Stein, 1997). On the other hand, misallocation of resources in diversified business groups might arise from agency conflicts (Rajan et al., 2000 and Scharfstein and Stein, 2000). This implies that the benefits of internal markets might be greater in less developed markets, whereas the associated cost might also be higher because of complex ownership structures (cross-holding) and weak institutions. They use the divergence between cash flow and control rights to measure the agency conflict between controlling and minority shareholders, as the controlling shareholders may channel firm resources to projects that benefit them and provide little or no benefit to minority shareholders. The results show higher valuation for older and slow-growing, group-affiliated firms when the divergence between cash flow and control rights is smaller. As firm age and growth are found to be positively associated with firm value for group-affiliated firms, younger and fast-growing firms do not benefit from group operation of an internal capital market. In contrast, financially constrained firms, proxied by interest coverage and dividend pay-out ratio, benefit from group affiliation. The results suggest that funds are misallocated among group firms, as mature, low-growth, and financially distressed firms are subsidized at the cost of other member firms (young and fast-growing). The results are even more significant when divergence between cash flow and control rights is more than 10 per cent.

The studies presented above suggest that there are fewer financing constraints for group firms, which might be a result of financial inter-linkages between member firms. It appears that an internal capital market tends to overcome the inefficiencies of the external market by funding member firms and benefiting the group as a whole. However, the personal interests of individual firms might be ignored and some firms might be benefitted at the cost of others. Studies like Khanna and Palepu (2000b) and Lensink et al. (2003) highlight the role of group-internal capital markets in improving firms' access to finance. On the other hand, Friedman, Johnson, and Mitton (2003) and La Porta et al. (2003) argue that group loans facilitate tunnelling of funds from minority shareholders. For example, Gopalan et al. (2007) report that the interest rate on group loans in India is 10 per cent lower than the market rate. It appears that the group loans involve a cost for firms which provide loans, and this might be a way for controlling shareholders to expropriate minority shareholders. The evidence also suggests that controlling shareholders transfer private resources to firms in financial difficulty.[11] For instance, the firm experiencing financial difficulty might be propped up with group loans at favourable terms to avoid bankruptcy. This signifies the effect of internal loans on firm value, as group loans have the potential to extract resources from one firm and prop into the other.

Friedman et al. (2003) suggest that the possibility of propping makes issuing debt more attractive when the legal system is weak. They argue that controlling shareholders prop up firms to avoid defaulting on existing debts. Burkart et al. (2003) outline incentives for controlling shareholders to maintain their control and avoid bankruptcy. The foremost incentive for controlling shareholders to inject funds is to preserve their options to expropriate in the future. In the Indian context, preserving a family reputation might be another incentive for controlling shareholders to prop up a weak firm. Friedman et al. (2003) hypothesize that tunnelling and propping are symmetric behaviours and, therefore, a pyramid structure should also facilitate propping. They find that during the Asian financial crisis of 1997–1998, firms with more debt suffered larger declines in stock price and this outcome was significantly greater for non-pyramid firms. This is consistent with the market expecting firms controlled through cross-holding and pyramid structures to be propped up during periods of financial distress. The finding above suggests some relationship between external funds and propping behaviour in firms controlled through cross-holdings and pyramids.

The group firms might have better access to funds from internal or external markets, but there is the possibility that one class of investors (controlling shareholders) benefits at the expense of others (minority shareholders). The internal market tends to impose costs on the minority shareholders of lending firms, as group loans are often issued on favourable terms. If the group firms have better access to external markets, one of the main motivations for external lenders to provide funds to group firms is the image of group firms as a more secure investment. Group firms are much less likely to default and the literature suggests that they are propped up by member firms in financial distress (Friedman et al., 2003). This process imposes costs on the minority shareholders of firms which prop up other financially distressed member firms.

Studies that looked at the international context reveal the inefficiency of internal capital markets. Shin and Park (1999) find that operations of an

---

[11] See, Friedman et al. (2003) and Hoshi et al. (1991) for evidence on propping.

internal capital market within the Korean *chaebol* are inefficient. *Chaebol* firms are found to invest more than non-*chaebol* firms despite their poor growth opportunities, which suggest value loss for *chaebol* firms. This finding is consistent with that of Kook et al. (1997), who showed that *chaebols* follow a group-oriented approach and firms' interests at the individual level might be compromised.

Family firms

As group-affiliated firms are often controlled and managed by founding families, it is important to review the literature on family control.

Starting from Jensen and Meckling (1976), studies show that controlling owners not only extract pecuniary private benefits but also derive non-pecuniary benefits. Pecuniary benefits are referred to as tunnelling in the literature. Non-pecuniary benefits are not limited to, but include, charitable contributions to establish social reputation, business transactions with friends, personal relationships such as friendship and respect with employees. Demsetz and Lehn (1985) named such benefits as 'amenity potential'. A recent definition by Coffee Jr (2002) clarified that private benefits of controlling shareholders include all those benefits which are not shared with other shareholders.

The controlling families of Indian business groups, which started as family businesses, tend to have the incentives (amenity potential, family reputation, and expropriation of outsiders) to maintain their control over the relevant entities. Amenity potential refers to non-pecuniary benefits of control, in the form of pleasure, derived by the founding family from running the company which bears their family name. It may also be in the form of power to influence social or political arrangements. Amenity potential and family reputation are likely to play a significant role in Indian society where people are always conscious of their status relative to other people. For example, the leading business group Tata has established numerous sports and cultural institutes such as Tata Cricket Academy, Tata Football Academy, and the National Centre for Performing Arts. Establishing such institutions aims at influencing social arrangements and improving family reputation.[12] The controlling shareholders might even indulge in value-destroying activities to influence social and political arrangements. The controlling owners make constant efforts

---

[12] Ehrhardt and Nowak (2003) report that amenity potential motivates founding-families around the world to retain control of their businesses.

to stay close to the government, which might also involve costs for outside shareholders. For example, the Tata group maintained close relations with the former government of West Bengal to acquire land for their new project to manufacture the Nano car. However, the newly elected government reversed the land expropriation programme due to concerns regarding expropriation of valuable agricultural land by Tata. Firm resources might be misused to establish connections in the political environment. Tata group and many other firms were accused of providing bribes to the former telecommunication minister, Mr A. Raja, to obtain preferential benefits in the license allotment. This was later revealed in the 2G spectrum scam. The appointment of family members on the board to maintain family control might further hurt firm performance and, again, result in value loss for outside investors. Consistent with the findings of Perez-Gonzalez (2006), family board members are less likely to break implicit contracts with local associations and employees, which might be a cost for the firm.

Ehrhardt and Nowak (2003) investigate the nature of private benefits of control among family-controlled German firms. They find substantial evidence of private benefits of control, and the nature of private benefits not only is limited to pecuniary benefits but also includes non-pecuniary benefits. The enjoyment through association with luxury brands and the reputation benefits are found to be prominent reasons to maintain control of firms. They argue that any private benefits, pecuniary or non-pecuniary, which are not shared with minority shareholders prove to deviate controlling shareholders from the maximization of firm value. They also identify the use of dual-class shares to retain family control in order to preserve such private benefits. The market appears to be aware of such value-destroying arrangements and, therefore, significant underperformance is found for firms with dual-class shares.

Perez-Gonzalez (2006) investigates whether inherited control in family firms hurts firm performance. He examines 162 CEO successions in the US to establish any link between family successions and firm performance and reports that family heirs hurt firm performance. This happens because the inheriting CEOs lack the ability and motivation on the part of inheriting CEOs. The educational background also helps to explain the underperformance of CEOs, particularly those who failed to attend selective institutions, compared to more highly educated peers. The cost of underperformance of the firm is likely to be borne by outside investors.

Family successions might not be in the best interest of the firm because of the following reasons:

- Limited quality to choose from: the heirs of the family may lack the adequate skills and expertise to manage the firm, and choosing a family heir means potentially forgoing a higher quality match. This leaves the firm with a limited quality of people to choose from. According to Warren Buffet's analogy, family successions are like 'choosing the 2020 Olympic team by picking the eldest sons of the gold-medal winners of the 2000 Olympics'.
- Continuation of existing arrangements: it might be hard for a family CEO to break pre-existing implicit contracts with related stakeholders like local associations or employees. Conversely, a professional CEO will not have the pressure to follow the existing approach or the tradition of honouring implicit contracts.
- Monitoring intensity: unrelated CEOs will be subject to severe scrutiny and monitoring by the founding family, but a family CEO may use firm resources for personal needs because of less or no monitoring.

Burkart et al. (2003) examine the crucial issue of succession in family firms. They present three incentives for families to maintain their control: amenity potential, family reputation, and expropriation of outside investors. Jensen and Meckling (1976) describes that family shareholders get these private benefits at the expense of outside investors. They highlight three options for a founder to retire in the absence of an outright buyer: sell out the shares in the stock market, hire a professional, or pass control to a family member. This study concludes that the decision to sell off the entire ownership or hire a professional manager depends upon the legal protection of minority shareholders. The level of expropriation of minority shareholders is determined by legal protection and monitoring. Since family owners own the majority of shares, minority shareholders do not have incentives to monitor actively because of the additional cost involved. In this context, monitoring is costly whereas reliance on law is free. Therefore, it leaves only legal protection as a controlling measure. Strong shareholder protection makes it costly for family shareholders to expropriate the wealth of outside investors and, therefore, the best possible solution for the founder is to hire a professional manager or sell off the ownership stake in the stock market. Morck et al. (2004) argue that family-controlled groups in countries with weak investor protection impose the threat of expropriation of minority shareholders. Similarly, La Porta et al. (1999) and Claessens et al. (2000) explain why family firms are such an enduring phenomenon in nations with weak legal protection of investors. Increased reliance on law makes it important to put stricter rules and disclosure requirements in place. This finding implies that firms with significant needs for outside financing would benefit from legal reform, but family firms would generally oppose it because it limits their capacity to expropriate the wealth of outsiders.

The moral hazard conflict between controlling and minority shareholders might also affect firm diversification and financing decisions. Shleifer and Vishny (1986) suggest that controlling shareholders can impose costs on the firm. First, families can diversify the firm's operations to reduce the firm risk. Second, families may prefer equity financing to reduce the probability of default. These risk aversion strategies may impose costs on the firms or minority shareholders. However, Anderson, Mansi, and Reeb (2003) report that family ownership does not have any significant effect on financing and diversification decisions.

The presence of controlling shareholders not only makes family firms unique in regard to the conflict of interest between the shareholders (controlling and minority), these firms are also distinct when it comes to conflicts between shareholders and debtholders. Diversified shareholders have incentives to expropriate the wealth of debtholders by investing in risky projects (Jensen and Meckling, 1976). As a result, debtholders impose covenants and monitoring devices to protect themselves from risk shifting. However, this behaviour of shifting risk to debtholders cannot be monitored completely with the help of debt covenants and other monitoring devices. For instance, the attempts to restrict investments into negative NPV projects are difficult to enforce, as these investment decisions involve personal judgment. Debtholders, anticipating such incentives, demand higher return compensation which leads to a higher cost of debt.

Undiversified firms have strong incentives to mitigate agency conflicts with bondholders. Founding family shareholders are more likely to choose a long term firm strategy, as they face family reputation concerns. Thus, firm survival is an important concern for families, which implies that they are more likely to maximize firm value. They are less likely to indulge in expropriation of bondholders' wealth because of their long-term survival approach and the family reputation that is at stake. If families seek to maintain a good reputation, we expect the cost of debt to be lower for founding family firms.

Anderson, Mansi, and Reeb . (2003) examine the effect of equity ownership on the agency cost of debt. They find that family firms experience a lower cost of debt in comparison to non-family firms. However, the greater family ownership leads to an incremental increase in debt costs, but family firms still enjoy lower costs of debt than non-family firms. Furthermore, they report that firms with family CEOs are associated with higher costs of debt in comparison to outside CEO firms. This finding is consistent with the notion that family CEOs get positions through family ties rather than job qualifications, and this leads to a higher agency cost of debt.

Gomez-Mejia, Larraza-Kintana, and Makri (2003) examine the compensation of CEOs of 253 family-controlled public firms over a four year period (1995–1998). They find that CEOs with family ties receive significantly lower compensation than professional executives. This is consistent with the notion that a family CEO is emotionally attached to the firm and, consequently, more likely to accept a lower remuneration package. Family CEOs are unlikely to compete in the external labour market. Furthermore, the greater family ownership concentration further decreases the compensation of family CEOs. However, family member CEOs are protected from bearing excessive personal risk when systematic business risk increases. Amenity potential or expropriation of minority shareholders might also be incentives for family CEOs to accept lower compensation. A key management position being held by a family member might facilitate the expropriation of outsiders or non-pecuniary benefits of control and, thus, compensation might not be the primary concern for family CEOs.

It is evident from the arguments presented above that controlling shareholders of family firms might adversely affect a firm's performance. The appointment of family members to management positions, irrespective of their skills and expertise, and less or no monitoring of family members, tends to impose costs on minority shareholders. However, the long-term approach and commitment of family members is likely to benefit the firm. Similarly, the lower compensation of family CEOs and the lower cost of debt for family firms should aid in maximizing firm value. Therefore, it is an empirical question to examine the effect of family ownership on firm value.

Ownership and firm value

Starting with Fama and Jensen (1983b) and Shleifer and Vishny (1997), several studies provide evidence of entrenchment effects of controlling shareholders. The separation between cash flow and control rights is critical in understanding the incentives for controlling shareholders to expropriate outside investors. The conflict between controlling shareholders and minority shareholders is likely to be more prominent than the conflict between a diversified spread of owners and management in the Asian context (La Porta et al., 1999). Conflict between investors, together with inadequate regulation in emerging countries, generates an environment best suited for extraction of firm resources. Claessens et al. (2002), Lemmon and Lins (2003), Lins (2003), Joh (2003), and Bertrand et al. (2002) provide evidence of expropriation of minority shareholders when controlling shareholders have lower cash-flow rights and higher control rights.

Claessens et al. (2002) examine the positive incentive effect of cash-flow rights and the negative entrenchment effect of controlling rights held by large shareholders on firm value. They investigate in East Asia, where corporations are generally controlled by promoter families. They find that firm value, measured by the market-to-book ratio of assets, increases with the share of cash-flow rights held by the largest shareholder. They also report that firm value decreases when the control rights of the largest shareholder exceed its cash-flow rights. Upon investigating ownership types, the results appear to be driven by family firms. Claessens et al. (2002) provide evidence consistent with the entrenchment effect that controlling shareholders are more likely to expropriate the wealth of minority shareholders, especially when they have lower cash-flow rights, which consequently results in lower firm valuation.

Joh (2003) examines the performance of South Korean firms before the economic crisis. He investigates whether controlling shareholders with more control rights than cash-flow rights expropriate firm resources before the crisis. Consistent with the hypothesis, the results reveal that a firm's profitability is less when the controlling rights exceed cash-flow rights, which suggests a greater incentive for controlling shareholders to expropriate. Similarly, firm profitability declines when the divergence between control and cash-flow rights is higher. Furthermore, the level of financial investment in affiliated firms is negatively associated with firm performance, suggesting resources are being allocated ineffectively among group firms. The results indicate the adverse effects of ownership concentration on the financial health of firms, and it has been suggested that this has helped cause the economic crisis.

Bertrand et al. (2002) measure the extent of tunnelling activities amongst Indian business groups. They argue that family members control several independent member firms[13] and this raises fears of expropriation of minority

---

[13] Khanna and Palepu (2000b) assert that business groups in India are family owned and controlled by family members through board memberships, recruiting top management and coordinated actions among member firms.

shareholders.[14] The controlling shareholders have greater incentives to expropriate the wealth of shareholders when they have lower cash-flow rights. The existing literature provides evidence of higher q-ratios and superior performance of group firms where the controlling shareholders have higher cash-flow rights.[15] The poorer performance of firms where controlling shareholders have lower cash-flow rights may result from tunnelling activities. Therefore, they focus on the movement of resources from firms where controlling shareholders have low cash-flow rights to firms where they have high cash-flow rights. The resources can be tunnelled from one firm to the other by group loans, transfer pricing, asset acquisitions, and so on. This study examines the sensitivity of earnings to profit shocks through a business group in order to quantify tunnelling. The cash-flow rights of controlling shareholders include direct rights and indirect rights. The two proxies used to measure direct rights are director ownership and other shareholder ownership. As Indian families control the firms by board membership and voting control, director ownership serves as the proxy for direct cash-flow rights of controlling shareholders. The equity held by other shareholders determines minority shareholders and also captures the cash-flow rights which controlling shareholders do not have. Consistent with the hypothesis, they find that fewer resources are tunnelled out of the group firms where the controlling shareholders have higher cash-flow rights and fewer minority shareholders to expropriate. Furthermore, the results suggest that firms within a group are sensitive to each other's shocks and firms with the highest level of director equity (which is the proxy for cash-flow rights of controlling shareholders) benefit most from the shocks to the other firms in the group. The means of tunnelling is examined further, and the tunnelling of resources both into and out of firms is found to occur through non-operating profits.

Lemmon and Lins (2003) investigate whether differences in ownership structure explain differences in East Asian firms' performance during the financial crisis. The use of pyramid structures, which allow for controlling shareholders to maintain a high degree of control while reducing cash-flow rights, are associated with lower firm value. They find that divergence between cash flow and control rights results in lower firm value when controlling

---

[14] The entrenchment effect presents the view that controlling owners have incentives to expropriate the wealth of minority shareholders.

[15] See Bianchi, Bianco, and Enriques (2001), Claessens et al. (1999), and Claessens et al. (2000). The Kumar Mangalam Committee raised similar concerns.

shareholders have high levels of control rights. There is no association between the divergence of rights and firm performance when controlling shareholders have low levels of control rights. This finding suggests that control is necessary to expropriate outside shareholders.

Lins (2003) investigates how the effect of management ownership on firm value could be influenced by large non-management shareholders. The analysis involves three sets of tests. First, he examines the relationship between managerial ownership and firm value after controlling for firm-specific variables. The results provide evidence of firm value loss when the control rights of the management group exceed their cash-flow rights. Second, the role of non-management blockholders in mitigating the valuation discount of controlling shareholders is examined. The ownership level of large non-management blockholders is positively associated with firm value. Unlike management blockholders, non-management blockholder control rights are not associated with a reduction in firm value when they are the largest blockholders. Finally, the effect of shareholder protection on the level of expropriation of minority shareholders is tested. Both the findings specified above are found to be more pronounced in economies with low investor protection. These results suggest that large non-management shareholders may act as a substitute for missing institutional governance mechanisms in countries with poor investor protection.

Morck et al. (1988) examine the relationship between management ownership and firm value to disentangle convergence-of-interest and entrenchment effects. Managerial ownership and Tobin's Q, which is a proxy for market valuation, is found to be positively associated in the 0 to 5 per cent ownership range, but this association becomes negative in the 5 to 25 per cent range, and a further positive association is found beyond a 25 per cent ownership level. The initial rise in firm value suggests management's greater incentive to maximize firm value as their share rise. The ownership rights above 5 per cent seem conducive with greater control being linked to the entrenchment effect, as is evident from the negative association between ownership and firm value. The incentive effect might also be operative in the specified range; it is just dominated by the entrenchment effect. They argue that entrenchment is not only a consequence of voting power because a 5 to 10 per cent stake might not be enough to win proxy contests or to single-handedly elect directors. Other aspects are just as important, such as family dominance on the board, longer tenure, and founder status of managers. The results reveal lower values for older firms which are run by the founding family in comparison to firms run by an officer unrelated to the family. The non-linear relationship between ownership and firm value signifies that sufficient control is necessary for entrenchment to take place. An ownership level below 5 per cent does not appear to provide sufficient control to extract private benefits and, thus, there is no evidence of a negative impact on firm value. The rise in ownership beyond 5 per cent provides greater control to extract benefits. The entrenchment effect might also be enhanced with higher management positions and longer tenure of managers.

Bae, Kang, and Kim (2002) follow a different approach to identify the tunnelling behaviour of South Korean groups by investigating the acquisitions of poorly performing firms by other member firms within the group. They find that within-group takeovers are associated with a decline in the stock price of the bidder; however, they enhance the value of other firms in the group. The controlling shareholders benefit from the increase in value of other member firms at the cost of minority shareholders of bidder firms in the form of acquisition loss. Another study by Baek, Kang, and Lee (2006) examines equity-linked private securities offerings to seek evidence of tunnelling. They find that intra-group deals are offered at prices well below the fair value, and this causes negative market and firm value reaction.

Selarka (2005) investigates the influence of blockholders on firm value in the Indian context. She explores the unique situation by examining the role of outside blockholders in challenging controlling shareholders. One body of literature recognizes blockholders as a disciplinary mechanism, as these blockholders have voting rights to prevent controlling shareholders from extracting private benefits. As most blockholders are institutional investors and corporate bodies, they are able to make informed decisions and, thus, they are more likely to challenge value-destroying activities of controlling shareholders. Another body of literature show that substantial control and ability to influence corporate decisions by these outside blockholders enables them to extract private benefits (Burkart et al., 1997; Grossman and Hart, 1980).Selarka (2005) investigates this trade-off between incentive and entrenchment effects, examining a sample of 1,397 manufacturing firms listed on the BSE in 2001.

The results indicate a U-shaped relationship between firm value and the ownership of insider blockholders, which supports the entrenchment effect. Controlling shareholders are more likely to expropriate the wealth of minority shareholders until their ownership reaches a substantial level, where their incentives to extract private resources decreases due to stronger alignment incentives. Outside blockholders have no effect on firm value at lower and higher levels of control; however, a moderate level (10 to 15 per cent) of outside ownership is negatively associated with firm value. Selarka (2005) further examines the cause of the negative entrenchment effect associated with outside ownership, and pressure-sensitive institutional investors are found to drive these results. The results suggest that financial institutions, banks, and insurance companies are more likely to support management due to business relationships, instead of challenging them.[16] This study also examines the interaction effect between the two largest outsiders. The interaction effect is positive when both outsiders have ownership levels of between 5 to 10 per cent. An ownership level above 15 per cent reverses the effect. The difference between the ownership of the top two outsiders is quite large at this level and this may result in a lack of incentives to coordinate.

Douma et al. (2006) examine the ownership structure in order to explain the performance of Indian listed firms. They primarily examine the impact of foreign and domestic shareholders on firm performance. According to the resource-based theory, firm competitive advantage is an outcome of the possession of tangible and intangible resources. Resource heterogeneity arises from shareholders being domestic or foreign and financial or strategic. For instance, financial foreign shareholders are equipped with good monitoring skills but their emphasis on liquidity and the stock market index reveals their unwillingness to commit to a long-term relationship. The decisions to buy or sell shares of domestic firms by foreign institutional investors (FIIs) are made by fund managers, whose performance is measured by comparing their results with a stock market index and/or with competing institutions. Therefore, ownership by foreign financial institutions is expected to be positively associated with market-based firm performance (Tobin Q) and not necessarily accounting-based return (ROA). In fact, foreign corporate ownership goes beyond immediate financial returns and extends to managerial expertise and technical collaborations. Since firms with foreign corporate shareholders are endowed with superior managerial, technical, and financial resources, foreign corporate ownership is expected to be positively associated with firm performance. According to the alignment effect, insider ownership provides an incentive for managers to reduce agency costs which results into better performance. However, excessive control might provide them with powers to expropriate the wealth of minority shareholders. Therefore, insider ownership is expected to be positively associated with firm performance up to a particular threshold, and ownership rights beyond a certain level affects firm performance negatively.

---

[16] This is consistent with Pound (1988).

Douma et al. (2006) use a sample of 1005 firms listed in the BSE for one year, 1999–2000, to test their hypothesis. After controlling for sales and age, foreign ownership is found to be positively associated with both measures of performance (Return on Assets and Tobin Q). Furthermore, foreign institutional ownership is only positively associated with Tobin Q, but not significantly correlated with ROA. Foreign corporate ownership is positively associated with both measures of performance, Tobin Q and ROA. This finding supports the hypothesis and provides support to the resource-based theory. Director ownership is positively associated with the accounting measure of firm performance (ROA), but the results are insignificant for Tobin Q. Furthermore, the coefficient estimate for the squared term of director ownership is statistically insignificant, which does not provide any support for the entrenchment effect.

Heugens, Van Essen, and Van Oosterhout (2009) did a meta-analysis on the relationship between concentrated ownership and firm performance in nine Asian countries. Using accounting and market measures, they find that the relationship between ownership concentration and firm performance is positive and significant. They suggest that concentrated ownership is an effective remedy against familiar agency problems in countries where legal protection of shareholders is weak. However, the positive association between firm performance and ownership concentration is significant at lower levels of ownership. As the ownership stake increases, owners can extract full control over the firm, and the effect on performance becomes negligible and insignificant. Furthermore, the association between concentrated ownership and firm performance is more strongly positive when the concentrated owner is a market investor, as opposed to an insider. This supports the view that firms suffer from self-control and sub-optimal decisions under the control of inside investors (which consist of corporate founders and their immediate family).

RPTs

In the above section, it is suggested that controlling shareholders extract private benefits at the cost of outside investors when their control rights exceed their level of cash-flow rights. The most widely used method by controlling shareholders to expropriate the wealth of minority shareholders is RPTs. Such transactions can tunnel firm resources to related-parties by non-arm's-length transactions, that is, purchases at a premium, sales at a discount, interest-free loans, and guarantees. Prior studies have provided evidence on the expropriation of minority shareholders through RPTs.

Wong, Kim, and Lo (2013) examine the issue of whether RP sales transactions increase or reduce the market value of the firm. Using a sample of 4,520 firm-year observations (565 firms) during the period of 2002–2009, they examine three issues. First, they investigate whether RP sales by Chinese listed firms are value adding or value reducing. Second, they examine whether and how the influence or power of controlling shareholders affects the association between firm value and RP sales. Finally, they investigate if the RP sales are motivated by tax incentives. To test the above hypotheses, they decompose RP sales into normal and abnormal components by regressing RP sales against size, debt, and book-to-market ratio. The residual of this regression is measured as abnormal RP sales. After controlling for size, age, debt, ROA, liquidity, tax, book-market, year, and industries, abnormal RP sales are found to be positively associated with firm value, measured by Tobin's Q. They further divide the sample into two categories representing large and small portions of parent directors on the board based on the median percentage. For the subsample of firms with a low proportion of parent directors, RP sales are positively associated with firm value at the 1 per cent level. However, the results are insignificant for firms with a high percentage of parent directors. They also divide the sample into two groups based on high and low government ownership. Related-party sales are positively associated with firm value for firms with low government ownership; however, this association becomes insignificant for firms with high government ownership. These findings suggest that the RP sales are not viewed as efficient for firms with a high percentage of parent directors and high levels of government ownership.

Peng, Wei, and Yang (2011) examine the timing and extent of tunnelling by controlling shareholders of Chinese firms. They argue that tunnelling and propping are two major forms of expropriation by controlling shareholders through connected transactions between affiliated firms. The ownership of listed firms in China is highly concentrated and the majority of shares are not tradable. Therefore, controlling shareholders could not benefit from share value appreciation and this leads to their tunnelling behaviour through connected transactions. The inability to trade shares suggests that tunnelling incentives increase when firms are in a strong financial position. The controlling shareholders are strongly motivated to prop up firms in a poor financial state to avoid delisting and losing the right to issue new shares. The firms are categorized as being either financially sound or financially in trouble. The connected transactions by firms that are financially sound are considered to be tunnelling activities, while the connected transactions by firms in a poor financial position are deemed propping activities. It is the financial position (strong or poor) of the firm which determines the nature of the transaction, namely, whether it is tunnelling or propping, rather than the terms of the transaction.

Consistent with their hypothesis, Peng et al. (2011) find a negative market reaction to the announcement of connected transactions by firms in a strong financial position. This suggests that the market perceives such connected transactions as tunnelling behaviour and it reacts unfavourably. They find a positive reaction to the announcement of connected transactions by firms with poor financial position, which suggests that the market perceives such transactions as propping behaviour. The results of this study are consistent with Jian and Wong (2010) and Liu and Lu (2007). Peng et al. (2011) contribute to the literature by identifying both the timing and extent of tunnelling and propping through connected transactions. The focus of previous studies was on sales and group loans, whereas Peng et al. (2011) focus on asset and equity transactions. In particular, this study includes asset acquisitions, asset displacements, asset sales, cash transfers, and equity transfers.

Jian and Wong (2010) investigate propping through RPTs. In particular, they examine the use of RP sales to prop up earnings. Furthermore, they examine if RP sales are accrual-based or also cash-based, in order to understand the role of discretionary accruals in earnings management. They find that related sales to controlling shareholders are used to prop up earnings. The discretionary accruals are not positively associated with incentives to achieve earnings targets, which suggests no use of accrual-based earnings management. Jian and Wong (2010) find evidence of the use of cash-based RP sales for propping purposes. This is consistent with auditors paying greater attention to accrued sales which results in receivables and bad debts, whereas cash-based transactions are less likely to be detected. Moreover, cash sales are less costly for group firms because cash can be transferred back from the seller through loans. These findings are consistent with Graham, Harvey, and Rajgopal (2005) who identified that managers prefer real earnings management over accrual-based earnings management to avoid the attention of auditors. This suggests that the focus should not only be limited to accruals, but also include cash-based transactions.

Cheung, Rau, and Stouraitis (2006) examine the tunnelling or propping effect of RPTs in Hong Kong. They first investigate what type of connected transactions lead to expropriation of minority shareholders. Second, they examine which firms are more likely to expropriate outsiders. Finally, they examine whether the market anticipates such expropriation transactions. Cheung et al. (2006) include variables on disclosure quality, corporate governance, and ownership structure to examine whether the expropriation of outsiders takes place and what determines the magnitude of expropriation activity. They report that RPTs are associated with negative returns. The lack of disclosure about RPTs is also associated with negative abnormal returns. Furthermore, the larger the ownership by the controlling shareholder, the larger is the negative reaction experienced by the firm engaging in RPTs, which suggests a greater level of expropriation. The results suggest that less tunnelling occurs through operating activities, that is, purchases and sales, which implies that tunnelling occurs through non-operating activities such as asset acquisitions and cash payments involving loans. There is little evidence provided that corporate governance attributes affect the likelihood of engaging in RPTs. They also did not find any evidence to support market anticipation of the expropriation by *ex-ante* discounting of firms undertaking RPTs.

Cheung et al. (2009) investigate RPTs between Chinese listed firms and their controlling shareholders. The announcement of RPTs is associated with reductions in firm value which are not present in similar arm's-length transactions and, therefore, RPTs are unlikely to be motivated by purely economic reasons. They find evidence of more tunnelling than propping in their sample. They report that tunnelling and the propping phenomena are more profound in firms with high levels of state ownership. Propped-up firms are found to operate very poorly in the fiscal year following the announcement of RPTs. This supports those studies which argue that controlling shareholders transfer wealth and resources from profitable firms to distressed and non-profitable firms (Shin and Park, 1999; Rajan et al., 2000; Cornell and Liu, 2001).

Jian and Wong (2003) examine the use of RPTs to manage earnings in Chinese listed firms. In addition to the efficiency argument, the selected companies might conduct RPTs to avoid reporting losses and to inflate earnings. This study examines the RP sales which affect the operating earnings. Group firms are found to report higher levels of RPTs. Furthermore, the RP sales are used to manipulate earnings upward to meet government requirements for issuing new shares or to avoid delisting. The increase in free cash flows leads to higher lending to related parties, which is indicative of tunnelling behaviour. This behaviour is more pronounced in group firms. The market reacts less positively to RP sales than arm's-length sales transactions suggesting that the market predicts the underlying incentives of RPTs. However, the market does not discriminate the RPTs of group-affiliated firms from non-group firms.

Srinivasan (2013) analyses RPTs using a small sample of 171 Indian companies for the period between 2009 and 2011. Firms with high RPTs related to income and sales were found to report lower return on assets compared to firms with low RPTs. Further, Big 4 auditors were found to have a restraining effect on RPTs. However, ownership structure failed to offer any explanation for the magnitude of RPTs.

Research gap

Previous research has examined the effect of ownership structure on the performance of Indian firms. Most of these studies have focused on a particular shareholding, that is, directors' shareholding. Recently, however, more interest has been directed at multiple-owner groups to examine both the individual and joint effects of various shareholder groups on the magnitude of agency cost (see Douma et al., 2006 for ownership rights and Peng and Jiang, 2010 for governance quality). In this study, we similarly adopt the view that useful insights into the extent of resolution of the principal–principal conflict are obtained by examining the multiple control mechanisms. We note that a key aspect of much of the prior research is that the ownership rights of the controlling group are assumed to operate to alleviate or aggravate agency cost in isolation,[17] and the role of other blockholders, such as institutional investors, is often ignored. Our point of departure from the extant work is as follows: we suggest that important linkages should not only exist among the shareholdings of different groups, but also among other governance mechanisms such as board members and CEOs.

Prior studies on the expropriation of minority shareholders of Indian business groups provide indirect evidence only. For example, Bertrand et al. (2002) and Kali and Sarkar (2011) provide evidence of tunnelling through shock sensitivity. This study contributes to limited literature which examines RPTs to seek evidence of expropriation of minority shareholders in Indian context. Studies such as Wong et al. (2013), Peng et al. (2011), and Cheung et al. (2009) examine RPTs of Chinese firms. However, we examine the value relevance of RPTs in the presence of indirect ownership rights of controlling

---

[17] Bertrand et al. (2002), Joh (2003), and Lemmon and Lins (2003) examine the cash-flow and control rights of controlling families only and the role of other blockholders is ignored in mitigating agency cost Type 2.

shareholders, which extends our knowledge on the RPT phenomenon in a unique setting. The findings of Cheung et al. (2006) and Cheung et al. (2009) might be appropriate in the context of Hong Kong and China where there are many state-owned entities. However, different transactions could favour tunnelling in different settings and the underlying incentives for expropriation may differ between different controlling shareholders (for example, government versus family controlling shareholders).

Related studies

This section presents earlier studies which are closely related to our study. The conflict between controlling and minority shareholders has been explored in the studies mentioned below. However, this study contributes significantly to the existing knowledge by exploring the new avenues of principal–principal conflict. In this section, we draw attention to the limitations of earlier studies and mitigate these weaknesses, which justifies the contribution that our analysis makes.

This study is different from Bertrand et al. (2002) in several aspects. Bertrand et al. (2002) examine the tunnelling behaviour which involves the transfer of resources from a firm where controlling shareholders have lower cash-flow rights to firms where controlling shareholders have greater cash-flow rights. In contrast, we examine RPTs which involve non-arm's-length transactions of buying and selling among intra-group firms. Related-party transactions are often legal and require disclosure in annual reports, whereas tunnelling is an illegal and hidden phenomenon. It is not possible to measure the magnitude of tunnelling because the information is not made available to the public and, therefore, Bertrand et al. (2002) provide indirect evidence of tunnelling by isolating firm-specific shocks from industry shocks. The firms with lower cash-flow rights of controlling shareholders are found to be less sensitive to their own industry shocks and this is interpreted as evidence of tunnelling because they argue that some of the profits are diverted to other firms in the group; this leads to the under-response to their own industry shocks. If the firm shows greater sensitivity to shocks affecting the low cash-flow right firms in the group, then it is considered as evidence of tunnelling from firms with low cash-flow rights of controlling shareholders to firms with high cash-flow rights of controlling shareholders. This represents indirect evidence of tunnelling. On the other hand, we use the direct measure, the magnitude of RPTs, which is publically available to record the market reaction.

Our study is also different from Srinivasan (2013) in that we used a much larger sample, a later period of 2008–2012, and examined the effect of RPTs on a market measure (market value of equity – MVE).

Second, the proxy used by Bertrand et al. (2002) seems to be an inappropriate measure of cash-flow rights of controlling shareholders. The proxy (director ownership) used to capture direct cash-flow rights of controlling shareholders will overstate direct rights if directors are not family members. Third, Bertrand et al. (2002) do not examine how the relationship between controlling family ownership and tunnelling behaviour could be affected by other large blockholders which are not part of the family group. This study separates the ownership of other large blockholders and examines the effect of their ownership rights on market valuation.

Another study which links the diversification of Indian business groups with tunnelling motives is Kali and Sarkar (2011). Similar to Bertrand et al. (2002), Kali and Sarkar (2011) provide indirect evidence of tunnelling through shock sensitivity, whereas our study provides direct evidence through RPTs . We also consider the challenges to the controlling family in extracting firm resources from other large blockholders by including blockholder ownership and corporate governance mechanisms such as board independence, audit committee, and the presence of a non-family CEO. However, Kali and Sarkar (2011) do not make any attempt to control for firm-specific corporate governance attributes. Overall, Kali and Sarkar (2011) explore a different perspective, that is, group diversification in seeking evidence of tunnelling. This study overcomes many shortcomings of their approach and follows a more direct and rigorous strategy.

Jian and Wong (2003) examine RPTs of Chinese listed firms. The small proportion of firms included in the sample reduces the power of the tests. Because their study consists of a sample of 131 firms only in the raw material industry, the findings might not be valid in other settings. This study also examines only one type of RPT (RP sales), and undertaking the study of other RPTs such as asset acquisition, loans, and equity transfers can enhance our understanding of the issue. Our sample includes 1,530 firm-year observations and examines four types of RPTs (trading, asset transfers, investments, and loans).

Villalonga and Amit (2006) examine the impact of family ownership, control and management on firm value. The existence of family control in excess of ownership rights through pyramid structure and cross-holding is associated with lower firm value. Family management enhances firm value when the founder serves as CEO or chairperson, whereas the existence of a descendant CEO or chairman destroys value. This study examines US firms where investor protection is strong and, thus, outcomes in the weak investor protection economies such as India may be different. Some of the firms in Villalonga and Amit (2006) are controlled through pyramid structures and cross-holdings and the remainder are directly controlled, which reduces the risk of expropriation, whereas this study focusses on group firms which are solely controlled through cross-holdings and pyramids. Therefore, the incentives to expropriate outside investors would be higher in India because of weak investor protection and indirect ownership.

Despite the fact that Joh (2003) and Lemmon and Lins (2003) investigate the economic crisis period and we examine the behaviour of controlling shareholders under normal economic conditions, our study is also different from these in a number of other ways. Joh (2003) and Lemmon and Lins (2003) do not study the role of large non-management blockholders, whereas we investigate the presence of large blockholders (other than controlling family) in family-controlled firms. In contrast to Claessens et al. (2002), Lemmon and Lins (2003), and Lins (2003), which attempt to draw inferences from data across countries, this study focuses on a particular country (India) where the risk of shareholder extraction is high.

To examine the impact of controlling shareholders, the three fundamental elements must be distinguished, that is, ownership, control, and management. The studies such as Bertrand et al. (2002), Claessens et al. (2002), Lins (2003), and Lemmon and Lins (2003) examine the effect of controlling shareholder ownership and control but they ignore the role of management. Villalonga and Amit (2006) show the importance of distinguishing ownership, control, and management to examine the incentives of controlling shareholders. Therefore, we investigate the impact of founding-family ownership, control, and management on earnings-market valuation. In particular, we exploit the interaction between founding-family control and the magnitude of non-arm's-length transactions to examine the extent of any entrenchment effects.

Summary

This chapter provides the theoretical framework and literature review. Agency theory reveals that family-controlled firms suffer from principal–principal conflict and family firms are subject to severe Type 2 agency cost problems. It had also highlighted that the self-control problems of family firms undermine the external control mechanisms, and this in turn facilitates the expropriation of minority shareholders. It can be concluded from the literature review that divergence between control and cash-flow rights provides controlling shareholders with the incentives to extract private benefits, and RPTs provide the means for such expropriation.

Current studies provide indirect evidence on expropriation of minority shareholders. Not much effort has been made to provide direct evidence on entrenchment effects in the context of India. Therefore, our study contributes significantly to the literature by providing direct evidence on market valuation of RPTs in group-affiliated firms.

Chapter 4

Hypotheses Development

Introduction

This chapter develops hypotheses based on the theoretical and institutional settings presented in previous chapters. Chapter 2 outlined the institutional background in India, which is characterized by concentrated ownership, or family dominance and weak investor protection. Cross-holdings and indirect control rights of founding families provide controlling shareholders the incentive to extract private benefits. In a weak investor protection environment, it becomes easier for controlling shareholders to extract firm resources for their own personal benefits.

Chapter 3 reviewed literature on the behaviour of business groups, family firms and RPTs, and highlighted several motivations for controlling shareholders to indulge in value destroying activities. Consequently, the disclosure of RPTs might be valued negatively. Ownership rights of different groups are expected to affect firm value differently. RPTs between subsidiary and holding firms are likely to be valued on the basis of the nature of the transaction, whereas indirect rights of controlling shareholders are likely to play a key role in the valuation of RPTs with member firms. The presence of indirect ownership presents benefits for controlling shareholders to extract private benefits, and it is likely to influence the valuation of RPTs with member firms in the group.

This chapter is structured in two parts. The first section predicts the effects of ownership rights on firm value to seek evidence of expropriation of minority shareholders. In particular, we hypothesize the effect of direct and indirect rights of controlling shareholders on firm value. This is followed by hypotheses on the valuation effect of minority shareholdings. The second section predicts the value transfer potential of RPTs. The association between RPT disclosure and firm value is predicted to be influenced by the relationship with the party involved in the RPT, the nature of the transaction, and the indirect rights of controlling shareholders.

Firm value and ownership structure

The effect of ownership structure on firm value has been examined extensively in the literature. In particular, several studies have examined the role of large investors in resolving the conflict between shareholders and managers.[18] Shleifer and Vishny (1997) argue that concentrated ownership provides both incentives and power to the controlling shareholders to mitigate agency problems. Therefore, the investors with large ownership stakes are viewed as value-adding. However, the other body of literature investigates the cost associated with the concentrated ownership. The presence of large investors gives rise to conflict between controlling and minority shareholders (Demsetz and Lehn, 1985). Fama and Jensen (1983b) and Shleifer and Vishny (1997) indicate that controlling shareholders may pursue their own interests, which deviate from the interests of outside investors. As the ownership structure of firms in Asia exhibit greater concentration (La Porta et al., 1999), a number of studies in that region associate concentrated ownership with value loss, suggesting that controlling shareholders extract firm resources for private benefits (Bertrand et al., 2002; Claessens et al., 2002).

Research studies have attempted to measure the expropriation of minority shareholders using different proxies for the likelihood of it occurring. An important branch of literature employs the legal system as a proxy for the likelihood of expropriation of outsiders. Johnson et al. (2000) focus on the legal treatment of minority shareholders in different legal systems with respect to expropriation. Brockman and Chung (2003) report that firms operating in legal systems with lower investor protection have wider bid-ask spreads. A second branch of literature employs dividend payouts as a proxy for expropriation. La Porta et al. (2000) show that investors in countries with poor legal protection receive lower dividends because of their incapacity to force firms to distribute cash flows. Faccio et al. (2001) also examine expropriation through dividend payouts. A third branch of literature employs the divergence between cash flow and control rights as a proxy for the possibility of expropriation.

---

[18] Jensen and Meckling (1976) explain the agency cost resulting from the conflict of interest between shareholders and managers of modern corporations.

Lemmon and Lins (2003) provide evidence supporting the view that ownership structure plays a vital role in the likelihood of expropriation of minority shareholders. Claessens et al. (2002) report a positive association between firm value and cash-flow rights held by controlling shareholders and a negative association between firm value and the divergence between cash flow and control rights. Another study which examines the divergence between cash flow and control rights is Joh (2003). It is not possible, however, to determine the divergence between cash flow and control rights of Indian firms due to the unavailability of data. Indian disclosure laws do not mandate the release of information concerning indirect cash-flow rights (Bertrand et al., 2002). Information about the ownership of controlling shareholders is available in two broad categories: first, ownership obtained through individuals and Hindu Undivided Family (HUF); second, through corporations. The first category represents the direct shareholding of controlling groups and the cash-flow and control rights are equal in this category. Corporations in the second category are not fully owned by controlling families and, therefore, the ownership obtained through these corporations serves as a proxy for indirect cash-flow rights.

The distinction between direct and indirect ownership is important in the Indian context, if one is to investigate the potential for expropriation of minority shareholders, where control is often maintained through indirect ownership, that is, cross-holdings and pyramids (Claessens et al., 2002; Gopalan et al., 2007). Bertrand et al. (2002, p. 121) identify that 'a single shareholder (or a family) completely controls several independently-traded firms and yet has significant cash flow rights in only a few of them.' La Porta et al. (1999), Claessens et al. (2000), and Lins (2003) raised concerns about indirect cash-flow rights in the Asian context. The controlling shareholders, who are promoting families, generally are able to exercise effective control of all the firms in the group, whereas they bear only a fraction of the cost of exercising their control.[19] This environment provides an excellent opportunity to examine the extreme agency problems arising due to controlling interest.

To disentangle the alignment and entrenchment effects of controlling shareholders, we examine the valuation of publicly traded Indian group firms relative to their ownership structures. The existing literature suggests that positive incentive effects are associated with direct ownership rights of large shareholders and that negative entrenchment derives from indirect

---

[19] Jensen and Meckling (1976) explain agency cost as a result of divergence between controlling and outside shareholders.

rights of large shareholders. Shleifer and Vishny (1997) highlight the profit maximization goal of large shareholders and also raise concerns about their self-serving behaviour at the cost of outsiders. Morck et al. (1988) report an inverse U-shaped relationship between inside ownership and firm valuation, which suggests that firm value increases with higher inside ownership, but after a point managers pursue their private benefits at the cost of outside investors which results into lower firm value. Stulz (1988) formalizes the effect of cash flow and control rights on firm valuation. McConnell and Servaes (1990) provide the supporting empirical evidence. The divergence between cash-flow rights and control rights is suggested as being more prominent in Asian countries.[20] The situation is similar in India where family groups dominate the market and family members often maintain their control with relatively small cash-flow rights.[21] Control is often maintained through pyramid structures and cross-holdings among member firms in the group (Bertrand et al., 2002). However, dual-class shares which enhance the control rights of major shareholders are not allowed in India.

To seek evidence on the effects of ownership and control rights of the promoter group on firm market valuation, we test the following hypotheses.

Family ownership and firm value

On the one hand, greater direct ownership in the hands of controlling shareholders increases the incentives of controlling shareholders to run the firm properly and not get involved in expropriation activities. Consistent with the alignment effect proposed by Shleifer and Vishny (1997), concentrated cash-flow rights align the interest of controlling shareholders with the firm and the incentives to extract private benefits diminish. Claessens et al. (2002) report a positive association between cash-flow rights of controlling shareholders and firm value, which supports the view that direct cash-flow rights reduce the entrenchment effect and result in higher firm value. Similarly, Lemmon and Lins (2003) argue that incentives for controlling shareholders to divert resources for their personal benefit decreases with proportional increase in cash-flow ownership.

On the other hand, Fama and Jensen (1983b) and Morck et al. (1988) suggest that greater controlling rights in the hands of large shareholders provide them

---

[20] See Claessens et al. (2002).
[21] Similarly, Claessens et al. (2000) report that more than two-thirds of Asian firms are controlled by a single shareholder.

with increased incentive to expropriate the wealth of minority shareholders. Claessens et al. (2002) report a negative association between the magnitude of controlling rights of the largest shareholder and firm value, which supports the entrenchment behaviour of controlling shareholders.

Studies on firm performance have extensively examined the non-linear association between ownership structure and firm performance. McConnell and Servaes (1990) document a curvilinear relationship between insider ownership and corporate value. Similarly, Morck et al. (1988) report that firm value first increases and then declines with management ownership. While the ownership of controlling shareholders is expected to be positively associated with firm value, we choose to examine if the association remains linear for all levels of ownership rights or if it becomes curvilinear after a particular threshold. Morck et al. (1988) propose that managers respond to two opposing forces, convergence of interest and entrenchment effects. The effect of ownership on firm value depends on which force dominates. As individuals are self-interested, the natural tendency of controlling families is to allocate firm resources in their own interest, which may conflict with the interest of outsiders.

As controlling groups' ownership increases, their interests are likely to align with the interests of outside shareholders. However, this alignment effect might not be equally effective for direct and indirect ownership. Rising direct ownership rights might reflect the controlling group's greater incentive to maximize firm value as their stake rises. However, the increase in indirect ownership rights might be associated with conditions conducive to expropriation by incumbent controlling shareholders for two reasons. First, they bear only a fraction of the cost of their decisions when the control is obtained through indirect rights. The large portion of the cost of their inefficient decisions might be allocated to outsiders when they bear only a marginal share. The conflict of interest arises with fractional ownership of the firm because every owner's ability to bear risk varies with the relative size of their stake in the firm (Fama and Jensen, 1983a, 1983b). This may result in loss of firm value. Second, they might be encouraged to reallocate resources from a firm where they have lower cash-flow rights to a firm where they have higher cash-flow rights, given that they have effective control over both the firms. For instance, a controlling family owns 30 per cent of the shares of A Ltd and 5 per cent of B Ltd. Further, A Ltd owns 25 per cent of the shares of B Ltd, which gives the controlling family effective control of B Ltd through A Ltd. In this case, the controlling family gains only 12.5 per cent (5+7.5[25x0.3]) of the profits of B Ltd, whereas they earn 30 per cent of the profits of A Ltd. This could encourage the controlling group to transfer the resources of B Ltd to A Ltd through RPTs or tunnelling. If outside shareholders expect the entrenchment effect to dominate alignment effect, they will value the shares of B Ltd downward.

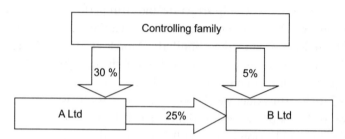

Direct rights

As the direct ownership of the controlling group increases, their interests are more likely to align with the interests of outside shareholders. They are more likely to manage the firm effectively because it increases their wealth too. Studies such as Douma et al. (2006) and Bertrand et al. (2002) find a positive association between inside-ownership and firm value of Indian listed firms. Similar evidence is provided by Claessens et al. (2002) and Lemmon and Lins (2003) who examine the data of East Asian countries. As a result, we expect the alignment effect to dominate the entrenchment effect with increasing levels of direct ownership of the controlling group. This expectation results in the following hypothesis.

H1: The association between direct ownership rights and the MVE is expected to be positive and linear.

Indirect rights

When controlling shareholders do not bear the full cost of their control activities, minority shareholders might be disadvantaged (Jensen and Meckling, 1976). Indirect rights, by their very nature, are smaller than direct rights because they are diminished as they pass through the chain of ownership (Bertrand et al., 2002). The higher the proportion of indirect rights, the higher the separation between cash flow and control rights. The higher the separation between cash flow and control rights, the greater the incentives for controlling shareholders to extract firm resources and vice versa. Claessens et al. (2002)

find that firm value falls when the control rights of the largest shareholder exceed its cash-flow ownership. Douma et al. (2006) report that positive influence attributed to corporate ownership (indirect ownership) is reduced in the case of group-affiliated firms, which provides evidence consistent with the use of indirect ownership as a vehicle by controlling families to extract private benefits. Johnson et al. (2000) also argue that indirect rights obtained through corporate holding can be used to form pyramids that facilitate the tunnelling of resources.

Indirect ownership is very common amongst group-affiliated firms in India and corporate control is maintained by founding families either through direct or indirect ownership or both. Indirect ownership may not necessarily influence the firm value negatively; however, an excessive level of indirect ownership is expected to affect firm value negatively for the following reasons. First, the indirect rights undermine the importance of direct rights in maintaining effective control. Second, indirect ownership provides increased incentives for minority expropriation. Therefore, the indirect ownership rights of controlling shareholders are expected to influence firm value negatively after a certain threshold, resulting in the second hypothesis proposed for testing as follows:

H2: The association between indirect ownership rights and the MVE is expected to be curvilinear.

Minority ownership and firm value

The equity held by 'non-promoter individuals', where these individuals are defined as shareholders that are not promoters, nor foreigners, nor financial institutions, nor government, nor corporate bodies, provides a valid proxy for the ownership share available for the controlling group to expropriate. Bertrand et al. (2002) also employ a similar approach to capture the amount of cash-flow rights the family does not own. In the Prowess database, there are two classes of shareholders under this category of non-promoter individuals: first, shareholders with a face value of total holding less than INR 100,000; and second, shareholders with a face value of total holding above INR 100,000. INR 100,000 is equivalent to less than US$1,700 and, therefore, the first class of non-promoter individuals represents obvious minority shareholders. Conversely, the second class of shareholders might include some blockholders other than the controlling group. By no means is anyone with a shareholding of face value above INR 100,000 a blockholder, and will have the power to challenge the controlling group. However, any blockholder (for example, with

5 or 10 per cent of shares) will not be included in any other category except 'non-promoter individuals'. For instance, a non-promoter shareholder holding 5 per cent of the shares of a firm will not be included in the promoters group, nor in financial institutions, nor in government, nor in corporate bodies, nor in non-promoter individual class 1 (shareholding worth up to INR 100,000). Therefore, the presence of any blockholder in the firm will be captured by the non-promoter individual class 2.

An institution-based view suggests that the relationship between governance mechanisms and firm value may vary under different institutional settings. Rediker and Seth (1995) propose that the effect of a particular mechanism should be influenced by the levels of other mechanisms which simultaneously operate in the firm. Consistent with this proposition, Peng and Jiang (2010) argue that external governance mechanisms may substitute for internal mechanisms in contributing to the effectiveness of corporate governance. For instance, in countries with well-developed legal and regulatory systems, the external mechanisms help to govern firms and the incentives and power of controlling shareholders becomes less important in determining firm value. However, in countries with less developed legal and regulatory institutions, controlling shareholders play a vital role in maintaining firm value. When family ownership is considered to be positively associated with firm value in the literature, shareholdings of minority shareholders might be negatively associated with firm value under these institutions. First, minority shareholding reflects the number of shares not owned by controlling shareholders. The minority shareholding in family firms represents the cost of the decisions of controlling families which will not be borne by families and, thus, higher levels of minority ownership provide controlling shareholders the incentive to expropriate the wealth of minority shareholders. Second, the protection of minority shareholders in India is not very strong and the legal system is prone to corruption (Dutta, 1997; OECD, 2012). As a result, the market realizes that controlling families' interests diverge from theirs and they respond by discounting the shares of such firms.

Minority 1

This category is the percentage ownership of non-promoter individuals holding nominal share investments worth up to INR 100,000, which is equivalent to less than US$1,700. A shareholder holding shares with a nominal value of up to US$1,700 is not likely to take part in the management of the company or challenge the controlling shareholders. Class 1 of non-promoter individuals represents shareholders in the complete minority and, therefore, the higher the proportion of holdings of this class, the higher the incentive for controlling shareholders to extract benefits. This also represents the share of the cost of decisions which will not be borne by the controlling group. Bertrand et al. (2002) find that more resources are tunnelled out of the group firms where there are higher minority shareholders to expropriate. The higher the proportion of shares held by minority shareholders, the lower the share of any cost associated with expropriation activities which is allocated to the controlling group, which suggests that controlling shareholders are more likely to make inefficient decisions. Diffused ownership also suffers from the free-rider problem. Coffee (1991) argues that dispersed outside investors have limited ability to effectively monitor as a result of higher coordination costs and information asymmetry. Douma et al. (2006) also argue that shareholders holding a miniscule proportion of shares have very little incentives to devote their time and effort. As a result, we develop the following hypothesis:

H3a: The proportion of class 1 minority shareholders is expected to be negatively associated with firm value.

Minority 2

Minority 2 is the percentage ownership of non-promoter individuals holding nominal share investments worth above INR 100,000, which is equivalent to a shareholding worth above US$1,700. While such a shareholding is not necessarily significant ownership and does not necessarily provide incentives to manage the firm effectively, this category might include some non-promoter blockholders. As there might be some blockholders in Class 2 of the non-promoter individual category, they might challenge the controlling group to protect their interests. Lins (2003) reports that large non-management blockholders are positively associated with firm value. Furthermore, unlike management blockholders, non-management blockholders are not associated with a reduction in firm value when they are the largest blockholders. Significant holdings of shares discourage these individuals to free-ride and they have greater incentives to protect their interests. Furthermore, unlike the Minority 1 group, we expect this category to be less vulnerable and they should have monitoring incentives. This leads to the development of the following hypothesis:

H3b: The proportion of class 2 minority shareholders is expected to be positively associated with firm value.

RPTs

It is documented in the literature that RPTs provide the potential for controlling shareholders to expropriate the wealth of outsiders.[22] The RPTs can be in the form of the sale and purchase of goods and services, loans, asset acquisitions, equity transfers, asset sales, and other complex strategic transactions. Related-party transactions cannot be assumed to be equivalent to arm's-length transactions and, therefore, firms are subject to certain regulations. For instance, in the UK, firms are required to obtain shareholder approval and an independent evaluation to enter into RPTs. In the US, shareholder approval is not required but the full disclosure of RPTs is mandatory. Similarly, the Indian Companies Act, 1956 imposes certain restrictions on RPTs under Sections 297, 299, and 300. Section 297 of the Companies Act, 1956 requires board approval to enter into RPTs, and central government approval might be required for companies with a paid-up capital of more than INR 10 million(US$0.17 million).

However, the effectiveness of such requirements may be questionable when the boards of Indian group firms are generally dominated by family owners. Section 297 (2) provides an exemption from government approval if the transaction is for cash and at prevailing market prices. The firms might get an exemption opportunistically when there is no prevailing market for RP goods and services.[23] It is evident that the RPT raises serious concerns for outsiders. As per Ball, Kothari, and Robin (2000), Leuz,Nanda, and Wysocki (2003) and DeFond,Hung, and Trezevant (2007), economic institutions can determine financial reporting properties. Therefore, the level of market development can shape firms' decisions to trade in the external market or form an internal market. Previous investigations such as Strachan (1976) and Pan (1999) recognize that group structure enables member firms to share risk by smoothing income flows and reallocating money from one member firm to the other. Yafeh (2003) suggests that risk sharing might be the most prominent

---

[22] Jensen and Meckling (1976) explain that an insider who owns less than 100 per cent of shares does not bear the full cost of his consumption of firm benefits. Recent papers byJian and Wong (2010) and Peng et al. (2011) came to similar conclusions.

[23] Kohlbeck and Mayhew (2010) present the view in reference to FAS 57 that RPTs might lack prevailing markets.

factor behind reduced variance in profitability among affiliated firms. Studies such as Myers and Majluf (1984) and Greenwald and Stiglitz (1993) suggest that firms might be constrained in the presence of capital market imperfections and, thus, they rely on internal resources. Khanna and Yafeh (2005) provide some support to the notion that intra-group loans are used to smooth earnings in the Indian context. In India, group firms are more likely to rely on RPTs to overcome the inefficiencies of external markets,[24] which give rise to more opportunities for tunnelling.

The Accounting Standard 18 (Related Party Disclosures) issued by the ICAI further requires the disclosure of RPTs. Despite these regulations, RPTs form a significant part of business activities, especially in the case of group firms. The RPTs are routed through other firms indirectly controlled by family promoters (*Business Line*, 8 December 2002). For instance, Reliance Industries provided loans of INR 140,000 million to associated firms (*Business Line*, 8 December 2002). Gillette India, P&G Hygiene, and Novartis acquired significant portions of their raw materials from their sister firms (*Business Line*, 8 December 2002). The expropriation of minority shareholders has been a concern in India because of corruption and poor legal enforcement. The Kumar Mangalam committee raised concerns about conflicts between the controlling shareholders and the wider interests of the company, including the effect of RPTs (Bertrand et al., 2002). The recommended measures include the establishment of audit committees to review RPTs.

The audit committee is a sub-committee of the board and, therefore, it becomes vital to understand the role of independent directors when they are given the duty to stop the abusive use of RPTs. However, the mere title 'independent' is not enough to fulfil the assigned duty, when they could be under enormous pressure from controlling shareholders. First, these independent directors are appointed by controlling shareholders and this might impair their independence. Independent directors of these family firms often view their role as strategic advisors to controlling shareholders, which undermines their ability to effectively monitor family managers (Khanna and Mathew, 2010). Second, the independent directors acknowledge their reliance on promoter families because of the directorships in other group affiliate firms. Sarkar and Sarkar (2009) report that independent directors hold 67 per cent of their directorships in group affiliates and about 43 per cent of their directorships are concentrated in the same business group.

---

[24] See Khanna and Palepu (2000b) for more discussion about market inefficiencies in India.

The argument presented above suggests that potential wealth transfer can occur through RPTs. Kohlbeck and Mayhew (2010) examine the market valuation of firms that disclose RPTs and report lower valuations for firms that engage in RPTs. However, the market response is different for different transactions. Simple transactions involving directors, officers, or shareholders lead to negative valuation by the market. Transactions of a complex nature and those relating to investments are not valued negatively by the market.

Similar to accounting accruals, RPTs can be either normal or abnormal for any firm. RPTs might have a value-enhancing effect as a result of strategic partnerships, the risk-sharing phenomenon, and efficient contracting. Khanna and Palepu (2000b) argue that the superior performance of Indian group firms is a result of efficient internal markets. We examine RPTs to evaluate whether market valuations are consistent with: (*a*) extraction of private benefits, which results in lower valuation; (*b*) RPTs being value enhancing; or (*c*) RPTs being relatively benign transactions and their disclosure having little or no association with market valuation (Kohlbeck and Mayhew, 2010). We expect that the valuation of RPTs, whether negative, positive, or no reaction, depends on the relationship with the other party involved in the transaction, the nature of the transactions, and the incentives of the controlling shareholders.

The Accounting Standard 18 (AS-18) issued by the ICAI, which is applicable for RP disclosures, includes subsidiaries or holding companies, associates, individuals with significant control, their relatives, and firms where controlling shareholders have significant influence as RPs. Consistent with the definition above, any transactions within the group are considered to be between RPs in this study. We distinguish transactions with subsidiary or holding firms from transactions with other parties. The transactions with subsidiary and holding firms might be viewed as part of the normal course of the business and, therefore, these transactions might not attract abnormal market valuation. On the other hand, transactions with parties where controlling shareholders have significant influence, member firms in the group, might be a result of efficient contracting or entrenchment effects. In this case, the efficient transactions are expected to be valued positively, and transactions with the aim of extracting private benefits are expected to be valued negatively. Cheung et al. (2006) identify asset sales, asset acquisitions, loans, equity sales, and trading activities (that is, purchases or sales) as transactions that are likely to result in expropriation of minority shareholders. Therefore, we examine the market valuation of these transactions to find any evidence of entrenchment or alignment effects.

Trading

This category involves the sale and purchase of goods and services to related parties. The business group firms might conduct RP trading to minimize transaction costs.[25] Shin and Park (1999) provide evidence of better performance of group firms with the use of internal transfers of products and services. The counter-argument is that RP sales might be a way to entrench private benefits. Studies such as Jian and Wong (2003) and Cheung et al. (2006) provide evidence of expropriation of minority shareholders through trading transactions.

Trading with member firms in the group

Group-affiliated firms might benefit from transactions involving the sale and purchase of goods and services when external markets are not fully developed and formal/informal ties between group firms tend to overcome the imperfections of external markets (Khanna and Palepu, 2000b). Kohlbeck and Mayhew (2010) argue that connected transactions involve less information asymmetry between the two parties (RP and firm), in comparison to the transaction between the firm and a third party conducted at arm's length. The other body of literature suggest that RPTs may impose costs on group-affiliated firms. Related-party transactions are more likely to result in expropriation of minority shareholders when the control rights of controlling shareholders exceed their cash-flow rights. Bertrand et al. (2002) find evidence of tunnelling when controlling shareholders have lower cash-flow rights. As discussed above, controlling shareholders bear only a fraction of the cost of their control decisions when they own only a marginal proportion value of shares. Wong et al. (2013) report a positive association between RP sales and firm value; however, the positive association disappears for firms with a high percentage of parent directors and highly concentrated ownership. In the Indian context, RP trading transactions can benefit the firms where controlling shareholders have higher cash-flow rights at the cost of firms where they have higher indirect rights. Therefore, we develop the following hypotheses:

H4a: RP trading with member firms is likely to be viewed as entrenchment and therefore, negatively associated with firm value.

---

[25] Khanna and Palepu (1997) argue that internal markets can facilitate resource allocation in emerging markets where external markets are not fully developed.

H4b: RP trading with member firms is likely to affect the value relevance of earnings negatively in the presence of indirect–ownership rights of controlling shareholders.

Trading between subsidiary and holding firms

The reliance of subsidiary and holding firms on each other for raw material is part of the normal course of business and disclosure of such transactions is not expected to affect the market valuation. Cheung et al. (2006) argue that transactions involving subsidiary/holding relationships are not expected to result in value loss for the firm. They find supportive results for transactions involving trading, asset transfers, and equity stakes between subsidiary and holding firms. Kohlbeck and Mayhew (2010) also argue that some RPTs are relatively benign where their disclosure has little or no association with firm valuation. As these transactions are a result of the subsidiary–parent relationship and not necessarily motivated by personal benefits, indirect-ownership rights should not influence the valuation of trading transactions between subsidiary and holding firms. This results in the following two hypotheses:

H4c: RP trading with subsidiary and/or holding firms are likely to be benign transactions and, therefore, their disclosure is not likely to be associated with market valuation.

H4d: RP trading with subsidiary and/or holding firms are not likely to influence the value-relevance of earnings in the presence of indirect ownership rights of controlling shareholders.

Asset transfers

Another form of transaction that must be examined is RP asset sales and asset acquisitions. These asset transfers might be aimed to minimize transaction costs by group firms. On the contrary, asset transfers also have the potential to lead to the expropriation of minority shareholders. For instance, assets sold below the fair value and assets acquired above fair value cause value loss for the firm.

Asset transfers with member firms

Asset transfers have been extensively examined as a potential source of expropriation of minority shareholders (Cheung et al., 2009; Cheung et al.,

2006). These transactions can be value-reducing as well as value-enhancing (Friedman et al., 2003). While Khanna and Palepu (2000b) argue that group firms benefit from internal markets, Cheung et al. (2006) report that considerable shareholder value is destroyed following the announcement of asset acquisitions and asset sales to connected parties. We expect group-affiliated firms to benefit from asset transfers; however, this could result in expropriation of minority shareholders in the presence of indirect rights of controlling shareholders. Therefore, we develop the following two hypotheses:

H5a: Asset transfers with member firms are likely to be viewed as efficient and, therefore, positively associated with firm value.

H5b: Asset transfers with member firms are likely to affect the value-relevance of earnings negatively in the presence of indirect ownership rights of controlling shareholders.

Asset transfers with subsidiary and/or holding firms

Asset transfers with subsidiary and holding firms are likely to be normal transactions and, therefore, they are not likely to influence the market valuation. Furthermore, we expect these transactions to be driven by their subsidiary–parent relationship and indirect ownership rights of controlling shareholders are less likely to play a key role in the valuation of these transactions. We develop the following two hypotheses:

H5c: Asset transfers with subsidiary and/or holding firms are likely to be benign transactions and, therefore, their disclosure is not likely to be associated with market valuation.

H5d: Asset transfers with subsidiary and/or holding firms are not likely to influence the value-relevance of indirect ownership rights of controlling shareholders.

Investments

This category includes the sale and purchase of shares with related parties. Cheung et al. (2006) argue that the sale of equity stakes in the listed company to connected parties might result in expropriation of the listed firm's minority shareholders and they record a negative market reaction to the disclosure of equity sales. On the contrary, Kohlbeck and Mayhew (2010) report that RP investments are not associated with valuations or returns. In fact, they suggest that complex transactions, including investments, are not well understood by the market, whereas simple RPTs including loans are valued negatively. Therefore, investments might not be valued negatively by the market.

Investment transactions with member firms

Transactions involving the sale and purchase of equity with a connected party are likely to result in expropriation of minority shareholders (Cheung et al., 2009; Cheung et al., 2006). Joh (2003) states that the level of investment in group-affiliated firms is negatively associated with firm performance. It is suggested that group-affiliated firms allocate resources inefficiently. However, these transactions are not well understood by the market (Kohlbeck and Mayhew, 2010) and, therefore, their disclosure might not influence the market value negatively. We expect that controlling shareholders are more likely to extract benefits through other transactions, such as asset transfers, cash guarantees, and loans, with the use of investments likely to be less prevalent. Given the mixed evidence on the valuation of investment transactions, the directional association between the magnitude of investment transactions and MVE is not predicted. However, the effect of RP investments on earnings-market valuation is expected to be negative in the presence of indirect ownership rights. Therefore, we develop the following two hypotheses:

H6a: The association between the magnitude of investments involving member firms and the MVE could be either positive or negative.

H6b: RP investments with member firms are likely to affect the value-relevance of earnings negatively in the presence of indirect ownership rights of controlling shareholders.

Investment transactions with subsidiary and/or holding firms:

Rajan et al. (2000) examine inefficient investment decisions of diversified firms. It is expected that funds will transfer from divisions with poor opportunities to divisions with good opportunities; however, resources can flow towards the most inefficient division. The inefficient allocation of resources is profound in subsidiary/holding firms as well (Cornell and Liu, 2001). Therefore, the sale and purchase of shares between subsidiary and holding firms might facilitate the allocation of resources from a cash-generating enterprise to inefficient parent operations. As such, we develop the following hypotheses:

H6c: Investments involving subsidiary and/or holding firms are likely to be inefficient and, therefore, their disclosure is likely to be negatively associated with market valuation.

H6d: RP investment transactions with subsidiary and/or holding firms are not likely to influence the value-relevance of earnings in the presence of indirect ownership rights of controlling shareholders.

Loans

The literature suggests that corporate loans are an important means of expropriating minority shareholders.[26] For example, Kalyani Steels, a group firm, had more than two-thirds of its net worth invested in other member firms, which yielded less than a 1 per cent rate of return (Bertrand et al., 2002). Gopalan et al. (2007) also report that a significant amount of loans are provided across group firms in India. The firms in better financial positions tend to provide loans to weak firms and the group loans are provided at an interest rate that is significantly lower than the market borrowing rate. The interest on group loans is almost 10 per cent lower than the market rate. Gopalan et al. (2007) further examine the subsequent performance of firms that receive loans. They show that receiver firms significantly underperform in the subsequent two years, which is inconsistent with the notion that loans are used to finance profitable investment opportunities. Furthermore, the results suggest marginally greater support, in the form of loans, to higher insider holdings firms in a group. The support provided by group loans is found to be an important factor in avoiding weak firms going bankrupt. The findings mentioned above suggest that group loans are often provided on favourable terms and for unprofitable investments, which reveals the cost for firms which provides the loans. In other words, these group loans involve costs for the firms which provide loans, and a means of expropriating the wealth of minority shareholders might be by transferring funds from firms with lower cash holding rights to firms with higher cash holdings.

On the contrary, Khanna and Palepu (2000b) argue that RP lending might benefit group firms when the external market is not fully developed. Related lending might benefit the group as a whole by making funds available when required; however, it may impose a cost on the minority shareholders of lending firm. Since we analyze these transactions at the firm level, it is likely to capture the lower valuation of firms lending to other member firms in the group. Controlling shareholders might not see related lending as value destroying because of their stake in all firms in the group. However, minority shareholders of a lending firm might not have any financial stake in the firm where this money is channelled and, therefore, the outside investor value is reduced for firms which disclose RP lending.

---

[26] La Porta et al. (2003) and Claessens et al. (2006) provide evidence on misallocation of funds by controlling shareholders through related lending.

Loans to member firms

Cheung et al. (2006) report that firms providing cash assistance to related parties experience value loss. Jiang, Lee, and Yue (2005) provide direct evidence on tunnelling through corporate loans by controlling shareholders. They find that companies with large amounts of loans are associated with poor performance in the future and are more likely to face the risk of delisting. Firms with a large number of loans experience lower market valuation, which suggests that the market correctly predicts the adverse impact of these loans on firm performance. Thus, we develop the following hypothesis:

H7a: RP loans to member firms in the group are likely to be perceived as expropriation of minority shareholders and, thus, result in value loss for the firm.

Prior studies report that firms in which controlling shareholders have lower cash-flow rights or higher indirect rights tend to provide higher loans (Claessens et al., 2002; Sarkar and Sarkar, 2000). This suggests that more funds in the form of loans are likely to be tunnelled out when controlling shareholders have higher indirect ownership rights. As a result, we develop the following related hypothesis:

H7b: RP loans to member firms are likely to be negatively associated with value-relevance of earnings in the presence of indirect ownership of controlling shareholders.

Loans to subsidiary or holding firms

If loans between subsidiary and holding firms are used to channel money from profitable firms to unprofitable operations, this is likely to result in value loss (Cornell and Liu, 2001). In earlier RPT studies, cash loans are viewed as minority expropriation regardless of the relationship between the connected parties (Cheung et al., 2009; Kohlbeck and Mayhew, 2010; Cheung et al., 2006). These arrangements are viewed as a misallocation of resources, which enable the following hypothesis to be made:

H7c: RP loans to subsidiary or/and holding firms are likely to be viewed as a misallocation of funds and, thus, cause value loss for the firm.

The loans between subsidiary and holding firms are likely to be driven by the relationship between the two firms (subsidiary–parent relationship) and indirect ownership rights of controlling shareholders are less likely to dominate. Therefore, we develop the following hypothesis:

H7d: The valuation of RP loans to subsidiary and/or holding firms are not likely to influence the value-relevance of earnings in the presence of indirect ownership of controlling shareholders.

Summary

This chapter presents testable hypotheses with the support of agency theory. Seven hypotheses regarding the determinants of expropriation of minority shareholders are developed. Hypotheses 1 and 2 predict the association between family ownership and MVE, whereas the influence of minority ownership on MVE is predicted in Hypothesis 3. Furthermore, the influence of RPTs disclosure on MVE is hypothesized. Hypothesis 4 presents the predicted association between RP trading (sale and purchase of goods and services) and MVE. The association between RP asset transfers and MVE is presented in Hypothesis 5. Hypothesis 6 predicts the market valuation of RP investments. Lastly, the association between RP loans and MVE is predicted by Hypothesis 7. Furthermore, the next chapter provides a detailed discussion on research methods employed to test the above-mentioned hypotheses.

Chapter 5

Research Methods

This chapter presents a detailed discussion of the research methods used in the study. This chapter is organized as follows. The first section explains the procedures employed to select the data sample. The next section provides the description of the data, which includes the selection of firms based on group membership and industry classification. The last section explains the empirical models employed to measure the valuation of the effects of group membership, ownership structure, and RPTs.

Sampling procedures

Sample selection

The Prowess database developed by the Centre of Monitoring Indian Economy (CMIE) is used to identify the sample firms. We identify two parameters to select firms for the analysis. These are: (*a*) firms belonging to Indian Business Groups, and (*b*) firms that are listed on the BSE. On 20 November 2012, the initial search using the Prowess database identified 8,420 group firms, of which, only 1,640 firms were found to be listed. As financial firms are subject to different regulation, we chose to exclude financial firms from the sample. After excluding them, 1,443 firms remained. We randomly selected 400 firms from them. The data we require for the analysis (financial, ownership, and corporate governance) was not available for all 400 firms. There were 83 firms with missing information in the Prowess database. After deleting those firms from the sample, there were 317 firms, which is approximately 22 per cent of the total population (1,443 firms). The details of sample firms are provided in Panel A of Table 5.1. Appendix 1 provides names of firms included in the sample. Information on RPTs and corporate governance is hand collected.

TABLE 5.1
Sample firms and firm-year observations

Panel A: Sample firms	
	Number of firms
Total population	1,640
Financial	197
Total non-financial firms	1,443
Randomly selected	400
Firms with mission information	83
Final sample	317

Panel B: Firm-year observations	
Year ending	*Observations*
2008	298
2009	301
2010	311
2011	314
2012	306
Total observations	1,530

Source: Authors.

Total sample firms belong to 156 business groups. The average firms per group is two, with a minimum of one firm per group and a maximum of eight firms per group. Appendix 2 provides the names of these groups and the number of firms per group.

We examine the group firm ownership structure and RPTs for sample firms for the recent five-year period from the year ending in March 2008 to March 2012. Our sample contains 1,530 firm-year observations. The number of individual year observations varies because of missing variables for some firms in particular years during the selected period and details are provided in Table 5.1 (Panel B).

Sample firms are classified into eight industries (see Table 5.2). Manufacturing firms represent almost 37 per cent of the total firms, followed by the service industry which is just under 20 per cent. Approximately 18 per cent of the total firms belong to the chemical industry. Electricity and mining firms represent a very small portion of the sample, which is less than one per cent individually. Manufacturing firms are over-represented in the sample, and this should be considered when generalizing the results of this study.

TABLE 5.2
Industry classification

Industry	Number	Proportion
Chemical	57	18%
Construction and real estate	20	6%
Electricity	3	1%
Manufacturing	119	37%
Metal and metal Products	29	9%
Mining	2	1%
Services	60	19%
Textiles	27	9%
Total	317	100%

Source: Authors.

Data type and collection

Data collection involves obtaining information on: (*a*) financial, (*b*) stock market, (*c*) ownership, (*d*) corporate governance, and (*e*) other firm-specific information. Financial information comprises items such as assets, liabilities, book value of equity, earnings, and RPTs. Collection of stock market data involves gathering share price information on specific dates. Ownership data comprises direct and indirect ownership of controlling families, ownership of domestic and foreign institutional shareholders, and ownership of minority shareholders. Corporate governance data includes information about the number of members on the board, the proportion of independent members on the board, proportion of independent members in the audit committee and CEO/chairperson identity for the sample firms. Other firm-specific information includes gathering information about group affiliation, industry affiliation, and the name of the auditor.

All the information is collected from the Prowess database maintained by the CMIE. Prowess is a very comprehensive source and provides information about various aspects of Indian firms. However, all of this information is not downloadable. Prowess extracts information from annual reports and it is placed in different segments of the database. Consequently, it is not always available in a form which meets the research design requirements. Data collection involved much going back and forth to gather information. Information on the book value of assets, liabilities, and shareholders' equity and earnings is available to download, whereas the profile of each sample firm is examined individually to collect information on RPTs, auditor, and other governance variables. For instance, information on the proportion of independent members on the audit committee is not provided in Prowess and audit committee independence is determined by gathering information about the independence status of each member on the committee.

The identification of business groups is based on the classification by CMIE. The same group classification was previously used in Khanna and Palepu (2000b), Bertrand et al. (2002), Gopalan et al. (2007), and other research studies. They classify firms into either groups or stand-alone (non-group) categories. CMIE group classification is not only based on equity ownership, with company announcements and qualitative aspects of corporate behaviour also considered to identify business groups. The identification of group firms in India is relatively easy compared with other countries. First, firms in India are members of only one group, which eliminates the possibility of any confusion. Second, unlike Japanese *keiretsu*, Indian groups are easily identifiable because of the family ties. Further, there is no movement of firms across the groups.

This study analyzes the variables at firm level, rather than group level. The analysis at firm level has several benefits. First, every firm is a separate legal entity and the financial information is readily available at firm level. Second, the variation evident at firm level would be lost if we aggregate the quality measures at the group level. Furthermore, groups differ in terms of their social and economic ties, which would influence their reporting incentives, and ignoring such differences would be unwise.

Statistical analysis

This study uses several statistical techniques for the data analysis and hypotheses testing. Descriptive statistics are presented so that useful insights into data are generated. Correlation analyses are used to identify the extent of association between independent and control variables and to determine if there is high level of multicollinearity. Regression analysis is employed as the main form of statistical test. The regression method is considered appropriate for testing the proposed hypotheses and it is widely used in studies of ownership structure and RPTs (Cheung et al., 2006; Douma et al., 2006; Khanna and Palepu, 2000b; Kohlbeck and Mayhew, 2010). Therefore, we use (OLS) multiple regressions and fixed-effect models to address our research questions.

Value relevance model

The value relevance model is extensively used in the literature to test the relevance of accounting information. Many studies show that both equity book value and net income are priced in the share price.[27] Watts (1974) suggests that the balance sheet and income statement have different roles in explaining the variation in the MVE. The fundamental role of the income statement is for equity valuation, and the income statement reflects information about a firm's growth opportunities and unrecognized net assets. The balance sheet provides information on liquidation values[28] and, thus, facilitates loan decisions and debt covenants. Therefore, the MVE is a function of both.

$$MVE_{it} = \alpha_0 + \alpha_1 \, BVE_{it} + \alpha_2 \, EARN_{it} + e_{it}$$

The literature also examines whether the variation in the MVE is explained relatively better by the book value of equity or net income for a set of firms. Barth, Beaver, and Landsman (1998) report that the explanatory power of equity book value increases as financial health decreases. This suggests that liquidation values in the balance sheet becomes increasing important for equity valuation as the risk of default increases and income statement values lose their value relevance. On the other hand, the income statement has higher value relevance for healthy firms because investors place more valuation weight on net income when there is no risk of default.

This study employs three sets of OLS regression models to test the various hypotheses. First, regression analysis will be employed to examine the effect of controlling shareholders' ownership on firm value. Second, the valuation consequences of minority shareholdings are examined. Third, regression analysis is used to determine the market valuation of various types of RPTs.

Ownership of controlling shareholders

This section outlines the regression model developed to test hypotheses 1 and 2. Two independent variables, named DIROWN and INDOWN, are added in the basic value relevance model presented above. We expect that there are other factors which could have an effect on firm value. Therefore, we develop our model by including additional variables to control for institutional investors, corporate governance, and audit quality differences. Brown, Beekes, and Verhoeven (2011) suggest that the construction of corporate

---

[27] See Easton and Harris (1991), Kothari and Zimmerman (1995), Ohlson (1995), and Francis and Schipper (1999) to name a few.

[28] It is expected that book values approximate liquidation values and assets are written down when book value is higher than market value. However, firms might not consistently recognize asset impairments.

governance indices should be sensitive to local institutional settings and both internal and external aspects of governance should be captured. The variables to represent the holdings of institutional investors include mutual funds, financial institutions, government, and FIIs. Conventional governance mechanisms, such as performance-based compensation and takeovers, are less effective in dealing with conflicts between shareholder groups (Gomez-Mejia et al., 2003; Kole, 1997). Therefore, we include Big 4 auditors, board size, independent directors,[29] audit committee independence, and non-family CEO/chairperson to account for the role of corporate governance in monitoring and/or challenging controlling shareholders. We also control for firm size, firm age, growth, debt, risk, industry, and year.

Variables measurement

Institutional investors are considered to be a means of improving corporate governance by taking active part in the management of corporations they own. The Cadbury Report (1992) expects institutions to consider themselves as owners and adopt a proactive approach. It would be reasonable to assume that shareholders owning significant blocks (other than promoting families) may restrict controlling family members from expropriating the wealth of minority shareholders. There is some evidence in the US context that blockholders improve corporate governance. Mikkelson and Ruback (1991) find a positive and significant association between blockholders and firm value. Similar results were evident in the studies by Holderness and Sheehan (1988) and Barclay and Holderness (1991).

These institutional investors have both the incentives and power to challenge any acts of controlling shareholders which aim to extract resources from the firm. In fact, like controlling shareholders, large blockholders might also choose to extract funds from the firm. However, the interests of institutional investors are less likely to be aligned with controlling families to extract resources from the firm. Villalonga and Amit (2006) argue: if the large blockholder is a financial institution or widely held corporation, the private benefits on control are diluted among several owners. As a consequence, the blockholder's incentives for the expropriation of minority shareholders are small. In the Indian setting, Bertrand et al. (2002) provide evidence of

---

[29] Westphal (1998) argues that the composition of board of directors can contribute significantly to firm performance when alternative mechanisms are less effective.

tunnelling from firms with lower cash-flow rights to firms with higher cash-flow rights by controlling shareholders. Studies such as Claessens et al. (1999) and Claessens et al. (2000) also provide evidence of superior performance of group firms where controlling shareholders have higher cash-flow rights. This is consistent with the group level structure facilitating controlling families to extract funds, whereas institutional investors have no involvement at the group level. If indirect rights provide controlling shareholder incentives to divert resources from firms with low cash-flow rights to firms with high cash-flow rights, then institutional investors are most likely to oppose it as they do not benefit from such expropriation. In this case, large blockholders would play a challenging role to controlling family shareholders. Lins (2003) finds that large, non-management blockholder rights are positively associated with firm value. This is consistent with a positive monitoring role in mitigating extreme agency problems.

However, differences in identity, concentration, and resource endowments among these investors determine their relative incentives, power, and ability to monitor family managers. For instance, financial investors might be interested in short-term returns, whereas corporate investors might be more inclined towards long-term growth. The sustainability of these advantages is also linked to the institutional context. For example, in countries with less developed economies, FIIs are expected to have better monitoring skills than domestic institutional investors. Sarkar and Sarkar (2000) report that foreign investors are positively associated with firm value in India, whereas domestic institutional investors do not play an active role in governance. Similarly, Douma et al. (2006) indicate that domestic institutional investors are negatively associated with firm performance measured by ROA. However, domestic institutional investors do not significantly influence market-based performance (measured using the Tobin's Q ratio) in India.

Therefore, we distinguish domestic institutional investors from FIIs. Furthermore, we classify domestic institutional investors into three categories: (*a*) mutual funds; (*b*) financial institutions; and (*c*) central and state government. Development financial institutions and mutual funds might be state-owned; however, the type of holding and resultant incentives to monitor them might be different between the two groups (Sarkar and Sarkar, 2000). Financial institutions hold both debt and equity, whereas mutual funds hold only equity. These dual holdings might reduce the conflict between shareholders and debtholders and these financial institutions might not be in the same position as mutual funds (Mulbert, 1997; Prowse, 1990). Overall, we expect these four categories of institutional investors (mutual funds, financial institutions, government, and FIIs) to possess different monitoring skills and, thus, the ownership of each class should be associated with firm value differently based on their distinct objectives.

Mutal funds: Mutual funds hold a significant level of equity in the Indian market. Existing literature documents that mutual funds in India are negatively associated with firm value, highlighting the ineffective monitoring of these funds. However, the studies examining performance of mutual funds were conducted in the 1990s. For instance, Sarkar and Sarkar (2000) find that ownership of mutual funds is negatively associated with firm value, using data for 1995–1996. There have been many reforms in the mutual fund industry in the last two decades aiming at greater growth. The Securities and Exchange Board of India (Mutual Funds) Regulation, 1993 was introduced by SEBI to allow the entry of private firms in the mutual fund industry. In 2010, SEBI formulated a draft to permitting mutual funds to invest in real estate. The restrictions on foreign investments have been relaxed under the Foreign Exchange Management Act, 1999. With India achieving the second highest growth rate worldwide in the last decade, mutual funds are expected to be competitive and possess better monitoring skills. These funds are expected to achieve market returns and, therefore, the association between mutual funds ownership and the MVE is expected to be positive.

Financial institutions: These development financial institutions are predominantly government-owned, and they are considered to be passive monitors in India (Khanna and Palepu, 1999). Douma et al. (2006) find that domestic financial institutions are negatively associated with firm performance. However, Sarkar and Sarkar (2000) report that financial institution ownership is positively associated with firm value once they own a substantial stake in the firm. Moreover, these financial institutions are not only equity holders, but also debt holders. Because of their greater involvement, we do not expect these institutions to assess their investments entirely based on stock market performance. Instead, financial institutional ownership is expected to be stable and based on a long-term association, and they might continue their investments in poor-performing firms. Therefore, the association between financial institution ownership and firm value could be either positive or negative.

Government ownership: Megginson, Nash, and Van Randenborgh (1994) and Dewenter and Malatesta (2001) provide empirical evidence to support the view that government ownership is less efficient than private ownership. Government ownership suffers from a number of problems that reduce its monitoring ability. First, the government's nominees on the board are bureaucrats with minimal corporate knowledge. Second, even if government representatives are equipped with skills to oversee corporate matters, they do not have incentives to be active monitors. Their career prospects are not influenced by the performance of the firms in which they serve on the board of directors. Finally, government is oriented towards social welfare objectives, less profit driven, and, thus, less vigilant in monitoring corporate matters (Ramaswamy, Mingfang, and Veliyath, 2002). As a result, government ownership is likely to affect firm value negatively.

Foreign institutional investors: Foreign institutional investors are oriented towards stock-market based measures of return and they have incentives to sell their ownership stake of poor-performing firms. In the case of these institutions, the performance of fund managers, who are involved with buying and selling shares, is measured by the stock market index (Douma et al., 2006). However, FIIs are unlikely to act as a cohesive block in enhancing corporate governance for two reasons. First, these institutions manage a portfolio of shares in different industries to achieve a diversified portfolio. Second, the ownership stake of foreign investors in a single firm is constrained by the legal system of India. Therefore, the holdings of foreign institutions are relatively fragmented. Given the stock market perspective, foreign financial institutional ownership is expected to be positively associated with firm value, measured by MVE.

Corporate governance variables

Board size: Existing literature provides mixed evidence regarding the association between board size and corporate performance. Jensen (1993) argues that large boards are less effective in coordination, communication, and decision-making. Eisenberg, Sundgren, and Wells (1998) support Jensen's hypothesis that large boards result in lower firm value. Mak and Kusnadi (2005) support the negative association between board size and firm performance using data for Singapore and Malaysia. Board composition is, in fact, viewed as an effective measure in reducing environmental uncertainty by securing valuable resources (Aldrich, 2008). For example, inviting members with different kinds of knowledge and skills to join the board will strengthen the firm's ability to cope with the changing economic environment. As firms compete in an uncertain environment, these representatives increase in number and the board becomes larger. Pearce and Zahra (1992) support this view and report that board size is positively associated with firm performance. Therefore, the effect of board size on firm value is an empirical question and we do not predict any directional association between board size and firm value.

Independent directors and audit committee independence: In the presence of conflict between controlling and minority shareholders, independent directors may serve a protective role for minority shareholders to limit the expropriation of their wealth. Dalton et al. (1998) argue that independent directors contribute objectivity, which assists in minimizing managerial entrenchment and expropriation. Independent directors can impose a number of constraints on controlling owners, such as limiting their involvement in or influence over the audit committee, nominating committee, or compensation committee. The property rights literature also presents a similar view. It suggests that minority shareholders are only protected when they have power relative to controlling owners and are able to limit the opportunistic behaviour of controlling shareholders (Hart and Moore, 1990).

However, the self-control problem of family firms undermines the effectiveness of outside non-executive directors. In spite of the obvious advantages of outside directors in terms of expertise, monitoring skills, and diversity, family firms are less likely to use them for the following reasons (Schulze et al., 2001). First, they pose a challenge to family owners in terms of perceived loss of control. Second, while the independent status of these directors enhances their ability to provide advice on some matters, they have little influence on matters involving family members (Nelson and Frishkoff, 1991). Finally, 'hand-picking' independent directors for reasons other than effective supervision of the management can undermine their value (Rubenson and Gupta, 1996). For example, the tendency of controlling families to appoint outside members to their board who are friends or have a fiduciary relationship with them (their accountant or board member from another firm of the family group) compromises true independence. Sarkar and Sarkar (2009) report that independent directors hold 67 per cent of their directorships in group-affiliated firms and about 43 per cent of their directorships are concentrated in the same business group, which highlights their dependence on controlling groups. Furthermore, they find that the market discounts the incidence of multiple directorships held by independent directors in group-affiliated firms.

Since the audit committee is a sub-committee of the board, the shortcomings associated with independent board members are likely to hamper the effectiveness of the audit committee also. The reliance of audit committee members on the controlling group for their directorships is likely to impair their independence. Furthermore, independent directors often consider their role as being an advisor to controlling shareholders and not to monitor them so that the interests of outside shareholders are protected (Khanna and Mathew, 2010).

Non-executive independent directors are expected to enhance control mechanisms. However, in the context of this study, independent directors are less likely to be effective monitors for the reasons listed above. Therefore, we do not predict any directional association between independent board members and firm value.

Big 4 auditors: Big 4 auditors are expected to be associated with higher accounting quality because of their greater technical ability to identify accounting irregularities and frauds, which will be valued highly by the market. In addition, Big 4 audit firms exercise greater care and skill to maintain their reputation. DeAngelo (1981) notes that Big 4 audit firms should have more incentives to maintain their reputations than non-Big 4 firms. Prior literature provides evidence that Big 4 audit firms are associated with lower earnings management. Gallery et al. (2008) argue that audit quality, when measured by large audit firms, will constrain the amount of RPTs.

Big 4 audit firms include KPMG, Ernst & Young, Deloitte, and PricewaterhouseCoopers. These multinational firms have not as yet captured a large share of the Indian market and for this reason, they have formed local alliances to perform audit services. Bharat S. Rau & Co is the Indian associate of KPMG, Ernst & Young is associated with S R Batliboi and S. V. Ghatalia & Associates, the Indian associates of Deloitte are A. F. Ferguson Associates, S. B. Billimoria, C. C. Choksi, P. C. Hansotia, and Fraser & Ross, and Deloitte Haskins & Sells and PWC are associated with two firms: Lovelock and Lewis and Dalal & Shah.

Non-family CEO/chairperson: Villalonga and Amit (2006) argue that family firms with a family CEO are expected to have no Type 1 agency cost. However, the Type 2 agency cost might be higher when the family is empowered with top management positions. Specifically, family control is likely to facilitate expropriation of minority shareholders in environments where regulations fail to address the financial manoeuvres of controlling shareholders and legal systems are prone to corruption (Young et al. 2008). Anderson and Reeb (2004) show that limited levels of family involvement on the board provide benefits to the firm, but excessive power creates costs for the firm. The results also indicate that board independence is likely to be lower by 9.5 per cent when family members serve on the nominating committee. This suggests that family members prefer to limit board independence to better facilitate their ability to extract firm resources. The presence of a family chairperson signifies that greater control lies in the hands of the family, and the likelihood of expropriation of minority shareholders is expected to be higher when a family member serves on the board as chairperson.

However, the appointment of a capable employee to the top position may not necessarily result in a better outcome due to the constant influence of controlling shareholders on the management. If the CEO of the firm is an outsider, family members of the founding family often occupy the position of chairperson. Therefore, professional CEOs might not be as effective in family firms as they might prove in widely held firms.

We include a dummy variable to capture the appointment of a non-family person in one of the top two positions: CEO or chairperson, and we predict a positive association between non-family CEO/chairperson and firm value.

Other control variables

Firm size: One body of literature reports firm size to be positively associated with firm value. Larger firms are expected to have better disclosure, more diversified activities, and more liquid trading, resulting in lower risk of financial distress (Claessens et al., 2003). On the contrary, smaller firms may have more growth opportunities, which is shown to be correlated with higher firm valuation. Beedles et al. (1988) find that small firms consistently outperform large firms. Claessens et al. (1999) associate diversification with value discounts in Asia and, thus, small firms might experience lower value discounts because they have less diversified operations. Claessens et al. (2002), Lins (2003), and other studies on firm valuation control for firm size. Therefore, we control for firm size but do not predict any directional association between firm size and firm value. Firm size has been measured as natural logarithm of total assets.

Firm age: Consistent with the argument presented above, older firms are expected to have higher firm value because of their better reputation, liquid trading, and better disclosure. However, the older firms might lack growth opportunities, leading to lower firm value. Evans (1987) report that age is an important determinant of firm growth, variability of firm growth, and the probability of firm dissolution. Again, we do not predict any directional association between firm age and firm value. We measure firm age as a natural logarithm of firm age in years from the date of its registration.

Debt: Leverage (DEBT) is measured by total debt over total assets. While leverage plays a disciplinary role by limiting the excessive cash flow in hand and reducing profit diversion, leverage can also have a negative effect if it increases the financial distress and risk of bankruptcy (Maury and Pajuste, 2005). Therefore, we do not provide a clear prediction on the association between firm value and leverage.

Growth: The level of growth in the previous year serves as proxy for firms' growth prospects and is expected to be positively associated with firm value. This is measured by the market value of the firm at the beginning of the year over total assets.

Industry: We also include industry variables to account for possible valuation differences among industries. Industry is a vector of industry indicator variables based on the industry classification of the CMIE. Sample firms are classified into eight categories: chemical; construction and real estate; electricity; manufacturing; metal and metal products; mining; services; and textiles.

Year: Consistent with cross-sectional panel data, we include year dummy variables to control for differential effects of time (Mitton, 2002). Year is a vector of year indicator variables: 2008, 2009, 2010, 2011, and 2012.

Model

A base regression model has been developed to examine the market valuation of ownership rights and to test the proposed hypotheses, which is presented below:

$$MVE_{i,t} = \alpha_0 + \alpha_1 BVE_{i,t} + \alpha_2 EARN_{i,t} + \alpha_3 DIROWN_{i,t} + \alpha_4 INDOWN_{i,t} +$$
$$\alpha_5 NPMF_{i,t} + \alpha_6 NPFI_{i,t} + \alpha_7 GOVT_{i,t} + \alpha_8 FII_{i,t} + \alpha_9 BIG4AUD_{i,t} + \alpha_{10} ACIND_{i,t} +$$
$$\alpha_{11} BDIND_{i,t} + \alpha_{12} BDSIZE_{i,t} + \alpha_{13} NONFAMCEO_{i,t} + \alpha_{14} FSIZE_{i,t} + \alpha_{15} FAGE_{i,t}$$
$$+ \alpha_{16} DEBT_{i,t} + \alpha_{17} GROWTH_{i,t-1} + \Sigma_{i,j}^3 Year_{i,t} + \Sigma_{i,j}^4 Industry_{i,t} + \varepsilon_{i,t}$$

Where:

$MVE_{i,t}$ is the natural logarithm of MVE 90 days after the balance sheet end date, scaled by the beginning number of shares outstanding;

$BVE_{i,t}$ is the book value of shareholders' equity, scaled by the beginning number of shares outstanding;

$EARN_{i,t}$ is year-end income before tax and extraordinary items, scaled by the beginning number of shares outstanding;

$DIROWN_{i,t}$ is the percentage direct shareholding of controlling individuals and families;

$INDOWN_{i,t}$ is the percentage indirect shareholding of controlling families through corporations;

$NPMF_{i,t}$ is the percentage ownership of non-promoter mutual funds;

$NPFI_{i,t}$ is the percentage ownership of non-promoter financial institutions and banks;

$GOVT_{i,t}$ is the ownership of the central and state government;

$FII_{i,t}$ is the ownership of foreign institutional investors;

$BIG4AUD_{i,t}$ is an indicator variable equal to one if the firm is audited by a Big 4 auditor and/or their Indian associates, and zero otherwise;

$ACIND_{i,t}$ is the proportion of independent members to total members of the audit committee;

$BDIND_{i,t}$ is the proportion of independent directors to total board members;

$BSIZE_{i,t}$ is board size measured by the number of members of the board of directors;

$NONFAMCEO_{i,t}$ is an indicator variable equal to one if the CEO or chairperson position is occupied by a non-family person and zero otherwise;

$FSIZE_{i,t}$ is the natural logarithm of total assets;

$FAGE_{i,t}$ is the natural logarithm of firm age;

$DEBT_{i,t}$ is the ratio of total debt to total assets;

$GROWTH_{i,t}$ is the previous year's growth, calculated based on the market value of the firm at the end of year *t-1* divided by the ending book value of the total assets at *t-1*;

Year is a vector of year indicator variables for the 2008, 2009, 2010, 2011, and 2012 years;

Industry is a vector of industry indicator variables based on the CMIE industry classification.

Minority ownership

This regression is employed to test Hypothesis 4. The independent variables MINORITY1 and MINORITY2 replace IPIND and IPCORP in the model presented above. All other variables remain the same. The revised regression model is presented below:

$$MVE_{i,t} = \alpha_0 + \alpha_1 BVE_{i,t} + \alpha_2 EARN_{i,t} + \alpha_3 MINORITY1_{i,t} + \alpha_4 MINORITY2_{i,t} +$$
$$\alpha_5 NPMF_{i,t} + \alpha_6 NPFI_{i,t} + \alpha_7 GOVT_{i,t} + \alpha_8 FII_{i,t} + \alpha_9 BIG4AUD_{i,t} + \alpha_{10} ACIND_{i,t} +$$
$$\alpha_{11} BDIND_{i,t} + \alpha_{12} BDSIZE_{i,t} + \alpha_{13} NONFAMCEO_{i,t} + \alpha_{14} FSIZE_{i,t} + \alpha_{15} FAGE_{i,t}$$
$$+ \alpha_{16} DEBT_{i,t} + \alpha_{17} GROWTH_{i,t} + \Sigma^3_{i,j} Year_{i,t} + \Sigma^4_{i,j} Industry_{i,t} + \varepsilon_{i,t}$$

Where:

MINORITY1 is the percentage ownership of non-promoter individuals holding nominal share investments worth up to INR 100,000;

MINORITY2 is the percentage ownership of non-promoter individuals holding nominal share investments worth above INR 100,000;

Other variables are defined earlier.

RPTs

This regression analysis aims to test Hypotheses 5 to 8. As the purpose of this model is to examine the market valuation consequences of RPTs, the magnitude of the various types of RPTs are included in the model. Following Rediker and Seth (1995), firm performance depends on the efficiency of a bundle of mechanisms in controlling agency costs, rather than on the efficiency of a single governance mechanism. The consequences might be important if relevant independent variables are omitted from the model and this problem could worsen if the omitted explanatory variable is correlated with the included independent variable. In other words, different mechanisms work as substitutes and there is less likelihood of finding an association if a number of substitute mechanisms possess important explanatory power and are not measured. Therefore, we include some interactions in the model. In the value-relevance model, we include additional independent variables which represent interaction terms between the various RPTs type indicators and the BVE, EARN, and IPCORP variables to examine whether RPTs moderate the value relevance relationship and the influence of indirect ownership rights.

$$MVE_{i,t} = \alpha_0 + \alpha_1 BVE_{i,t} + \alpha_2 EARN_{i,t} + \alpha_3 INDOWN_{i,t} + \alpha_4 \Sigma^8_{i,j} RTYPE_{i,t}$$
$$+ \alpha_5 BVE_{i,t} * \Sigma^8_{i,j} RTYPE_{i,t} + \alpha_6 EARN_{i,t} * \Sigma^8_{ij} RPTYPE_{i,t} + \alpha_7 EARN_{i,t}$$
$$* \alpha_i INDOWN_{i,t} * \Sigma^8_{ij} RPTYPE_{i,t} + \alpha_8 DIROWN_{i,t} + \alpha_9 NPMF_{i,t} + \alpha_{10} NPFI_{i,t}$$
$$+ \alpha_{11} GOVT_{i,t} + \alpha_{12} FII_{i,t} + \alpha_{13} BIG4AUD_{i,t} + \alpha_{14} ACIND_{i,t} + \alpha_{15} BDIND_{i,t} +$$
$$\alpha_{16} BDSIZE_{i,t} + \alpha_{17} NONFAMCEO_{i,t} + \alpha_{18} FSIZE_{i,t} + \alpha_{19} FAGE_{i,t} + \alpha_{20} DEBT_{i,t}$$
$$+ \alpha_{21} GROWTH_{i,t} + \Sigma^3_{i,j} Year_{i,t} + \Sigma^4_{i,j} Industry_{i,t} + \varepsilon_{i,t}$$

Where:

$MVE_{i,t}$ is the natural logarithm of the market value equity 90 days after the balance sheet end date, scaled by the beginning number of shares outstanding;

$BVE_{i,t}$ is the book value of shareholders' equity, scaled by the beginning number of shares outstanding;

$EARN_{i,t}$ is year-end income before tax and extraordinary items, scaled by the beginning number of shares outstanding;

$INDOWN_{i,t}$ is the percentage indirect shareholding of controlling families through corporations;

$RPTYPE_{i,t}$ represents one of the following vectors describing a magnitude of

- TRAD: RP trading which involves the sale and purchase of goods and services, scaled by the beginning total assets;
- ASST: RP asset transfers, scaled by the beginning total assets;
- INVST: RP investments, scaled by the beginning total assets;
- NETLOAN: RP loans given, scaled by the beginning total assets;

$DIROWN_{i,t}$ is the percentage direct shareholding of controlling individuals and families;

$NPMF_{i,t}$ is the percentage ownership of non-promoter mutual funds;

$NPFI_{i,t}$ is the percentage ownership of non-promoter financial institutions and banks;

$GOVT_{i,t}$ is the ownership of central and state government;

$FII_{i,t}$ is the ownership of foreign institutional investors;

$BIG4AUD_{i,t}$ is an indicator variable equal to one if the firm is audited by a Big 4 auditor and/or their Indian associates, and zero otherwise;

$ACIND_{i,t}$ is the proportion of independent members to total members of the audit committee;

$BDIND_{i,t}$ is the proportion of independent directors to total board members;

$BSIZE_{i,t}$ is board size measured by the number of members of the board of directors;

$NONFAMCEO_{i,t}$ is an indicator variable equal to one if the CEO or chairperson position is occupied by a non-family person and zero otherwise;

$FSIZE_{i,t}$ is the natural logarithm of total sales;

$FAGE_{i,t}$ is the natural logarithm of firm age;

$DEBT_{i,t}$ is the ratio of total debt to total assets;

$GROWTH_{i,t}$ is the previous year's growth, calculated based on the market value of the firm at the end of year *t-1* divided by the ending book value of the total assets at *t-1*;

Year is a vector of year indicator variables for the 2008, 2009, 2010, 2011, and 2012 years;

Industry is a vector of industry indicator variables based on the CMIE industry classification.

Sensitivity tests

This study conducts additional sensitivity tests to check the findings' robustness. These include fixed-effect models serving as an alternate to the pooled OLS regression models. Furthermore, the regression analysis is also run on partitioned samples. Results from these samples offer comparisons to the main findings for the full sample and generate further insights on the market valuation of RPTs. The substitution effect of audit committee and board independence is also examined in more detail. In addition to having a non-family CEO, the CEO effect on firm value is examined further based on the existence of CEO/chairperson duality. Finally, the generalized method of moments (GMM) estimation models are employed to control for endogeneity issues.

Summary

A large sample of 1,530 firm-year observations is gathered for the period from 2008 to 2012 to seek evidence on the expropriation of minority shareholders within Indian business groups. In particular, the use of RPTs among group firms is examined. Predictive variables include family ownership and the magnitude of various RPTs. Additional tests are conducted to confirm the robustness of the main findings. The next chapter provides descriptive statistics on the sample set.

Chapter 6

Descriptive Statistics

Introduction

This chapter presents descriptive statistics and other preliminary statistical tests to provide insights into the ownership structure and the RPTs disclosure of sample firms. First, the descriptive statistics of the entire sample comprising 1,530 firm-year observations are presented. This is followed by division of the sample into two categories: (*a*) firms which have disclosed RPTs, and (*b*) firms which have not disclosed any RPTs. Further analysis is then conducted by dividing RPTs based on the association with the related party. RPTs with subsidiary and holding companies are separated from RPTs with other group member firms. These analytical steps provide an important overview of firm characteristics and RPT disclosure. Finally, the Pearson correlation matrix is presented to identify any potential multicollinearity problems.

Descriptive statistics of the full-sample

This section provides descriptive statistics for all research variables, including firm-specific characteristics of the sample. Independent variables consist of direct and indirect ownership of controlling shareholders, minority ownership, and the magnitude of RPTs, whereas the dependent variable is the MVE. Table 6.1 provides descriptive statistics for the full sample of 1,530 firm-year observations.

The dependent variable, MVE, has a mean value of INR 211 with a maximum value of INR 8,799 and a minimum of INR 0.42. The average book value of equity is INR 127, with a maximum value of INR 5,051 and a minimum of INR -497. Average earnings per share amount to INR 20 and median earnings are INR 7, with a maximum of INR 1,436 and a minimum of INR -1,297. Average direct ownership of controlling families (DIROWN) amounts to 15 per cent only, with a median ownership level of 7 per cent. Indirect ownership of controlling families (INDOWN) averages 34 per cent of the total ownership, with a maximum value of 88 per cent and a minimum ownership level of zero. The minimum value of zero represents no indirect ownership, which suggests that such firms are controlled through direct ownership only. The results suggest that the proportion of indirect ownership through cross-holding is significantly higher than direct ownership, as the average holding of indirect ownership is more than double the proportion of direct ownership. This explains the prominence of cross-holdings in the context of the study. The average shareholding of minority shareholders with minimal holding (MINORITY1) is 16 per cent, whereas the average shareholding of minority shareholders with significant holding (MINORITY2) is 5 per cent. The average holding of institutional investors ranges from 0.1 per cent to 5 per cent, which suggests that institutional shareholdings in our sample are low, and this is consistent with other studies of India (Douma et al., 2006). The average holding of mutual funds is 2 per cent, with a maximum ownership level of 22 per cent. This is followed by domestic financial institutions with an average holding of 1 per cent. Government share holdings average only 0.1 per cent with a maximum value of 8 per cent. With an average holdings of 5 per cent, FIIs top the list.

TABLE 6.1
Descriptive statistics of the full sample

	Mean	Median	Std. Dev.	Maximum	Minimum	Observations
MVE	211.755	73.350	516.945	8799.336	0.420	1,530
BVE	127.146	64.626	291.324	5051.471	-497.335	1,530
EARN	20.706	7.165	76.807	1436.765	-1297.059	1,530
DIROWN	0.153	0.074	0.182	0.756	0.000	1,530
INDOWN	0.342	0.361	0.204	0.881	0.000	1,530
MINORITY1	0.161	0.148	0.099	0.634	0.000	1,530
MINORITY2	0.058	0.046	0.051	0.327	0.000	1,530
NPMF	0.020	0.000	0.037	0.222	0.000	1,530
NPFI	0.014	0.000	0.034	0.373	0.000	1,530
GOVT	0.001	0.000	0.006	0.087	0.000	1,530
FII	0.052	0.001	0.094	0.574	0.000	1,530
BIG4AUD	0.188	0.000	0.391	1.000	0.000	1,530
ACIND	0.824	0.800	0.187	1.000	0.000	1,530
BIND	0.536	0.539	0.138	1.000	0.000	1,530

Contd.

	Mean	Median	Std. Dev.	Maximum	Minimum	Observations
BSIZE	9.115	9.000	3.028	20.000	3.000	1,530
NONFAMCEO	0.316	0.000	0.465	1.000	0.000	1,530
FSIZE	18,808.060	4,628.650	45,688.790	557,974.700	20.800	1,530
FAGE	36.255	30.000	21.884	141.000	2.000	1,530
DEBT	0.331	0.308	0.278	1.87	0.000	1,530
GROWTH	0.875	0.474	1.179	8.960	0.026	1,530
TRADMF	0.060	0.000	0.233	1.630	0.000	1,530
TRADSH	0.023	0.000	0.096	1.460	0.000	1,530
ASSTMF	0.003	0.000	0.025	0.593	0.000	1,530
ASSTSH	0.001	0.000	0.013	0.374	0.000	1,530
INVSTMF	0.005	0.000	0.026	0.410	0.000	1,530
INVSTSH	0.013	0.000	0.076	1.270	0.000	1,530
NETLOANMF	0.001	0.000	0.110	1.570	-1.910	1,530
NETLOANSH	0.006	0.000	0.052	1.120	-0.330	1,530

Source: Authors.

Notes: The data is winsorized at the top and bottom 1 per cent level; the independent variables comprise INDOWN, DIROWN, MINORITY1, MINORITY2, TRADMF, TRADSH, ASSTMF, ASSTSH, INVSTMF, INVSTSH, NETLOANMF, NETLOANSH, whereas the dependent variable is MVE. Control variables include NPMF, NPFI, GOVT, FII, BIG4AUD, ACIND, BIND, BSIZE, NONFAMCEO, FAGE, FSIZE, GROWTH, DEBT, and RISK. MVE=market value of equity 90 days after year end scaled by number of shares outstanding; BVE= book value of equity at the year end scaled by number of shares outstanding; EARN=earnings before tax and extraordinary items scaled by number of shares outstanding; DIROWN=percentage direct shareholding of controlling individuals and families; INDOWN=percentage indirect shareholding of controlling families through corporations; MINORITY1=percentage ownership of non-promoter individuals holding nominal share investments worth up to INR 100,000; MINORITY2=percentage ownership of non-promoter individuals holding nominal share investments worth above INR 100,000; NPMF=percentage ownership of non-promoter mutual funds; NPFI=percentage ownership of non-promoter financial institutions and banks; GOVT=percentage ownership of central and state government; FII= percentage ownership of foreign institutional investors; BIG4AUD=dummy variable for Big 4 auditors; ACIND=audit committee independence; BDIND=board independence; BSIZE=board size; NONFAMCEO=dummy variable for non-family CEO or chairperson; FSIZE=total assets; FAGE=firm age; DEBT=ratio of total debt to total assets; GROWTH=previous year growth; TRADMF=magnitude of RP trading with member firms; TRADSH=magnitude of RP trading with subsidiary and holding firms; ASSTMF=magnitude of asset transfers with member firms; ASSTSH=magnitude of asset transfers with subsidiary and holding firms; INVSTMF=magnitude of investments with member firms; INVSTSH=magnitude of investments with subsidiary and holding firms; NETLOANMF=magnitude of net loans given to member firms; NETLOANSH=magnitude of net loans given to subsidiary and holding firms.

The average for BIG4AUD is 0.18, which suggests that 18 per cent of firm year observations are audited by Big 4 auditors. Audit committee independence averages 82 per cent with a maximum value of 100 per cent. Average board independence is 53 per cent, with a maximum value of 100 per cent. The maximum value of 100 per cent suggests that all directors on the board of some firms are independent. These results demonstrate that listed firms in India follow good governance guidelines and the majority of the board members are non-executive independents. The proportion of independent members on the audit committee is even higher, which is consistent with the requirements of the SEBI. It requires that the audit committee should comprise at least three members, of which at least two should be independent. However, it is unknown if the appointed members are truly independent and play their role effectively in monitoring the controlling shareholders. The average for the non-family CEO or chairperson variable is 0.31, which indicates that about one third of firm-year observations have a non-family CEO or chairperson.

Total assets' average is INR 18,808 million, with a maximum value of INR 557,974 million and a minimum value of INR 20.8 million. These statistics suggest that the sample represents a reasonable spread across the size spectrum of firms. The median firm age is 30 years with the average of 36 years. The maximum value of age is 141 and minimum value of 2. The debt to assets ratio averages 0.33, and the percentage of debt to assets ranges from 0 to 187 per cent. The highest leverage level, with the ratio of 1.87:1, indicates that a few firms might be on the verge of insolvency. The average of the previous year's growth ratio is 0.87.

Trading transactions with member firms average 6 per cent of the total assets, with some firms disclosing RP trading up to 163 per cent of the total assets and some firms without such transactions. This suggests excessive reliance on RP trading by some firms. The difference between the maximum value (1.630) and the average (0.06) appears to be very large, and this is contributed by the fact that more than 600 firm-year observations do not report RP trading with member firms. The average RP trading after excluding non-RPT firms will be significantly higher, and it should improve the normality of the sample distribution. Average RP trading with subsidiary and holding firms is 2 per cent only, with a maximum value of 146 per cent of total assets. Again, more than 800 firm-year observations do not disclose RP trading with subsidiary and holding firms. These results also indicate that the sale and purchase of goods and services involving member firms are significantly greater than such trading with subsidiary and holding firms.

Asset transfers with member firms in the group average 0.3 per cent of total assets, with a maximum value of 59 per cent of total assets and a minimum value of 0 per cent. Average asset transfers with subsidiary and holding firms amount to 0.1 per cent only, with the maximum value being 37 per cent of total assets. Again, almost half of the sample firm-year observations do not have asset transfers with related-parties, which results in the huge variance between mean and maximum values. Consistent with the RP trading data, asset transfers with member firms amount to more than asset transfers with subsidiary and holding firms.

Investments with member firms average 0.5 per cent of total assets, with a maximum value of 41 per cent. Average RP investments with subsidiary and holding firms amount to 1.3 per cent of total assets, with a maximum value of 127 per cent. In contrast to previous RPTs, investments with subsidiary and holding firms are greater than investment transactions with member firms. Average investments with subsidiary and holding firms are more than double the magnitude of average RP investments with member firms.

Net loans given to member firms amount, on average, to only 0.1 per cent of the total assets. The maximum value of net loans is 157 per cent of total assets and the minimum value is -191 per cent. The negative value represents that loans received from member firms are greater than loans given, which indicates propping. Average net loans given to subsidiary and holding firms are 0.6 per cent of total assets, with a maximum value of 112 per cent and a minimum value of -33 per cent. Again, the negative value suggests excessive cash loans received. This is indicative of the fact that cash loans are higher among subsidiary and holding firms, on average. Nevertheless, the cases of these cash loans are more extreme in relation to member firms (tunnelling up to 157 per cent and propping up to 191 per cent of total assets).

Descriptive statistics of RPT and non-RPT firms

This section presents descriptive statistics using the group category form of analysis for the full 1,530 firm-year observations. Categorization of firms into groups is based on the disclosure of RPTs and the relationship with the other party involved in the transactions. Transactions with subsidiary and holding firms are separated from transactions with other member firms.

RP transactions involving member firms

The firms with disclosure of RPTs involving member firms are reported in Table 6.2. Firms which have disclosed at least one type of RPTs with member firms are categorized as RPT firms and firms without RPTs disclosure are termed as non-RPT firms.

TABLE 6.2

Panel A: Firms with disclosure of RPTs with member firms

	Mean	Median	Std. Dev.	Maximum	Minimum	Observations
MVE	258.345	93.012	620.725	8,799.336	0.42	908
BVE	151.568	77.268	360.520	5,051.471	-497.335	908
EARN	24.091	8.298	94.587	1,436.765	-1,297.059	908
INDOWN	0.353	0.380	0.204	0.881	0	908
DIROWN	0.144	0.060	0.181	0.756	0	908
MINORITY1	0.147	0.133	0.093	0.608	0.0078	908
MINORITY2	0.055	0.042	0.049	0.321	0	908
NPMF	0.024	0.001	0.040	0.222	0	908
NPFI	0.014	0.001	0.036	0.373	0	908
GOVT	0.000	0	0.003	0.034	0	908
FII	0.064	0.008	0.103	0.574	0	908
BIG4AUD	0.206	0	0.405	1	0	908
ACIND	0.827	0.800	0.188	1	0	908
BIND	0.531	0.531	0.138	1	0	908
BSIZE	9.663	9	3.151	20	3	908
NONFAMCEO	0.319	0	0.466	1	0	908
FAGE	37.362	31	23.151	141	2	908
FSIZE	25,145.550	6,358.350	5,5770.92	5,57974.7	20.800	908
GROWTH	0.934	0.515	1.201	8.960	0.042	908
DEBT	0.336	0.320	0.256	1.76	0	908

Panel B: Firms without disclosure of RPTs with member firms

	Mean	Median	Std. Dev.	Maximum	Minimum	Observations
MVE	143.744	47.975	295.659	3760.2	0.5	622
BVE	91.494	51.477	130.318	1013.177	-428.437	622
EARN	15.765	5.812	37.642	510.679	-83.423	622

Contd.

	Mean	Median	Std. Dev.	Maximum	Minimum	Observations
INDOWN	0.325	0.343	0.202	0.750	0	622
DIROWN	0.164	0.090	0.184	0.735	0	622
MINORITY1	0.182	0.169	0.105	0.634	0	622
MINORITY2	0.063	0.050	0.054	0.327	0	622
NPMF	0.015	0.000	0.033	0.191	0	622
NPFI	0.014	0.000	0.032	0.256	0	622
GOVT	0.002	0	0.009	0.087	0	622
FII	0.035	0	0.075	0.501	0	622
BIG4AUD	0.161	0	0.368	1	0	622
ACIND	0.818	0.750	0.185	1	0	622
BIND	0.542	0.546	0.137	1	0	622
BSIZE	8.315	8	2.644	20	3	622
NONFAMCEO	0.312	0	0.464	1	0	622
FAGE	34.639	29	19.796	138	2	622
FSIZE	9,556.545	2,844.050	2,1268.16	2,28086.9	21	622
GROWTH	0.938	0.437	3.289	71.314	0.026	622
DEBT	0.321	0.288	0.298	1.87	0	622

Source: Authors.

Panel A in Table 6.2 presents attributes of firms involved in at least one kind of RPT with member firms, which is followed by firms which were not involved in any type of RPT with member firms during 2008–2012. Out of 1,530 firm-year observations, 908 firm-years disclosed at least one of the four RPTs, whereas 622 firm-year observations were without any RPTs. The MVE is INR 258 million, on average, for firms with RPTs and INR 143 million for firms without RPTs. Similarly, the average book value of equity is INR 151 million for firms with RPTs and INR 91 million for firms without RPTs. The average total assets are INR 25,145 million for RPT firms and INR 9,556 million for Non-RPT firms. The results suggest that firms with RPT disclosure are larger in size than firms without RPT disclosure in terms of MVE, book value of equity, and total assets.

In terms of ownership, the average indirect rights of controlling shareholders are 35 per cent for RPT firms and 32 per cent for non-RPT firms. On the contrary, direct rights of controlling shareholders are lower in RPT firms with 14 per cent in comparison to 16 per cent in non-RPT firms. The higher level of indirect ownership of controlling shareholders might provide expropriation incentives. The shareholdings of minority shareholders are slightly lower in RPT firms, on average. As RPT firms are larger in size, they have more domestic and FIIs. This is consistent with Kang and Stulz (1997) who report that FIIs are likely to invest in firms which are large, familiar, and actively traded.

The governance attributes of both sets of firms appear to be similar. Average board independence is above 50 per cent for both set of firms and audit committee independence is above 80 per cent, on average. The board size and non-family CEO variables are similar, on average, for RPT and non-RPT firms. The only distinct attribute of RPT firms is the nature of the audit firm used. These firms are more likely to be audited by Big 4 auditors relative to non-RPT firms. This could be associated with firm size too, as RPT firms are larger in size, and large firms are likely to be more inclined to select reputable audit firms.

Table 6.3 presents results for tests of mean difference between the two groups of firms (RPT firms and non-RPT firms). The average MVE is significantly higher for firms involved in RPTs than firms without RPTs. The book value of equity (BVE) averages INR 151 million for firms with RPTs, whereas the average BVE for non-RPT firms is INR 91 million. The mean of these two groups is statistically different at the 1 per cent level. Similarly, the average total assets are significantly higher for RPT firms in relation to non-RPT firms.

As mentioned previously, firms involved in RPTs exhibit a greater level of indirect ownership and lower level of direct ownership of controlling shareholders compared to non-RPT firms. These ownership differences are statistically significant at the 1 per cent level. Firms involved in RPTs have a significantly lower level of minority shareholder ownership than non-RPT firms. Overall, the results indicate that controlling shareholders have greater indirect ownership in RPT firms, which might encourage them to extract private benefits through RPTs. Minority shareholders might be aware of the potential abuse of controlling shareholders and prefer buying shares in firms where controlling shareholders have lower indirect ownership and higher direct ownership.

The governance differences between RPT and non-RPT firms are not statistically significant. The mean variance of board independence (BIND) and audit committee independence (ACIND) between two groups is statistically insignificant. However, firms involved in RPTs are found to have larger boards than non-RPT firms and these results are statistically significant at the 1 per cent level.

TABLE 6.3
Mean variance: *t*-test of two groups

	Related-party transactions between group-member firms			
	RPT firms	Non-RPT firms		
	Mean	Mean	t-statistics	p-value
MVE	258.345	143.744	4.283	0.000***
BVE	151.567	91.493	3.981	0.000***
EARN	24.090	15.765	2.084	0.037**
INDOWN	0.353	0.325	2.676	0.007***
DIROWN	0.144	0.164	-2.100	0.035**
MINORITY1	0.147	0.181	-6.779	0.000***
MINORITY2	0.055	0.062	-2.770	0.005***
NPMF	0.023	0.014	4.584	0.000***
NPFI	0.013	0.013	0.116	0.907
GOVT	0.000	0.001	-3.335	0.000***
FII	0.063	0.034	5.993	0.000***
BIG4AUD	0.205	0.160	2.225	0.026**
ACIND	0.827	0.818	0.902	0.367
BIND	0.531	0.542	-1.498	0.134
BSIZE	9.662	8.315	8.762	0.000***
NONFAMCEO	0.319	0.311	0.309	0.757
FAGE	37.362	34.639	2.393	0.016**
FSIZE	25,145.550	9,556.545	6.647	0.000***
GROWTH	0.933	0.788	2.368	0.018**
DEBT	0.336	0.321	0.635	0.525

Source: Authors.

Note:***$p<0.01$; **$p<0.05$.

RPTs involving subsidiary and holding firms

Panel A of Table 6.4 provides attributes of 643 firm-year observations which disclosed RPTs with subsidiary and holding firms, whereas Panel B reports the attributes of firms not providing disclosure of RPTs with subsidiary and holding firms.

TABLE 6.4

Panel A: Firms with disclosure of RPTs with subsidiary and holding firms

	Mean	Median	Std. Dev.	Maximum	Minimum	Observations
MVE	230.856	109.950	356.460	3768.133	0.420	643
BVE	135.420	91.050	158.905	1051.545	-43	643
EARN	21.577	9.261	41.911	375.742	-84	643
INDOWN	0.342	0.351	0.204	0.881	0	643
DIROWN	0.130	0.052	0.175	0.749	0	643
MINORITY1	0.135	0.114	0.090	0.458	0.009	643
MINORITY2	0.047	0.035	0.044	0.299	0	643
NPMF	0.029	0.010	0.041	0.205	0	643
NPFI	0.013	0.001	0.031	0.373	0	643
GOVT	0.001	0	0.008	0.087	0	643
FII	0.088	0.036	0.114	0.574	0	643
BIG4AUD	0.269	0	0.444	1	0	643
ACIND	0.861	1	0.157	1	0.333	643
BIND	0.533	0.529	0.118	1	0	643
BSIZE	10.187	10	2.874	20	3	643
NONFAMCEO	0.393	0	0.489	1	0	643
FAGE	36.123	30	22.696	141	2	643
FSIZE	30,967.630	9,163.100	60,807.76	557,974.7	78.7	643
GROWTH	1.079	0.576	1.357	8.960	0.055	643
DEBT	0.309	0.316	0.182	0.910	0	643

Panel B: Firms without disclosure of RPTs with subsidiary and holding firms

	Mean	Median	Std. Dev.	Maximum	Minimum	Observations
MVE	193.342	44.500	634.040	8799.336	0.420	887
BVE	121.341	52.264	357.747	5,051.471	-497.335	887
EARN	20.119	5.830	94.318	1,436.765	-1297.059	887
INDOWN	0.342	0.368	0.204	0.750	0	887
DIROWN	0.169	0.090	0.186	0.756	0	887
MINORITY1	0.181	0.171	0.101	0.634	0	887
MINORITY2	0.066	0.055	0.054	0.327	0	887
NPMF	0.014	0.000	0.033	0.222	0	887

Contd.

	Mean	Median	Std. Dev.	Maximum	Minimum	Observations
NPFI	0.015	0.000	0.036	0.373	0	887
GOVT	0.001	0	0.004	0.049	0	887
FII	0.026	0	0.064	0.441	0	887
BIG4AUD	0.129	0	0.335	1	0	887
ACIND	0.796	0.750	0.201	1	0	887
BIND	0.538	0.556	0.151	1	0	887
BSIZE	8.338	8	2.898	20	3	887
NONFAMCEO	0.260	0	0.439	1	0	887
FAGE	36.382	30	21.085	139	2	887
FSIZE	7,085.548	2,115.100	16,051.78	228,086.9	20.800	887
GROWTH	0.832	0.412	2.774	71.314	0.026	887
DEBT	0.344	0.300	0.323	1.87	0	887

Source: Authors.

On average, firms which disclose RPTs with subsidiary and holding firms have MVE of INR 230 million in comparison to INR 193 million for firms without RPTs. However, Table 6.5 indicates no statistical differences in the means of the MVE variable across the two groups of firms. Average BVE is also marginally larger for RPT firms than non-RPT firms, but the difference is statistically insignificant. There are some differences in the ownership structure of the two groups. Indirect ownership of controlling shareholders is equal at 34 per cent in both groups; however, the direct rights of controlling shareholders are lower in firms with RPTs. The variance in average direct ownership of controlling shareholders is statistically significant at the 1 per cent level. The minority ownership level is higher for non-RPT firms in comparison to RPT firms and these differences are statistically significant. While ownership level of domestic institutional investors appears to be higher, on average, for RPT firms, government ownership differences across the two groups are statistically insignificant. Table 6.5 indicates that the ownership level of FIIs is greater in firms with RPTs. This might be a result of the larger firms undertaking RPTs.

Firms which disclose RPTs with subsidiary and holding firms appear to have governance attributes that differ from firms without RPTs. Firms with RPTs have significantly greater average Big 4 auditor usage, board size, and audit committee independence. Furthermore, the presence of non-family CEO also appears to be more prevalent in RPT firms. As reported in Table

6.5, the mean variances across RPT and non-RPT firms for the BIG4AUD, ACIND, BSIZE, and NONFAMCEO variables are statistically significant at the 1 per cent level. However, the difference in mean BIND levels is statically insignificant across the two groups of firms. Overall, the descriptive statistics indicates that RPT firms are larger in size in comparison to non-RPT firms and RPT firms appear to have better governance attributes.

TABLE 6.5
Mean variance: *t*-test of two groups

| | RPTs between subsidiary and holding firms | | | |
| | RPT firms | Non-RPT firms | | |
	Mean	Mean	t-statistics	p-value
MVE	230.856	193.342	1.419	0.156
BVE	133.316	121.196	0.813	0.416
EARN	21.146	20.282	0.219	0.826
INDOWN	0.341	0.342	-0.078	0.937
DIROWN	0.132	0.171	-4.198	0.000***
MINORITY1	0.140	0.182	-8.515	0.000***
MINORITY2	0.048	0.068	-7.769	0.000***
NPMF	0.027	0.013	7.635	0.000***
NPFI	0.011	0.015	-2.070	0.038**
GOVT	0.001	0.000	1.321	0.186
FII	0.080	0.024	12.355	0.000***
BIG4AUD	0.254	0.123	6.656	0.000***
ACIND	0.852	0.795	5.962	0.000***
BIND	0.531	0.539	-1.060	0.289
BSIZE	9.974	8.286	11.351	0.000***
NONFAMCEO	0.386	0.249	5.825	0.000***
FAGE	36.123	36.382	-0.231	0.817
FSIZE	30,967.630	7,085.548	10.586	0.000***
GROWTH	1.045	0.710	5.604	0.000***
DEBT	0.313	0.370	-3.080	0.002***

Source: Authors.
Note: ***p<0.01; **p<0.05.

TABLE 6.6
Correlation matrix

	BVE	EARN	INDOWN	DIROWN	MINORITY1	MINORITY2	NPMF	NPFI	GOVT	FII	BIGAUD	ACIND	BIND	BSIZE	NONFAMCEO	FAGE	FSIZE	GROWTH	DEBT	TRADMF	TRADSH	ASSTMF	ASSTSH	INVSTMF	INVSTSH	NETLOANMF	NETLOANSH
BVE	1																										
EARN	0.478	1																									
INDOWN	0.088	0.068	1																								
DIROWN	-0.070	-0.050	-0.631	1																							
MINORITY1	0.007	-0.062	-0.169	-0.028	1																						
MINORITY2	-0.118	-0.078	-0.105	0.037	0.286	1																					
NPMF	0.049	0.092	-0.053	-0.072	-0.230	-0.231	1																				
NPFI	-0.053	-0.043	-0.052	-0.075	0.020	0.013	-0.053	1																			
GOVT	0.008	0.040	0.059	-0.058	0.013	0.043	0.010	-0.001	1																		
FII	0.092	-0.097	-0.097	-0.156	-0.377	-0.343	0.395	-0.030	-0.006	1																	
BIGAUD	0.036	0.050	0.023	-0.160	-0.088	-0.119	0.222	0.033	0.004	0.235	1																
ACIND	0.069	0.043	-0.034	-0.054	-0.087	0.050	0.121	0.001	-0.102	0.185	0.129	1															
BIND	0.044	0.033	-0.019	0.002	0.017	0.097	-0.008	0.007	-0.041	0.005	-0.080	0.408	1														
BSIZE	0.038	0.090	0.098	-0.161	-0.240	-0.186	0.216	0.006	0.043	0.218	0.248	0.121	-0.111	1													
NONFAMCEO	-0.006	0.003	0.164	-0.185	-0.052	-0.100	0.037	0.038	0.034	0.154	0.094	-0.011	-0.084	0.098	1												
FAGE	0.160	0.063	-0.029	-0.029	0.156	0.034	0.058	0.123	0.036	-0.075	-0.027	0.038	0.084	0.044	0.012	1											
FSIZE	0.132	0.162	0.082	-0.150	-0.350	-0.242	0.348	-0.090	0.012	0.415	0.223	0.177	-0.024	0.473	0.088	0.031	1										
GROWTH	0.007	0.090	0.131	-0.063	-0.318	-0.196	0.182	-0.064	-0.017	0.241	0.181	0.054	-0.050	0.159	0.109	-0.218	0.068	1									
DEBT	-0.145	-0.105	-0.035	-0.035	0.073	0.048	-0.113	0.180	-0.022	-0.053	-0.042	-0.043	-0.025	-0.038	-0.062	-0.016	-0.062	-0.264	1								
TRADMF	-0.025	0.004	0.008	0.015	0.049	0.023	0.009	-0.033	-0.032	-0.025	-0.022	-0.013	-0.050	0.051	0.042	-0.015	0.017	0.015	-0.008	1							
TRADSH	-0.018	0.005	0.035	-0.070	-0.020	-0.037	0.038	-0.045	0.245	0.071	0.091	0.005	-0.008	0.116	0.127	0.002	0.118	0.059	-0.001	0.025	1						
ASSTMF	-0.006	0.005	0.017	0.006	-0.025	-0.029	-0.038	0.011	-0.006	0.004	0.026	0.017	-0.038	0.034	0.002	0.022	0.005	0.031	0.044	0.103	-0.019	1					
ASSTSH	-0.007	-0.003	-0.006	-0.045	-0.019	0.007	0.015	-0.017	-0.011	0.073	0.047	0.012	-0.036	0.027	0.018	-0.018	0.027	0.127	-0.004	0.003	0.136	-0.003	1				
INVSTMF	-0.021	-0.009	0.061	-0.045	-0.051	-0.004	-0.011	0.012	-0.022	0.015	0.018	0.042	0.032	0.025	-0.014	-0.047	0.000	0.089	-0.053	0.014	-0.026	-0.009	-0.008	1			
INVSTSH	0.014	-0.005	-0.013	-0.007	-0.103	-0.080	0.057	0.028	-0.009	0.139	0.123	0.048	-0.001	0.097	0.091	-0.023	0.035	0.156	-0.032	-0.026	0.107	-0.011	0.031	0.029	1		
NETLOANMF	0.070	0.015	-0.011	0.006	-0.021	-0.021	0.007	0.006	-0.004	0.037	-0.035	-0.030	0.028	-0.028	0.022	0.035	-0.026	0.011	-0.015	-0.030	0.004	-0.200	0.005	0.034	-0.005	1	
NETLOANSH	0.019	-0.013	-0.039	-0.003	-0.062	-0.032	0.089	0.018	-0.010	0.094	0.089	0.015	-0.042	0.040	0.061	-0.017	0.023	0.018	-0.040	0.014	-0.016	-0.027	0.014	0.037	0.098	0.006	1

Source: Authors.

Correlation analysis

The correlation matrix is provided in Table 6.6 and it reports the correlations based on the total sample (n=1,530). As shown in the table, the highest correlation exists between the direct ownership rights of controlling families (DIROWN) and indirect ownership rights through cross-holding (INDOWN) at -0.63. High negative correlation between direct and indirect ownership rights of controlling families seems to be plausible, as families maintain their control either by direct ownership or indirect ownership or both. If the founding family does not have significant direct ownership of a firm, it maintains control by having indirect ownership rights through cross-holdings. Firm size (FSIZE) is positively associated with MVE and board size (BSIZE) at 0.48 and 0.47 respectively. Earnings (EARN) are positively associated with BVE at 0.47 and MVE is positively associated with BVE at the same level (0.47). The correlations between all other variables are below 0.45. It is evident from Table 6.6 that the observed major correlations are moderate, which does not suggest any potential multicollinearity problems (Farrar and Glauber, 1967).

Summary

This chapter presents descriptive statistics for the 1,530 firm-year observations. First, it provides attributes of the full sample based on the dependent and independent variables used for empirical analysis. The descriptive statistics reveal a greater reliance on indirect rights through cross-holdings to control group firms by controlling families. Related-party transactions with member firms involve the sale and purchase of goods and services, and asset transfers, whereas RPTs with subsidiary and holding firms involve investments, loans, and guarantees. Second, the sample firms are divided into firms which disclosed RPTs to member firms and firms without such disclosure. This section aims to identify dissimilarities between the two groups of firms. Firms with RPTs involving member firms are larger in size and their ownership structure is represented by higher indirect rights of controlling shareholders in comparison to firms without RPTs involving member firms. Third, the sample firm-year observations are divided on the basis of RPTs with subsidiary and holding firms. Firms which disclosed RPTs with subsidiary and holding firms are distinguished from firms which did not disclose RPTs to examine firm attributes separately. Average indirect rights of controlling shareholders are equal across two groups. Firms with RPTs with subsidiary and holding firms appear to have better governance attributes than firms without such RPTs. Finally, the analyses incorporate a correlation matrix evaluation, which suggests that the independent and control variables did not have a high level of correlation.

After discussing the descriptive statistics for all variables used in the research design, the next chapter presents the main empirical analysis. Chapter 7 begins with the analysis of ownership rights using OLS regressions. This is followed by the value-relevance of RPTs with member firms in the group. Last, the chapter presents the value-relevance of RPTs with subsidiary and holding firms.

Chapter 7

Empirical Results

This chapter presents the results of the main analysis and hypotheses testing of the study, focusing on the value relevance of ownership structure and RPTs. Multivariate analysis is presented using OLS regressions. In the first section, the effect of direct and indirect ownership of controlling families on firm value is examined. The second part of this chapter presents results on the value relevance of RPTs and the impact of indirect ownership of controlling families on RPT valuation. First, the results of transactions with group member firms are presented. Second, the RPTs involving subsidiary and holding firms are examined. This is then followed by a discussion on the distinct market valuation for these RPTs.

Ownership structure and firm value

This section provides evidence on the influence of ownership rights on firm valuation. First, the results of OLS regression estimation are presented to determine the association between direct and indirect ownership rights and the MVE. This is followed by quadratic equation analysis to examine the non-linear relationship between ownership rights and MVE. Finally, the results on the relationship between minority shareholder ownership and MVE are provided.

Family ownership and firm value

Table 7.1 presents the results of the value relevance model for ownership rights of controlling families. This model shows a significant positive coefficient for direct and indirect ownership rights of controlling families. However, the direct ownership of controlling families variable has a higher coefficient than the indirect ownership rights variable (direct 0.925; indirect 0.761). This supports the view that cross-holding (indirect ownership) has a less positive influence than direct ownership. However, this evidence might not prove sufficient to draw any conclusions. Therefore, we examine this issue further in the next section with more analysis.

TABLE 7.1

Effects of family ownership and control on firm value

Variable	Estimated Coefficient	t–Statistic[a]
C	-0.116	-0.448
BVE	0.002***	18.801
EARN	0.001***	3.791
DIROWN	0.925***	4.973
INDOWN	0.761***	4.479
NPMF	2.640***	3.544
NPFI	-4.019***	-5.457
GOVT	-5.000	-1.251
FII	0.991***	2.881
BIG4AUD	0.151***	2.212
ACIND	-0.644***	-4.326
BIND	0.027	0.138
BSIZE	0.028***	2.908
NONFAMCEO	0.008	0.157
FSIZE	0.343***	16.222
FAGE	0.187***	4.384
DEBT	-0.401***	-4.180
GROWTH	0.307***	12.869
YEAR[b]	Included	
INDUSTRY[b]	Included	
R-squared	0.630	
Adjusted R-squared	0.623	
F-statistic	91.427***	
Prob(F-statistic)	0.000	
Included observations: 1,530		

Source: Authors.

Notes: ***$p<0.01$; **$p<0.05$.

[a] The t-statistic is computed as the ratio of an estimated coefficient to its standard error.

[b] Dummy variables are included in the regression to control for year and industry differences; however, results are not reported due to space constraints.

The effect of domestic institutional investors on the firm value varies across different categories of investors. Ownership of mutual funds is positively associated with firm value, whereas financial institutions and government ownership is negatively valued. Prior studies such as Douma et al. (2006) and Sarkar and Sarkar (2000) provide similar results that domestic financial institutional ownership negatively affects firm value. Ramaswamy et al. (2002) argue that financial institutions in developing economies, which are predominantly government owned, espouse social welfare objectives. Therefore, financial institutions are less likely to be vigilant in their monitoring role, which will be reflected in lower market value measured in financial term.

FIIs are found to be positively and significantly associated with firm value (coef 0.991; t = 2.881). Sarkar and Sarkar (2000) report a similar finding that foreign ownership has a beneficial effect on Indian firms' value.

Corporate governance variables reflect very interesting results. Firms audited by Big 4 auditors are valued higher than those which are audited by non-Big 4 audit firms. It supports the view that Big 4 auditors are associated with higher accounting quality because of their greater technical skills in identifying accounting irregularities and maintaining their reputation (DeAngelo, 1981; Krishnan, 2003a, 2003b), which results in higher valuation. Board size is positively associated with firm value, which is consistent with Pearce and Zahra (1992) who report that board size is positively associated with corporate financial performance. However, this finding is not consistent with Eisenberg et al. (1998), Mak and Kusnadi (2005), and many other corporate governance studies.

Audit committee independence is found to be negatively associated with firm value, which is not consistent with other studies undertaken in developed Western countries. This finding contradicts the proposition advanced by Beasley (1996) and Fama (1980) that board independence is an important mechanism for effective governance. As the audit committee is a subcommittee of the board, it is expected that the existence of independent directors on the board may be equally effective. However, the negative association between audit committee independence and firm value may not be surprising given that the monitoring role of independent directors might be marginal because of a lack of true independence, their directorships in other member firms within the same business group, and informal ties with controlling shareholders (Patton and Baker, 1987; Khosa, 2017). The effect of board independence is positive but not significant.

A non-family person being employed as either CEO or chairperson is not valued differently from a family member occupying the same position. There are only 16 firms out of the total sample (316) where a controlling family member does not occupy the position of CEO or chairperson. It is a normal practice for a family member to occupy the position of chairperson if an outsider CEO is appointed. This finding suggests that an outsider CEO/chairperson appears not to challenge or monitor controlling families, but instead works under the influence of controlling families because they occupy at least one of the two top positions (CEO or chairperson). This finding is consistent with the proposition explored by Peng and Jiang (2010) that the institutional setting is vital in understanding the role of the CEO. In the context of this study, non-family CEOs are not viewed as being any different from family CEOs because controlling families still exert control over the firm by occupying the position of chairperson.

Firm size, age, and growth are positively associated with the firm value, whereas the level of debt is negatively associated with the firm value. These results are consistent with the existing literature. For example, Evans (1987) also reports that firm age and size are important determinants of firm growth.

Non-linear relationship between family ownership and firm value

The first regression shows that ownership rights of controlling families are associated with higher firm valuation. An alternative view in the literature, however, is that concentrated inside ownership provides opportunities and the means for extracting private benefits (Claessens et al., 2000; Joh, 2003; Lemmon and Lins, 2003). Therefore, we try to disentangle the alignment and entrenchment effects of ownership rights.

The ownership rights of controlling families might have a non-linear relationship with firm value, which suggests that the alignment effect could be dominant up to a certain threshold only and entrenchment effects may prevail above that level. This is more likely to exist for indirect ownership of controlling families. To examine this possibility, we include squared terms in the regression for direct and indirect ownership rights of controlling families.

Consistent with our hypothesis, Table 7.2 shows that square term for direct ownership of controlling families is insignificant, but it is highly significant and negative for indirect ownership. This finding supports the proposition that excessive indirect rights of controlling families result in value loss. Similarly, we present the quadratic equation to examine the coefficients for the ownership variables, as follows:

$$Ax^2 + bx + c$$

TABLE 7.2
Non-linear effect of indirect ownership on firm value (MVE)

Variable	Estimated Coefficient	t-Statistic[a]
C	-0.175	-0.661
BVE	0.002***	18.807
EARN	0.001***	3.779
DIROWN	0.768*	1.659
INDOWN	1.978***	4.302
DIROWN^2	0.509	0.693
INDOWN^2	-1.744***	-2.851
NPMF	2.614***	3.511
NPFI	-4.048***	-5.497
GOVT	-5.103	-1.279
FII	0.952***	2.766
BIG4AUD	0.158***	2.330
ACIND	-0.647***	-4.354
BIND	0.022	0.114
BSIZE	0.028***	2.881
NONFAMCEO	0.016	0.292
FSIZE	0.338***	15.689
FAGE	0.171***	3.974
DEBT	-0.400***	-4.170
GROWTH	0.312***	13.078
YEAR[b]	Included	
INDUSTRY[b]	Included	
R-square	0.632	
Adjusted R-square	0.625	
F-statistic	85.952***	
Prob(F-statistic)	0.000	
Included observations: 1530		

Source: Authors.

Notes: ***$p<0.01$; **$p<0.05$; *$p<0.1$.

[a] The *t*-statistic is computed as ratio of an estimated coefficient to its standard error.
[b] Dummy variables are included in the regression to control for year and industry differences; however, results are not reported due to space constraints.

It should be noted that this equation is differentiated and set equal to zero to solve for the optimal ownership level (x). Table 7.2 shows that the coefficient of indirect ownership rights through cross-holding is 1.978 (INDOWN) and the coefficient of its square term is -1.744 (INDOWN^2). Therefore, the ownership threshold after which firm value starts diminishing is 0.56 (-1.978/ (2x-1.744)). It becomes evident that indirect ownership rights of controlling families result in value loss at levels above 56 per cent. Excessive indirect rights provide controlling shareholders with incentives to expropriate the wealth of minority shareholders, which results in lower firm value. All other results remain unchanged from the regression 1 (reported in Table 7.1). This finding is broadly in agreement with Douma et al. (2006), who report that domestic corporate ownership in Indian business groups is used as a vehicle by controlling families to extract private benefits. Indirect ownership of controlling shareholders is measured as ownership rights obtained through corporations (cross-holding) and the level of domestic corporate ownership used by Douma et al. (2006) represents the same.

Minority ownership and firm value

The first two sets of analysis in the preceding sections highlight significant differences in the market valuation of direct and indirect ownership rights of controlling families. There is some support for entrenchment effects and controlling families appear to enjoy greater levels of control through indirect ownership and cross-holding; however, they bear relatively less of the cost associated with the decisions. We cannot determine their actual level of ownership because of the unavailability of data, which means that we do not know what proportion of the cost of their decisions is borne by controlling families. However, we can determine what proportion of the cost of their decisions is not allocated to controlling families. In other words, we investigate the shares held by non-promoter individuals, which serves as a proxy for minority ownership in the firms. As these shareholders do not belong to controlling families and they are not part of major shareholders, they are more likely to be expropriated by controlling shareholders. We collect information on shares held by non-promoter individuals.

There are two categories of such individuals. First, shares held by non-promoter individuals with a face value of total holding less than INR 100,000, which is less than US$1,700. Second, shares held by non-promoter individuals with a face value of total holding above INR 100,000. The first category represents diffused ownership and serves as a proxy for minority shareholders considering their marginal holding level and having no involvement in management. Shareholders in the second category might not be completely minority investors and the category may include some blockholders who often have better monitoring incentives. Therefore, a greater ownership level in category 2 is expected to have a less severe negative effect or no negative effect on the firm value.

Table 7.3 presents results for ownership rights of minority shareholders. Consistent with the hypothesis, category 1 of minority shareholders (Minority1) is negatively associated with firm value (coef -2.057, t = -6.863). This finding supports the view that higher ownership of minority shareholders in family firms provides greater incentives to controlling families to expropriate the wealth of minority shareholders or extract private benefits at the cost of minority shareholders.[30] This finding is also consistent with the view that diffused ownership is associated with less effective governance and, thus, the ownership level of minority shareholders may negatively impact on firm value.

The Minority2 variable (representing the second category of minority shareholders) is negative but not significant. This is inconsistent with Hypothesis 3_B; however, the finding suggests that this second category of investors are not necessarily just minority shareholders with no involvement, and they might be in a better position to challenge controlling families and therefore, firm value does not decline as the ownership interest of this category of shareholders increases. All other results remain unchanged from the earlier regression models, except that the coefficient for FIIs has become insignificant. The results in Table 7.1 indicate that FIIs are positively associated with firm value. However, the association becomes insignificant after omitting variables representing the ownership rights of controlling families and including variables representing the ownership rights of minority shareholders in the regression model.

Previous findings suggest that the second category of outside investors is not statistically significant. We re-estimate the regression to confirm if these results remain stable at different thresholds of ownership. We classify the second category of outside investors (MINORITY2) into three: (*a*) outside investors' holding from 0 to 5 per cent (MINORITY 0–5); (*b*) outside investors' holding from 5 to 10 per cent (MINORITY 5–10); and (*c*) outside investors' holding more than 10 per cent (MINORITY>10). We argued in Hypothesis 3_b that this category might include some blockholders, who have monitoring incentives. The presence of those blockholders should be captured in category 2 and 3 (MINORITY 5–10 and MINORITY>10). If the shareholding of outside

---

[30] Bertrand et al. (2002) provide evidence of tunneling from firms where minority shareholders have higher ownership.

investors (MINORITY2) falls in the first category (MINORITY 0–5), these investors may not have any power to challenge controlling shareholders. In this case, they are in the same position as MINORITY1 and, consequently, their shareholding might be valued negatively.

TABLE 7.3
Effect of minority ownership on firm value (MVE)

Variable	Estimated Coefficient	t-Statistic[a]
C	1.093***	4.167
BVE	0.002***	19.550
EARN	0.001***	3.805
MINORITY1	-2.057***	-6.863
MINORITY2	-0.136	-0.258
NPMF	2.495***	3.374
NPFI	-4.474***	-6.166
GOVT	-5.096	-1.283
FII	0.251	0.752
BIG4AUD	0.151***	2.256
ACIND	-0.667***	-4.481
BIND	0.009	0.050
BSIZE	0.028***	2.948
NONFAMCEO	0.029	0.548
FSIZE	0.296***	13.288
FAGE	0.201***	4.721
DEBT	-0.417***	-4.387
GROWTH	0.284***	11.816
YEAR[b]	Included	
INDUSTRY[b]	Included	
R-squared	0.635	
Adjusted R-squared	0.629	
F-statistic	93.388***	
Prob(F-statistic)	0.000	
Included observations: 1530		

Source: Authors.
Notes: ***$p<0.01$; **$p<0.05$.
[a] The *t*-statistic is computed as the ratio of an estimated coefficient to its standard error.
[b] Dummy variables are included in the regression to control for year and industry differences; however, results are not reported due to space constraints.

Table 7.4 reports the results after categorizing MINORITY2 up to 5 per cent, between 5 per cent and 10 per cent, and 10 per cent and above. Shareholdings of outside investors up to 5 per cent are negatively associated with MVE at 1 per cent (t = 2.739). This supports the previous finding that a shareholding of outside investors who constitute a complete minority is valued negatively. The shareholding of outside investors from 5 to 10 per cent and above 10 per cent is positively associated with firm value, but is not statistically significant. This suggests that shareholding above the threshold of 5 per cent includes some blockholders, who have greater incentive to monitor management. Therefore, outside shareholdings above 5 per cent are not valued negatively by the market.

TABLE 7.4

Effect of minority (2) ownership on firm value (MVE)

Variable	Estimated Coefficient	t–Statistic[a]
C	1.071	3.964
BVE	0.002***	19.596
EARN	0.001***	3.944
MINORITY1	-1.818***	-5.860
MINORITY 0–5	-5.488***	-2.739
MINORITY 5–10	0.860	0.474
MINORITY>10	1.537	1.381
NPMF	2.794***	3.789
NPFI	-4.593***	-6.357
GOVT	-4.430	-1.118
FII	0.063	0.184
BIG4AUD	0.144**	2.146
ACIND	-0.660***	-4.442
BIND	0.048	0.247
BSIZE	0.030***	3.142
NONFAMCEO	0.040	0.739
FSIZE	0.325***	12.273
FAGE	0.197***	4.629
DEBT	-0.259***	-3.563
GROWTH	0.288***	11.858
YEAR[b]	Included	
INDUSTRY[b]	Included	

Contd.

Variable	Estimated Coefficient	t–Statistic[a]
R-squared	0.638	
Adjusted R-squared	0.631	
F-statistic	85.284***	
Prob(F-statistic)	0.000	
Included observations: 1530		

Source: Authors.

Notes: ***$p<0.01$; **$p<0.05$; *$p<0.1$.

[a] The t-statistic is computed as the ratio of an estimated coefficient to its standard error.

[b] Dummy variables are included in the regression to control for year and industry differences; however, results are not reported due to space constraints.

Valuation of RPTs

The previous section presented empirical results where the key focus on ownership rights of controlling and minority shareholders helped to examine the valuation effects. This section adds to this knowledge by investigating the role of different types of RPTs on the market valuation. This section provides a direct measure in the form of RPT magnitude, to record any resulting valuation consequences for sample firms.

This section begins with an overview of RPTs involving member firms. Four transactions in particular are examined separately: (*a*) trading: sales and purchases of goods and services; (*b*) asset transfers: sales and purchases of assets; (*c*) investments: sales and purchases of shares; and (*d*) loans: cash payments given to member firms minus loans received. First, it is examined if the disclosure of these RPTs affects firm value. Next, the magnitude of RPTs is interacted with the book value of equity (BVE) and earnings (EARN) variables to examine if the disclosure of RPT enhances or reduces the informativeness of BVE and EARN. Finally, the magnitude of RPTs is interacted with EARN and indirect ownership rights of controlling shareholders (INDOWN) to examine if the RPTs affect the value-relevance of earnings in the presence of indirect ownership rights.

The next section examines RPTs involving subsidiary and holding companies. The four types of RPTs are examined: (*a*) trading; (*b*) asset transfers; (*c*) investments; and (*d*) loans. Similarly, the magnitude of RPTs is interacted with the BVE and EARN variables, which helps to identify if the disclosure of RPTs impacts on the value relevance of those accounting numbers. Last, the RPT category variables are interacted with earnings and indirect ownership rights of controlling families to identify if using RPTs and ownership of controlling families moderates the relationship between earnings and firm value (MVE).

The objective is to identify any distinct valuation effects of RPTs involving member firms from RPTs concerning subsidiary and holding companies.

RPTs with member firms

Panel A of Table 7.5 presents the results for the relationship between RPTs with member firms in the group and firm value. This section aims to test hypotheses 5 to 8. The results for each RPT are discussed below.

Trading

Table 7.5 (Panel A) reports that the magnitude of RP trading is negatively associated with the firm value (coef -0.286; t = -2.259). Therefore, the sale or purchase of goods and services from other member firms might be viewed as a form of expropriation and, therefore, it has negative market valuation consequences. These transactions might have a potential efficiency effect too, but the finding suggests that the entrenchment effect dominates the efficiency view.

The effect of RP sales and purchases on the BVE variable is positive and significant at the 1 per cent level. Table 7.5 (Panel A) shows a coefficient of 0.010 on this variable and an accompanying t-statistics of 5.125 on the interaction term between RP trading and BVE. This is consistent with Kohlbeck and Mayhew (2010) and it suggests that the disclosure of RP sales and purchase of goods and services enhances the informativeness of the book value of equity. Similarly, the effect of RP sales and purchases on the value relevance of earnings is positive and significant at the 5 per cent level.

Another key finding is that the interaction between the magnitude of RP trading with earnings and indirect ownership of controlling shareholders affects firm value negatively (coef -0.070; t = -2.751). This strongly supports the existence of entrenchment effects in the context of this study. As we proposed in the previous section, indirect ownership rights might provide incentives to controlling shareholders to extract private benefits because they bear only a fractional consequence of such value destroying activities. This finding suggests that the disclosure of RP trading in the presence of indirect ownership rights of controlling shareholders reduces the value-relevance of earnings. Therefore, the market penalizes such firms by valuing their shares downwards as a governance mechanism. This finding is in agreement with Cheung et al. (2009) who report that minority shareholders might be subject to expropriation through trading of goods and services with related-parties. Peng et al. (2011) also report that all transaction types, including sales and purchases, can potentially be forms of expropriation depending on the incentives of controlling shareholders. However, Bertrand et al. (2002) suggest that tunnelling mainly occurs through non-operating activities such as asset acquisitions and cash payments, and they find no evidence that operating activities have been used for expropriation purposes.

Overall, the results support Hypothesis 5_B, which confirm that RP trading (sale and purchase of goods and services) with member firms results in value loss for firms where controlling shareholders have indirect ownership rights. While the magnitude of RP trading with member firms influences the value-relevance of earnings positively, the undertaking of RP trading for firms controlled through indirect ownership affects the value-relevance of earnings negatively.

Asset transfers

The magnitude of asset transfers is found to be positively associated with firm value at the 10 per cent level. This shows that sales and purchases of assets to member firms in the group are viewed as efficient transactions and firms which disclose such asset transfers are valued upwards. This finding supports the body of literature which focuses on the efficient perspective of RPTs. Khanna and Palepu (2000b) advocate the role of business groups in overcoming the imperfections of external markets. Emerging markets such as India are characterized by inadequate disclosures, weak governance, and weak enforcement of property rights due to overburdened courts and widespread corruption. Under these circumstances, firms may not have easy access to raw materials, labour, capital, and other inputs and they might need to incur higher cost to acquire these resources. Group firms, which rely more on social ties, may benefit from internal markets. If the cost of formal contracts is expected to be higher in less developed legal systems, group firms might prefer to procure these resources from other member firms within the group. Friedman et al. (2003) also argue that these transactions can be value-reducing as well as value-enhancing.

The interaction of the magnitude of asset transfers with the BVE variable does not produce any significant results, which suggests that disclosure of asset transfers has no influential impact on BVE value relevance. The interaction between RP asset transfers and earnings is positively associated with MVE (coef 0.392; $t = 2.106$). Again, the disclosure of asset transfers in the presence of indirect rights of controlling shareholders affects the value-relevance of earnings negatively (coef -0.757; $t = -2.108$). This finding is consistent with Bertrand et al. (2002) who reports that tunnelling activities take place through non-operating earning items in Indian business groups. This finding also provide support to Kali and Sarkar (2011), who reports tunnelling activities exist where the control rights are higher than the cash-flow rights of controlling shareholders. Indirect rights acquired through cross-holdings serve as a proxy for divergence between cash-flow and control rights and, therefore, provide incentives for controlling shareholders to extract private benefits.

Panel A of Table 7.5 reports that the magnitude of RP asset transfers is associated positively with MVE at the 10 per cent level. However, the magnitude of RP asset transfers for firms which are controlled through indirect ownership is associated negatively with the value-relevance of earnings, which supports Hypothesis 6_B.

Investments

Panel A of Table 7.5 reports results on the market valuation effect of sales and purchases of shares to member firms. The coefficient for the magnitude of investment related RPTs is negative and significant (coef -4.050; $t = -3.297$). This suggests that the sale and purchase of shares of member firms are viewed as entrenchment and is valued negatively by the market. Cheung et al. (2006) explain that the nature of the transaction is important in understanding the market valuation of RPTs. They also find that considerable shareholder value is lost as a result of equity sales announcements. Furthermore, using RP investments in the presence of indirect rights of controlling shareholders affects the value-relevance of earnings negatively. Table 7.5 (Panel A) shows significant negative results for the interaction between the magnitude of investment-based RPTs, earnings and indirect rights of controlling shareholders variables (coef -0.509; $t = -2.096$). The interaction of magnitude of RP investments and BVE variables is positively associated with MVE at the 5 per cent level (coef 0.036; $t = 2.376$). However, the coefficient of the interaction between the magnitude of RP investments and EARN is marginally significant at 10 per cent.

Overall, the results suggest that the sale and purchase of shares is viewed as entrenchment, and the degree of indirect rights of controlling families affects the value-relevance of earnings negatively.

Loans

Net loans given to member firms in the groups are not valued significantly by the market. This finding conflicts with most studies which argue that cash payments to related firms are used to expropriate minority shareholders (Cheung et al., 2006; Peng et al., 2011). While Khanna and Palepu (2000b) argue that group firms might benefit from internal financing in the absence of a fully developed external market, results show that internal loan arrangements are not valued by the market.

Furthermore, RP lending affects the value relevance of BVE adversely (coef -0.003; $t = -3.931$). The interaction between the RPT loans and EARN variables does not provide a statistically significant coefficient (coef 0.001; $t = 0.033$). Interestingly, the extent of indirect ownership of controlling shareholders does not appear to play any role in the valuation of RP lending and earnings. The interaction term of the earnings, indirect rights, and magnitude of loans given to member firms variables does not provide any significant results.

While RP loans are found to reduce the value relevance of BVE at a significant level (1 per cent), the coefficient for the RP loans variable itself is not significant. Therefore, the results do not support Hypothesis 8_A. The magnitude of loans to member firms continues to indicate insignificant results in the presence of indirect ownership of controlling shareholders and, thus, Hypothesis 8_B is also not supported.

Overall, the results reveal that all RPTs are not value-adding or value-destroying. Asset transfers with member firms in the group add value marginally; however, transactions involving trading and investments result in value loss. More importantly, RPTs affect the value-relevance of earnings negatively in the presence of indirect ownership of controlling shareholders.

RPTs involving subsidiary and holding companies

Trading

Panel B of Table 7.5 presents the results of RPTs with subsidiary and holding firms. Results for the magnitude of sales and purchases of goods and services to subsidiary and holding firms are insignificant. This supports the hypothesis that transactions of a trading nature between the subsidiary and holding firms are part of the normal course of business and, therefore, they might not be viewed as a way of tunnelling. It is evident from the results that the disclosure of trading transactions with subsidiary and holding firms does not attract any negative or positive market reaction. The interaction between the magnitude of trading and BVE is positive but statistically insignificant. As the interaction terms between the magnitude of RPT and EARN are insignificant, this suggests that the disclosure of RP trading does not affect the value relevance of earnings. Furthermore, the results confirm that indirect ownership of controlling shareholders does not affect the valuation effects of RP trading and earnings. The coefficient on the interaction term between the magnitude of RP trading, earnings and INDOWN is negative, but insignificant (coef -0.003; $t = -0.069$). This supports the hypothesis that RP trading with subsidiary and holding companies is not influenced by indirect ownership of controlling families. Instead, there might be a strategic rationale behind these transactions and, therefore, disclosure of such transactions is not valued any differently by the market.

TABLE 7.5
Effects of RPTs on MVE

Variable	Panel A		Panel B	
	RPTs involving group-member firms		RPT involving subsidiary/holding firms	
	Estimated coefficient	t-Statistic [a]	Estimated coefficient	t-Statistic [a]
C	-0.076	-0.296	-0.110	-0.422
BVE	0.002***	16.773	0.001***	18.334
EARN	0.001***	3.379	0.001***	3.609
INDOWN	0.882***	4.892	0.754***	4.371
TRAD	-0.286**	-2.259	-0.259	-0.720
TRAD*BVE	0.010***	5.125	0.007	1.452
TRAD*EARN	0.027**	2.133	-0.001	-0.028
TRAD*EARN*INDOWN	-0.070***	-2.751	-0.003	-0.069
ASST	2.486*	1.704	-2.897	-0.563
ASST*BVE	-0.022	-1.449	0.029	0.390
ASST*EARN	0.392**	2.106	-0.169	-0.337
ASST*EARN*INDOWN	-0.757**	-2.108	0.280	0.425
INVST	-4.050***	-3.297	-1.230**	-2.285
INVST*BVE	0.036**	2.376	0.003	1.281
INVST*EARN	0.263*	1.704	0.031	0.642
INVST*EARN*INDOWN	-0.509**	-2.096	-0.073	-0.724
NETLOAN	0.008	0.029	-3.075***	-3.766

Contd.

| Variable | Panel A | | Panel B | |
| | RPTs involving group-member firms | | RPT involving subsidiary/holding firms | |
	Estimated coefficient	*t-Statistic*[a]	*Estimated coefficient*	*t-Statistic*[a]
NETLOAN*BVE	-0.003***	-3.931	0.014***	3.391
NETLOAN*EARN	0.001	0.033	0.023	0.346
NETLOAN*EARN*INDOWN	-0.079	-1.165	-0.058	-0.400
DIROWN	0.900***	4.948	0.910***	4.866
NPMF	2.842***	3.863	2.917***	3.899
NPFI	-3.672***	-5.070	-3.943***	-5.365
GOVT	-4.912	-1.255	-7.384*	-1.667
FII	0.840**	2.483	1.051***	5.477
BIG4AUD	0.124*	1.852	0.167**	2.437
ACIND	-0.664***	-4.532	-0.662***	-4.178
BIND	0.108	0.561	0.046	0.234
BSIZE	0.021**	2.134	0.027***	2.794
NONFAMCEO	0.011	0.201	-0.006	-0.001
FSIZE	0.338***	16.038	0.334***	15.679
FAGE	0.169***	4.037	0.193***	4.533
DEBT	-3.323***	-3.394	-0.393***	-4.087
GROWTH	0.314***	13.352	0.314***	12.857
YEAR[b]	Included		Included	
INDUSTRY[b]	Included		Included	
R-squared	0.652		0.638	
Adjusted R-squared	0.642		0.627	
F-statistic	63.253***		59.636***	
Prob(F-statistic)	0.000		0.000	
Included observations: 1530				

Source: Authors.

Notes: ***$p<0.01$; **$p<0.05$; *$p<0.1$.

[a] The *t*-statistic is computed as the ratio of an estimated coefficient to its standard error.

[b] Dummy variables are included in the regression to control for year and industry differences; however, results are not reported due to space constraints.

Asset transfers

The sale and purchase of assets between subsidiary and holding firms affects the MVE variable negatively, but the coefficient is statistically insignificant.

Table 7.5 (Panel B) reports that the disclosure of asset transfers with subsidiary and holding firms is not associated with the MVE (coef -2.897; t = -0.563). The interaction terms between the RP asset transfers and BVE variables and RP asset transfers and EARN variables do not provide any significant results, which suggests that the disclosure of asset transfers does not affect the value relevance of the book value of equity and earnings. Furthermore, the interaction between indirect ownership rights of controlling shareholders, earnings, and RP asset transfers provides insignificant results, which suggests that: first, the indirect rights of controlling families do not appear to play any role in the value-relevance of earnings and RP asset transfers; and second, these transactions are driven by business ties. In fact, asset transfers with member firms, other than subsidiary and holding firms, are valued positively and the same transactions are valued negatively in the presence of indirect ownership of controlling shareholders. Such a phenomenon does not appear to prevail in the case of asset transfers with subsidiary and parent companies.

Investments

Table 7.5 (Panel B) reports that the sale and purchase of shares from subsidiary and holding firms is negatively associated with firm value (coef -1.230; t = -2.285). The disclosure of the sale and purchase of shares from RPs does not affect the valuation of earnings and book value of equity. More importantly, these RP disclosures do not influence the value-relevance of earnings in the presence of indirect rights of controlling shareholders. The interaction between the magnitude of RP investments, earnings, and indirect ownership of controlling families (IPCORP) does not provide any significant results. Consistent with the previous two findings, indirect ownership of controlling shareholders does not influence the valuation of RP investments and earnings.

Loans

RP lending is negatively associated with the MVE at the 1 per cent level (coef -3.075; t = -3.766), which suggests that loans given to subsidiary and holding firms are viewed as detracting from firm value. Cornell and Liu (2001) argue that if a subsidiary firm is a successful and cash generating firm and the parent company is siphoning off cash from the subsidiary to fund unprofitable parent operations, then this will reduce the value of the subsidiary firm. Furthermore, it reduces not only the value of the subsidiary's stock but also the parent firm's holding of the subsidiary stock. This finding strongly supports the hypothesis that loans given to subsidiary and holding companies might be seen as an inefficient allocation of funds. Consistent with Hypothesis 8_D, the indirect rights of controlling shareholders do not influence the valuation consequences of RP lending. Overall, RP lending is viewed as inefficient and, therefore, firms which disclose RP lending are valued downwards. However, the valuation of RP lending is not affected by indirect ownership rights of controlling families.

Summary

This chapter reports the empirical analysis on the ownership structure and valuation of RPTs. The analyses provide strong support for most of our hypotheses. The results reveal a curvilinear relationship between indirect ownership rights and firm value (MVE), which suggests that controlling shareholders extract private benefits at the cost of minority shareholders when their control rights exceed their level of cash-flow rights. Furthermore, minority ownership is found to be negatively associated with firm value. Domestic financial institution ownership is found to be negatively associated with firm value, whereas mutual funds ownership and foreign institutional ownership is positively associated with firm value. OLS regression models suggest that not all RPTs result in firm value loss. The market valuation of RPTs depends on the relationship with the party involved in the transaction and the nature of the transaction.

The next chapter provides additional analysis that supports the main findings. Specifically, fixed-effect regression models are run to assess RPTs valuation effects. Next, the sample is classified into firms which disclose RPTs and those without RP disclosure. The regression models are estimated for firms which disclose RPTs to check the robustness of the results. Finally, we use alternative measurements for size and some governance variables to confirm the robustness of these major control variables.

Chapter 8

Additional Tests

Introduction

The previous chapter presented the main empirical findings, which suggest that the market values RPTs not only on the basis of the nature of the transaction but also considering the relationship with the party involved in the transaction and the potential incentives of controlling shareholders measured on the basis of their indirect ownership. This chapter adds to the analysis by providing additional tests controlling for firm heterogeneity using fixed-effect models. Next, to affirm the strength of the role of RPTs and indirect rights in the earnings-market valuation, the regression models are re-estimated only for firms which disclose RPTs and on individual RPTs. Alternative measures of firm size and some governance variables are then added in the model to check the robustness of the results based on different definitions for these variables. This chapter concludes with the summary of the additional test findings.

Fixed-effect model

To supplement pooled regression results, we run a fixed-effect model to address the panel structure of the sample data. First, a fixed-effect model is estimated to examine the effect of direct and indirect ownership rights on the MVE. Second, the results of this fixed-effect model estimation to examine the relationship between minority shareholder ownership and MVE are presented. Finally, the results for the market valuation of RPTs using fixed-effect model estimation are presented.

Family ownership and firm value

Table 8.1 presents the results regarding the association between family ownership rights and MVE. Direct ownership (DIROWN) of controlling shareholders is positively associated with MVE (coef 1.594; t = 5.230), which is consistent with the pooled regression results reported in Chapter 7 Indirect ownership (INDOWN) is also positively associated with MVE (coef 1.387; t = 5.250); however, the coefficient for INDOWN is smaller than DIROWN. Overall, the fixed-effect model results are in agreement with the pooled regression model results.

TABLE 8.1
Effects of family ownership on firm value (MVE)

Variable	Estimated coefficient	t-Statistic[a]
C	1.027	0.940
BVE	0.002***	11.840
EARN	0.000	1.310
DIROWN	1.594***	5.230
INDOWN	1.387***	5.250
NPMF	2.038**	2.410
NPFI	-1.504**	-2.100
GOVT	-6.656	-0.990
FII	1.957***	4.480
BIG4AUD	0.350***	3.100
ACIND	-0.245*	-1.640
BIND	-0.132	-0.880
BSIZE	0.008	0.680
NONFAMCEO	-0.244*	-1.940
FSIZE	0.047	0.850
FAGE	0.453	1.590
DEBT	0.034	0.300
GROWTH	0.085***	3.890
R-square: overall	0.437	
F-statistic	28.890***	
Prob(F-statistic)	0.000	
Included observations: 1530		

Source: Authors.
Note: ***$p<0.01$; **$p<0.05$; *$p<0.1$.
[a] The t-statistic is computed as ratio of an estimated coefficient to its standard error.

Minority shareholder ownership and firm value

Table 8.2 presents the results for the association between the ownership of minority shareholders and MVE. Consistent with the pooled regression model results, the first category of outside investors (MINORITY1) is negatively associated with MVE at 1 per cent (coef -3.272; t = -6.420). The association between the second category of outside investors (MINORITY2) and MVE is statistically insignificant. These results agree with pooled regression model findings and support the view that higher ownership of minority shareholders in family firms gives controlling families the incentives to extract private benefits, which results in value loss.

Market valuation of RPTs

The results of fixed-effect model estimation for the market valuation of RPTs are presented in Table 8.3. Panel A of Table 8.3 presents results for the market valuation of RPTs involving group-member firms.

The results show that the value-relevance of earnings is reduced by the disclosure of RP tradings and asset transfers in the presence of indirect ownership rights of controlling shareholders. The magnitude of RP investments involving group-member firms is negatively associated with the MVE variable (coef -1.841; t = -2.550). Furthermore, the valuation of earnings is negatively associated with MVE when interacted with RP investments and indirect ownership rights (coef -0.416; t = -2.870), which is consistent with the pooled regression results. Related-party loans are negatively associated with MVE at 10 per cent. The interaction between RP loans and BVE is negatively associated with MVE, which is in agreement with earlier findings using the pooled regression model.

Panel B of Table 8.3 presents results related to the market valuation of RPTs involving subsidiary and holding firms. Consistent with the pooled regression model results, the association between RP trading and asset transfers and MVE is not statistically significant. The pooled regression model results showed a negative association between RP investments and MVE; however, the negative association between RP investments and MVE is statistically insignificant in the fixed-effect model. Net loans are negatively associated with MVE at the 1 per cent level (coef -2.192; t = -4.330), which is consistent with pooled regression results.

Overall, the results using fixed-effect model estimation are in agreement with the pooled regression model results. The value-relevance of earnings is reduced by RPTs involving member firms in the presence of indirect ownership rights, whereas the indirect ownership rights of controlling shareholders do not have any power in explaining the earnings-market valuation of RP transactions involving subsidiary/holding firms.

TABLE 8.2
Effects of minority ownership on firm value (MVE)

Variable	Estimated coefficient	t-Statistic[a]
C	2.320**	2.140
BVE	0.002***	12.050
EARN	0.000	1.210
MINORITY1	-3.272***	-6.420
MINORITY2	0.098	0.170
NPMF	0.892	1.050
NPFI	-1.906***	-2.700
GOVT	-0.970	-0.140
FII	1.081**	2.460
BIG4AUD	0.356***	3.160
ACIND	-0.236	-1.580
BIND	-0.111	-0.740
BSIZE	0.005	0.440
NONFAMCEO	-0.224*	-1.790
FSIZE	0.045	0.820
FAGE	0.460	1.620
DEBT	0.058	0.520
GROWTH	0.072***	3.320
R-square: within	0.341	
R-square: between	0.500	
R-square: overall	0.489	
F-statistic	29.380***	
Prob(*F*-statistic)	0.000	
Included observations: 1,530		

Source: Authors.

Note: ***$p<0.01$; **$p<0.05$; *$p<0.1$.

[a] The *t*-statistic is computed as ratio of an estimated coefficient to its standard error.

TABLE 8.3
Effects of RPTs on MVE

Variable	Panel A		Panel B	
	RPTs involving group-member firms		*RPTs involving subsidiary/holding firms*	
	Estimated coefficient	*t-Statistic*[a]	*Estimated coefficient*	*t-Statistic*[a]
C	0.647	0.600	1.049	0.970
BVE	0.002***	12.140	0.002***	11.180
EARN	0.000	0.310	0.000	1.350
INDOWN	1.340***	5.100	1.377***	5.240
TRAD	0.029	0.340	0.075	0.340
TRAD*BVE	0.002	1.110	0.002	0.710
TRAD*EARN	0.015*	1.710	0.024	1.430
TRAD*EARN*INDOWN	-0.029*	-1.680	-0.049	-1.380
ASST	-0.289	-0.330	-0.938	-0.310
ASST*BVE	0.006	0.620	-0.024	-0.570
ASST*EARN	0.014	0.120	-0.002	-0.010
ASST*EARN*INDOWN	-0.023**	-2.210	0.268	0.690
INVST	-1.841**	-2.550	-0.015	-0.040
INVST*BVE	0.008	0.910	0.001	0.520
INVST*EARN	0.233**	2.520	0.000	0.010
INVST*EARN*INDOWN	-0.416***	-2.870	-0.008	-0.120
NETLOAN	-0.301*	-1.850	-2.192***	-4.330
NETLOAN*BVE	-0.002***	-3.640	0.010***	3.960
NETLOAN*EARN	-0.008	-0.480	-0.004	-0.110
NETLOAN*EARN*INDOWN	0.103	0.600	0.017	0.210
DIROWN	1.597***	5.310	1.642***	5.420
NPMF	1.929**	2.320	2.438***	2.870
NPFI	-1.298*	-1.830	-1.348*	-1.890
GOVT	-7.132	-1.070	-10.105	-1.490
FII	1.782***	4.130	1.872***	4.300
BIG4AUD	0.307***	2.730	0.359***	3.180
ACIND	-0.288*	-1.950	-0.224	-1.500
BIND	-0.065	-0.440	-0.124	-0.830
BSIZE	0.007	0.590	0.008	0.720
NONFAMCEO	-0.226*	-1.830	-0.294**	-2.350

Contd.

Variable	Panel A		Panel B	
	RPTs involving group-member firms		*RPTs involving subsidiary/holding firms*	
	Estimated coefficient	*t–Statistic*[a]	*Estimated coefficient*	*t–Statistic*[a]
FSIZE	0.053	0.960	0.043	0.790
FAGE	0.536*	1.890	0.452	1.590
DEBT	0.075	0.680	0.039	0.350
GROWTH	0.097***	4.480	0.085***	3.750
R-square: overall	0.416		0.440	
F-statistic	18.760***		17.810***	
Prob(*F*-statistic)	0.000		0.000	
Included observations: 1,530				

Source: Authors.

Note: ***$p<0.01$; **$p<0.05$; *$p<0.1$.

[a] The *t*-statistic is computed as ratio of an estimated coefficient to its standard error.

Firms with RPTs only

We ran an additional analysis by excluding firms without RPTs to determine if the earlier findings are robust. At least one of the four RPTs (trading, asset transfers, investments, and loans) with group-member firms is disclosed in 908 firm-year observations. Panel A of Table 8.4 presents the results for the value relevance of RPTs involving group-member firms. At least one of the four RPTs (trading, asset transfers, investments, and loans) involving subsidiary/holding firms is disclosed in 643 firm-year observations. Panel B of Table 8.4 presents the results on the market valuation of RPTs involving subsidiary/holding firms.

The disclosure of trading with member firms is negatively associated with MVE and the interaction of RP trading magnitude, earnings and indirect ownership rights of controlling families has a negative and significant association with the MVE (coef -0.059; $t = -2.342$). Consistent with earlier findings, asset transfers are not significantly associated with firm value (MVE), but earnings are valued negatively when interacted with RP asset transfers and indirect ownership rights (coef -0.875; $t = -2.452$). The disclosure of RP investments is negatively correlated with firm market valuation. Furthermore, the interaction between RP investments, earnings, and indirect ownership of controlling shareholders is negative and statistically significant. Net loans continue to show insignificant results. Overall, the results are consistent with the prior findings, and the value-relevance of earnings continues to be influenced by RPTs types and indirect ownership of controlling shareholders.

The effects of RPTs involving subsidiary/holding firms on earning-market valuation, reported in Panel B in Table 8.4, show that RP trading, asset transfers, and investments are benign transactions. Transactions involving the sale and purchase of goods and services (trading), asset transfers, and investments continue to prove insignificant in explaining variation in MVE. Net loans are negatively associated with the MVE (coef -1.384; t = -2.061), which is consistent with earlier findings. Overall, the results continue to support the view that indirect ownership of controlling shareholders does not have any power in explaining the valuation of RPTs involving subsidiary and holding firms.

TABLE 8.4
Effects of RPTs on MVE (only RPT firms)

Variable	Panel A		Panel B	
	RPTs involving group-member firms		*RPTs involving subsidiary/holding firms*	
	Estimated coefficient	*t-Statistic[a]*	*Estimated coefficient*	*t-Statistic[a]*
C	-0.027	-0.078	1.552	4.246
BVE	0.002***	13.819	0.004***	13.753
EARN	0.001*	1.856	0.002*	1.959
INDOWN	0.712***	3.329	0.236	1.065
TRAD	-0.350***	-2.758	0.077	0.176
TRAD*BVE	0.010***	5.495	0.009*	1.831
TRAD*EARN	0.022*	1.747	0.007	0.306
TRAD*EARN*INDOWN	-0.059**	-2.342	-0.019	-0.430
ASST	1.066	0.737	-2.832	-0.338
ASST*BVE	-0.008	-0.510	0.031	0.474
ASST*EARN	0.455**	2.460	-1.791*	-1.810
ASST*EARN*INDOWN	-0.875**	-2.452	3.030	0.384
INVST	-4.533***	-3.710	-0.260	-0.592
INVST*BVE	0.043***	2.898	0.000	0.094

Contd.

Variable	Panel A		Panel B	
	RPTs involving group-member firms		RPTs involving subsidiary/holding firms	
	Estimated coefficient	t-Statistic[a]	Estimated coefficient	t-Statistic[a]
INVST*EARN	0.239	1.563	0.045	1.138
INVST*EARN*INDOWN	-0.476**	-1.976	-0.147	-1.342
NETLOAN	-0.176	-0.640	-1.384**	-2.061
NETLOAN*BVE	-0.004***	-4.623	0.005	1.423
NETLOAN*EARN	0.012	0.398	-0.037	-0.624
NETLOAN*EARN*INDOWN	-0.036	-0.536	-0.008	-0.064
DIROWN	1.205***	5.099	0.122	0.511
NPMF	2.928***	3.409	3.154***	3.744
NPFI	-4.418***	-4.899	-2.145**	-2.089
GOVT	-26.039**	-2.451	-9.830**	-2.204
FII	0.682*	1.712	0.771**	2.099
BIG4AUD	0.103	1.215	0.017	0.227
ACIND	-0.447**	-2.309	-0.611***	-2.908
BIND	-0.068	-0.269	0.032	0.117
BSIZE	0.028**	2.315	0.027**	2.143
NONFAMCEO	0.075	1.067	0.031	0.444
FSIZE	0.352***	12.947	0.172***	5.405
FAGE	0.070	1.355	-0.023	-0.433
DEBT	-0.263*	-1.926	0.635***	3.227
GROWTH	0.315***	10.134	0.366***	13.335
YEAR	Included		Included	
INDUSTRY	Included		Included	
R-square	0.679		0.722	
Adjusted R-square	0.663		0.701	
F-statistic	41.605***		35.338***	
Prob(F-statistic)	0.000		0.000	
Included observations	908		643	

Source: Authors.

Note: ***$p<0.01$; **$p<0.05$; *$p<0.1$.

[a] The *t*-statistic is computed as ratio of an estimated coefficient to its standard error.

Individual test of RPTs

We analyse further by regressing RP trading, asset transfer, investment, and loan transactions individually in regression models. These RPTs involving group-member firms are examined separately from RPTs involving subsidiary and holding firms. The results are not reported due to space constraints, but the results are consistent with the main findings.

Consistent with earlier findings, RP trading, asset transfer, and investment transactions affect the value-relevance of earnings negatively in the presence of indirect ownership rights. Related-party investment and loan transactions involving subsidiary and holding firms are associated with significantly lower market valuation. However, indirect ownership rights do not have any moderating influence on the earning-market valuation of RPTs.

Alternative measure of firm size

We further analyse by using an alternative measure of firm size for all regression models. Instead of the natural logarithm of total assets, we use the natural logarithm of total sales. Douma et al. (2006) use sales as a proxy for the size of a firm. The results are not reported but we find results that are consistent with the main findings. The adjusted R^2 figures are similar too.

Endogeneity

The observed association between RPTs and market valuation could be a symptom rather than a cause. However, the choice to engage in RPTs may be correlated with other factors that affect market valuation rather than reverse causality (Kohlbeck and Mayhew, 2010). For instance, RP disclosure could be correlated with growth, which often impacts firm valuation. Therefore, our estimation models control for growth. Furthermore, we consider conditions that increase the likelihood that controlling shareholders are able to act opportunistically and may therefore be associated with firm value. Indirect ownership rights of controlling shareholders create incentives and opportunities to enter into RPTs. We include the ownership rights of controlling shareholders to capture this influence. Previous studies such as Cheung et al. (2006), Cheung et al. (2009), Douma et al. (2006), and Ge et al. (2010) do not consider endogeneity as a problem. Nevertheless, RPTs and corporate governance variables are potentially endogenous in nature. Prior studies examining the relationship between corporate governance and firm performance employs the GMM estimation technique to control for endogeneity issues (Guest, 2009; Pathan and Faff, 2013). This study also employs the GMM and considers all RPT variables, ownership variables, and corporate governance variables as endogenous.

The results of system-GMM estimator regressions are reported in Table 8.5 and 8.6. Table 8.5 shows that direct ownership (DIROWN) and indirect ownership (INDOWN) rights of controlling shareholders are positively associated with MVE at the 5 per cent level; however, the coefficient for INDOWN is smaller than DIROWN. These results are consistent with the pooled regression results reported in Chapter 7. The first category of outside investors (MINORITY1) is negatively associated with MVE at the 1 per cent level. The association between the second category of outside investors (MINORITY2) and MVE is statistically insignificant. These results agree with pooled regression model findings and support the view that higher ownership of minority shareholders in family firms gives controlling families the incentives to extract private benefits, which results in value loss.

Panel A of the Table 8.6 reports the results associated with market valuation of RPTs between group-member firms. The value-relevance of earnings is reduced by RPTs involving member firms in the presence of indirect ownership rights. Net loans given to member firms reduce the value relevance of book value of equity (BE) and earnings (EARN). However, the magnitude of RP investments does not produce any significant results, which is inconsistent with earlier results. Panel B also confirms that magnitude of RP loans involving subsidiary/holding firms result in value-loss for the firm.

With regards to control variables, Big 4 auditors are positively associated with the firm value and audit committee independence is negatively associated with the firm value at the 5 per cent level. However, the board size provides statistically insignificant results, which is inconsistent with earlier reported findings. Similarly, domestic financial institutions (NMFI) provide insignificant results after controlling for endogeneity. Overall, most of the findings are consistent with earlier results even after controlling for endogeneity problems using system-GMM estimator approach.

TABLE 8.5

Effects of family ownership and minority ownership on firm value: System-GMM estimator

Variable	Model 1		Model 2	
	Estimated coefficient	t-Statistic[a]	Estimated coefficient	t-Statistic[a]
C	0.679	0.430	1.279	0.800
BVE	0.002***	8.190	0.002***	8.200
EARN	0.000	0.070	0.000	0.210
DIROWN	0.954**	2.180		
INDOWN	0.891**	2.510		
MINORITY1			-2.234***	-2.580
MINORITY2			0.412	0.490
NPMF	1.602	1.390	0.477	0.430
NPFI	-1.125	-1.210	-1.087	-1.180
GOVT	-5.942	-0.620	-4.831	-0.500
FII	1.034*	1.770	0.829	1.461
BIG4AUD	0.280**	2.080	0.278**	1.990
ACIND	-0.440**	-2.170	-4.112**	-1.980
BIND	0.078	0.420	0.107	0.570
BSIZE	0.008	0.550	0.008	0.580
NONFAMCEO	-0.261	-1.520	0.029	0.548
FSIZE	0.002	0.020	-0.017	-0.220
FAGE	0.585*	1.675	0.695*	1.650
DEBT	-0.054	-0.745	-0.071	-0.430
GROWTH	0.140***	3.220	0.141***	3.160
YEAR[a]	Included		Included	
INDUSTRY[a]	Included		Included	
Included observations: 1530				

Source: Authors.

Notes:***$p<0.01$; **$p<0.05$; *$p<0.1$.

[a] Dummy variables are included in the regression to control for year and industry differences; however, results are not reported due to space constraints.

TABLE 8.6
Effects of RPTs on MVE: System-GMM estimator

Variable	Panel A		Panel B	
	RPTs involving group-member firms		*RPT involving subsidiary/holding firms*	
	Estimated coefficient	*t–Statistic*	*Estimated coefficient*	*t–Statistic*
C	1.031	0.660	1.123	0.730
BVE	0.002***	9.430	0.002***	7.610
EARN	0.000	0.350	0.000	0.090
INDOWN	0.850**	2.430	1.014**	2.400
TRAD	0.064	0.072	-0.047	-0.180
TRAD*BVE	0.001	0.430	0.003	0.720
TRAD*EARN	0.000	0.020	0.005	0.310
TRAD*EARN*INDOWN	-0.010**	-2.110	-0.005	-0.130
ASST	0.403	0.430	-3.423	-1.110
ASST*BVE	0.001	0.050	0.025	0.530
ASST*EARN	0.137	0.930	0.370	1.200
ASST*EARN*INDOWN	-0.275**	-1.970	-0.523	-1.300
INVST	-3.230	-0.410	0.067	0.170
INVST*BVE	0.013	1.030	0.001	0.620
INVST*EARN	-0.013	-0.120	-0.027	-0.470
INVST*EARN*INDOWN	-0.020	-0.120	0.034	0.290
NETLOAN	0.183	0.770	-1.259**	-2.110
NETLOAN*BVE	-0.002**	-2.550	0.003	0.710
NETLOAN*EARN	-0.036*	-1.650	-0.023	-0.390
NETLOAN*EARN*INDOWN	-1.630***	-3.360	0.115	0.910
DIROWN	0.987**	2.320	0.919***	2.680
NPMF	1.534*	1.671	2.066*	1.680
NPFI	-1.030	-1.130	-0.977	-1.06
GOVT	-6.220	-0.670	-10.099	-1.060
FII	1.090**	1.970	1.276**	2.250
BIG4AUD	0.325**	2.430	0.230*	1.760
ACIND	-0.436**	-2.340	-0.416**	-2.090

Contd.

Variable	Panel A		Panel B	
	RPTs involving group–member firms		*RPT involving subsidiary/ holding firms*	
	Estimated coefficient	*t–Statistic*	*Estimated coefficient*	*t–Statistic*
BIND	0.125	0.690	0.041	0.230
BSIZE	0.013	0.910	0.008	0.610
NONFAMCEO	-0.152	-0.920	-0.226	-1.370
FSIZE	-0.014	-0.180	0.012	0.160
FAGE	0.510	1.190	0.536	1.270
DEBT	-0.046*	-1.690	-0.083*	-1.720
GROWTH	0.091**	2.250	0.143***	3.240
YEAR [a]	Included		Included	
INDUSTRY [a]	Included		Included	
Included observations: 1530				

Source: Authors.

Notes: ***$p<0.01$; **$p<0.05$; *$p<0.1$

[a] Dummy variables are included in the regression to control for year and industry differences; however, results are not reported due to space constraints.

Summary

This chapter's additional analysis confirms the validity of, and provides additional insight to, the main empirical findings. Consistent with the pooled regression model results, the fixed-effect models find that direct and indirect ownership rights of controlling shareholders are positively associated with MVE, whereas minority ownership is negatively associated with MVE. These findings are consistent with the main findings of the previous chapter. For RPTs involving group-member firms and subsidiary/holding firms, the results remain unchanged after excluding non-RPT firms. Furthermore, regression models are re-estimated for each RPT separately and the results remain consistent. The main results are also robust to alternative measure of firm size.

The next chapter discusses the empirical findings and key implications of the research. Furthermore, it advances avenues for future research and concludes the study with final remarks.

Chapter 9

─────

Implications of the Study and Conclusion

This last chapter discusses the key findings, the implications of the research findings, avenues for future research, and provides concluding remarks. The coverage begins with a summary of the key findings followed by the discussion on the implications of this study. The next section highlights the contributions of the study. The last section provides directions for future research and concluding remarks.

Key findings

One of the most important challenges to the governance structure of family-controlled firms is to limit controlling shareholders from extracting private benefits at the cost of the minority shareholders. This study investigates the influence of ownership structure on the MVE in Indian business groups. As for firm-level ownership structure, the study considers three main features: (*a*) direct ownership of controlling shareholders; (*b*) indirect ownership of controlling shareholders, and (*c*) minority ownership. Moreover, the use of RPTs as a means of entrenchment is examined.

Given the importance of principal–principal conflict in family-controlled firms, this study seeks to address those issues by providing answers to several critical questions. Table 9.1 highlights the key research questions and main findings of the study.

The finding of a non-linear association between the indirect ownership rights and firm value is broadly in agreement with the view that indirect ownership is employed as a vehicle by controlling families to extract private benefits in India. Bertrand et al. (2002) and Douma et al. (2006) critically analyse the role of cross-holding in group-affiliated firms. RPTs affect firm value negatively, especially in the presence of indirect ownership rights of the controlling shareholders. This finding raises questions on inadequate regulations pertaining to RPTs. OECD (2012) also raises concerns over inadequate regulatory requirements pertaining to RPTs and the role of independent directors in approving such transactions. Such concerns have led to significant changes under the Companies Act, 2013 and SEBI Listing Requirements, which include shareholder approval for all material RPTs and the availability of an e-voting facility for all shareholder resolutions.

TABLE 9.1

Summary of research questions and key findings

Research questions	Key findings
Main research questions	
1 Does ownership structure explain the variation in firm value (MVE) of Indian business groups?	Direct ownership of controlling shareholders and indirect ownership of controlling shareholders are positively associated with firm value, whereas minority ownership is negatively associated with firm value (Tables 7.1, 7.2, 7.3, and 7.4).
2 Whether the market valuation of RPTs is consistent with: (1) RPTs being relatively benign transactions, (2) RPTs resulting in value loss, (3) RPTs being value-enhancing?	It is evident that the market values RPTs based on the nature of the transaction and the relationship with the party involved in RPTs (Table 7.5).
Detailed research questions	
a Does indirect ownership (obtained through cross-holding and pyramid) of controlling shareholders affect firm value differently than direct ownership rights?	While the association between direct ownership rights and firm value is found to be positive and linear, the association between indirect ownership and firm value is curvilinear (Table 7.2).
b Whether RPTs involving subsidiary and holding firms are valued differently from RPTs involving member firms in the groups?	RP trading and asset transfers with subsidiary and holding firms are found to be benign transactions, whereas RP trading with member firms are viewed as opportunistic and result in a negative market reaction (Table 7.5).
c Does indirect ownership of controlling shareholders influence the earnings-market valuation of RPTs?	Indirect ownership of controlling shareholder is a key predictor of the earnings-market valuation of RPTs with member firms (Table 7.5).
d Does the nature of the transaction affect the valuation of RPTs	RP asset transfers are valued positively by the market, whereas transactions involving investment, trading, and loan are valued negatively by the market (Table 7.5).

Source: Authors.

The evidence on ineffective monitoring by the independent directors provides support for the concerns raised by OECD (2012). OECD (2012) emphasizes the importance of independent members in approving RPTs and raises questions if they are really independent. The disconcerting evidence suggests that independent members may become advisors to controlling shareholders in companies with concentrated ownership (Khanna and Mathew, 2010). Clause 49 of the Listing Requirements of SEBI has been amended to restrict the maximum number of independent directorships to seven and three in the case of individuals serving as a full-time director in any listed firm. However, there are still no guidelines on serving as an independent director in multiple firms in the same business group.

The results of hypotheses testing for the effect of ownership structure and RPTson firm value are summarized in Table 9.2. Table 9.2 reveals that statistical tests support the hypotheses regarding the earnings-market valuation estimation. There is strong evidence supporting a curvilinear association between indirect ownership rights of controlling shareholders and firm value (H2: Table 7.2), suggesting the use of cross-holding and pyramid structures for extracting private benefits. Furthermore, the indirect ownership of controlling shareholders possesses important explanatory power of RPT valuation. As presented in Table 9.2, regression analyses support most of the eight hypotheses. However, statistical analysis fails to support the proposed negative association between RP loans given to member firms and firm value ($H8_a$ and $H8_b$). Firm size, growth, leverage, audit committee independence, board size, and many other governance attributes consistently explain the market valuation of family-controlled group firms. The data has been subject to winsorization to constrain outliers and non-perfect normal distribution. The statistical results are robust to various additional tests, including the estimation of fixed-effect models as an alternative to pooled regression models.

TABLE 9.2

Summary of hypotheses testing

	Hypotheses	Description	Decision
Research question 1	H1	There is a positive and linear association between the proportion of direct cash-flow rights of controlling shareholders and firm value.	Accepted
	H2	There is a curvilinear association between the proportion of indirect cash-flow rights of controlling shareholders and firm value.	Accepted
	H3	There is a negative association between the ownership of minority shareholders and firm value.	Accepted

	Hypotheses	Description	Decision
Research question 2	H4a	There is a negative association between the magnitude of RP trading involving member firms and firm value (MVE).	Accepted
	H4c	There is no association between the magnitude of RP trading involving subsidiary and holding firms and firm value (MVE).	Accepted
	H5a	There is a negative association between the magnitude of RP asset transfers involving member firms and firm value (MVE).	Rejected
	H5c	There is no association between the magnitude of RP asset transfers involving subsidiary and holding firms and firm value (MVE).	Accepted
	H6a	The association between the magnitude of RP investments involving member firms and firm value (MVE) could be either positive or negative.	Accepted
	H6c	There is a negative association between the magnitude of RP investments involving subsidiary and holding firms and firm value (MVE).	Accepted
	H7a	There is a negative association between the magnitude of loans to member firms and firm value (MVE).	Rejected
	H7c	There is a negative association between the magnitude of loans to subsidiary and holding firms and firm value (MVE).	Accepted
	H4b, H5b, H6b, and H7b	RPTs involving member firms influence the value-relevance of earnings in the presence of indirect ownership rights of controlling shareholders.	Accepted
	H4d, H5d, H6d, and H7d	RPTs involving subsidiary and holding firms do not influence the value-relevance of earnings in the presence of indirect ownership rights of controlling shareholders.	Accepted

Source: Authors.

Implications of the study

Concentrated ownership is considered to be the best protection for shareholders in economies where legal protection is relatively weak (Denis and McConnell, 2003; Heugens et al., 2009). However, this study suggests that concentrated-inside ownership provides opportunities for expropriation of minority shareholders. While more concentrated direct ownership of controlling families results in a higher MVE, indirect ownership obtained through cross-holding provides incentives to extract private benefits and results in value loss. This finding requires the prompt attention of regulatory bodies, outside investors and other interested parties. Khanna and Palepu (2000b) and Kali and Sarkar (2005) highlight the benefits of group-affiliation, whereas the prevalent cost associated with group-affiliation should not be ignored.

There is strong evidence of family dominance in corporate management. Controlling families demonstrate their control by family appointments on the board. This study reveals that family members serve in at least one of the two key positions (CEO/chairperson) in most of the sample firms. There are only 19 firms out of a total of 316 firms where none of the key positions (CEO/chairperson) are occupied by controlling family members. While firms can benefit from family managerial and organizational capabilities, profound altruism in family firms imposes costs on the firms. This study does not find any evidence of different valuation of non-family CEOs from family CEOs, which raises questions about the independence of professional CEOs from founding families. It appears that non-family CEOs appointed on the basis of professional expertise continue to work under the influence of the founding family. A controlling family member often occupies the position of chairperson when the CEO is non-family.

Furthermore, a self-control problem is found to undermine the effectiveness of independent directors. We find that independent directors on the board and audit committee are ineffective in monitoring controlling shareholders and thus, valued negatively by the market. The tendency of controlling families to appoint outside members who are friends or have a fiduciary relationship (that is board member from another member firm in the group) undermines the ability of outside directors to effectively monitor the firm's management. This suggests that improvements in governance practices are not sufficient if the focus is on form rather than substance. Regulatory bodies might need to constrain the reliance of outside directors on controlling families for their directorships in the other member firms within the same group. There are some steps taken under the recent changes in Clause 49 of the Listing Requirements to curb this problem by restricting the maximum number of independent directorships to seven. However, the problem of multiple directorships of independent directors in the same business group is not addressed.

There is very limited evidence that RPTs minimize transaction costs in the less developed Indian economy, whereas RPTs facilitate entrenchment effects in the presence of tunnelling incentives. Therefore, it is important to understand the underlying incentives of founding families, instead of labelling RPTs merely as good or bad. To avoid the abusive use of RPTs, regulators in India introduced new laws and regulations to make this process more transparent. Consistent with developed countries such as Canada and the UK, it is required that all material RPTs must have shareholder approval under the Companies Act, 2013 .

Contribution of the study

This study provides several important contributions. First, it helps to gain a better understanding of business groups, which are characterized by unique governance structures. It extends the body of literature that focuses on the distinct valuation of indirect ownership rights of controlling shareholders. This study provides support to earlier studies such as Claessens et al. (2002), Lemmon and Lins (2003), Lins (2003), and Joh (2003). In addition to the ownership rights of controlling shareholders, this study examines the ownership of minority shareholders, blockholders, and various institutional investors. Furthermore, we highlight the dominance of controlling families on the board, which makes the external governance mechanisms (that is independent directors and non-family CEOs) ineffective.

This study adds to the limited literature on RPTs of group-affiliated firms in India. Earlier studies in India (that is Bertrand et al., 2002; Khanna and Palepu, 2000b; Douma et al., 2006) provide indirect evidence of costs and benefits involved with group membership. Therefore, it helps to fill the gap in the accounting literature by providing direct empirical evidence. Furthermore, it provides important implications for policy-makers. If the use of RP transactions is well understood, stringent rules and regulations might be employed to restrict their potential abuse. This becomes even more important in the context of India, when regulations associated with RPTs are well below worldwide standards.

This study enriches existing tunnelling literature by examining the conditions under which the benefits of family ownership and control outweigh their costs. A synthesized framework of the two competing forces (that is alignment effect and entrenchment effect) is developed in explaining the valuation of RPTs. The findings highlight the point that RPT examination may not achieve the goal of finding evidence on expropriation of minority shareholders. Hence, the incentives provided by indirect ownership should be considered so that a more complete understanding is achieved. This approach provides better knowledge of tunnelling determinants from the ownership and governance perspectives.

Avenues for future research

This study provides several important insights into the conflict between controlling and minority shareholders, whereas there are many other areas to be examined to obtain better understanding of principal–principal conflicts. Therefore, we suggest several avenues for future research.

This study identifies the pervasive use of RPTs in extracting private benefits. However, the literature provides evidence on the use earnings management to conceal the value-loss as a result of RPTs. Future research could explore the effect of RPTs on earnings management. The use of RPTs in extracting private benefits provides strong incentives to family managers to conceal the effect of tunnelling transactions by managing earnings. Therefore, it becomes vital to examine the linkage between RPTs and earnings management.

Family ownership seems to influence the use of RPTs in group firms, so there is a need for evidence on the use of RPTs in non-family or non-group firms. Stand-alone firms face different agency problems and the use of RPTs might be driven by different motives. Therefore, comparative studies might help us to draw more informative conclusions.

As the magnitude of RPTs is used as a proxy to capture expropriation of minority shareholders, there are other measures of tunnelling suggested by the literature. For example, the compensation received by family managers might be a way to extract private benefits at the cost of the firm (Gomez-Mejia et al., 2003). Dividend distribution patterns can also be used as a proxy to identify agency problems (Jensen et al. 1992; Rozeff, 1982). Lower dividend payments result in more retained profits being available for controlling shareholders to extract. Future researchers can explore other proxies to gain a more insightful understanding of tunnelling behaviour.

Limitations of the study

We use ownership rights of corporations belonging to promoter groups as a proxy for indirect ownership. The control rights are often above the cash-flow rights for indirect ownership, which provides incentive to extract private benefits. Studies such as Claessens et al. (2000) and Claessens et al. (2002) separate cash-flow and control rights to examine the tunnelling incentives of controlling shareholders. However, ownership information at this level is unavailable in the context of India. Many of these corporations forming part of promoter groups are unlisted and they are not required to disclose ownership information. Therefore, we use the shareholding of corporations as a proxy to capture the tunnelling incentives of the promoter group. This proxy is not as precise as separating cash-flow and control rights of ownership obtained through cross-holdings. In the absence of information about the divergence between cash-flow and control rights, Bertrand et al. (2002) and Kali and Sarkar (2011) use similar proxies for Indian firms. We expect this proxy to be equally effective in measuring tunnelling incentives of controlling shareholders.

This study examined a limited number of RPTs, that is, trading, asset transfers, loans, and investments. Other RPTs include credits given and received (accounts receivable and payable), salaries, and other payments. There might be some expropriation of minority shareholders through these transactions, which are not part of this study. Future researchers might examine these transactions, which are beyond the scope of this study, to gain a fuller understanding of the use of RPTs for expropriation purposes.

This study examines the presence of independent directors on the board and audit committee and its implications on firm value, but ignores the expertise and activities of audit committees. The expertise and activities of firms' audit committees would be more important than the mere presence of independent members. Bédard et al. (2004) find a negative association between earnings management and financial and governance expertise of audit committee members. This suggests that qualitative attributes of independent members restrict the effect of reporting incentives for management. In addition to the number of independent members on the board, future research might also control for the expertise of these members.

Concluding remarks

Restricting the controlling shareholders from extracting private benefits at the cost of minority shareholders is an ongoing corporate governance issue in emerging economies. This study provides an in-depth longitudinal analysis of group-affiliated family-controlled firms from one of the fastest emerging economies in the world. A synthesized framework of convergence-of-interest and entrenchment effects is used to understand the effect of ownership structure on firm value. Direct inside ownership provides incentives to manage the firm effectively, whereas excessive indirect ownership rights, obtained through cross-holdings, present opportunities for expropriation of minority shareholders.

Another useful insight that can be drawn from the findings is that the self-control problem of family-controlled firms undermines the effectiveness of external control mechanisms. Family-controlled firms are not found to effectively use outside non-executive directors. Given the principal–principal conflict in group-affiliated firms, independent directors are implicitly assigned the duty to monitor controlling shareholders. Specifically, independent directors are responsible for reviewing RPTs to avoid potential abuse. This study presents important implications for regulators to enforce the lawful duties of independent directors.

This study helps to fill the research gap in tunnelling in Indian firms by providing direct evidence of its presence in RPTs. This study also provides direct evidence on the earnings-market valuation of RPTs and reveals some interesting findings on the disclosure of RPTs. The valuation of the RPTs is not only based on the nature of the transaction but also on the relationship with the party involved in these transactions. The sale and purchase of goods and services and assets involving subsidiary and holding firms are found to be benign transactions, whereas the sale and purchase of goods and services with group member firms are found to represent entrenchment and results in negative market valuation. Furthermore, the sale and purchase of goods and services, asset transfers, and investments involving group member firms affect the value-relevance of earnings negatively in the presence of indirect ownership rights of controlling shareholders. This implies that concentrated indirect ownership provides opportunities to extract private benefits and RPTs appear to facilitate the expropriation of minority shareholders. Transactions of loans and investments involving subsidiary and holding firms result in value loss.

Overall, indirect ownership rights of controlling shareholders continue to influence the earnings-market valuation of various RPTs with group-member firms, including trading, asset transfers and investments. Significant firm value is lost for firms where controlling shareholders exhibit significant control through indirect ownership rights obtained through cross-holdings. On the contrary, RPTs involving subsidiary and holding firms are valued based on the merit of the transaction, and the indirect ownership rights of controlling shareholders do not influence the valuation of RPTs with subsidiary and holding firms.

Appendix 1

List of Sample Firms

Firm Name	Group Name
Adani Enterprises Ltd	Adani group
Adani Ports & Special Economic Zone Ltd	Adani group
Adani Power Ltd	Adani group
Amrit Banaspati Co Ltd	Amrit Banaspati group
Amrit Corp Ltd	Amrit Banaspati group
Ahmednagar Forgings Ltd	Amtek group
Amtek Auto Ltd	Amtek group
Amtek India Ltd	Amtek group
Ansal Housing & Construction Ltd	Ansal group
Ansal Properties & Infrastructure Ltd	Ansal group
Aurobindo Pharma Ltd	Aurobindo group
Autolite (India) Ltd	Autopal group
Ballarpur Industries Ltd	Avantha group
Bajaj Auto Ltd	Bajaj group
Bajaj Electricals Ltd	Bajaj group
Bajaj Finserv Ltd	Bajaj group
Bajaj Hindusthan Ltd	Bajaj group
Hercules Hoists Ltd	Bajaj group
Mukand Engineers Ltd	Bajaj group
Mukand Ltd	Bajaj group
I F G L Refractories Ltd	Bajoria B.P./K.K. group
Gloster Ltd	Bangur G.D. group
Joonktollee Tea & Industries Ld	Bangur P.D./B.G. group
Shree Cement Ltd	Bangur P.D./B.G. group
Jayshree Chemicals Ltd	Bangur Shreekumar group
West Coast Paper Mills Ltd	Bangur Shreekumar group
India Glycols Ltd	Bharatia group
Jubilant Life Sciences Ltd	Bharatia group
Binani Industries Ltd	Binani group

Aditya Birla Chemicals (India) Ltd	Birla Aditya group
Aditya Birla Nuvo Limited	Birla Aditya group
Grasim Industries Ltd	Birla Aditya group
Hindalco Industries Ltd	Birla Aditya group
Idea Cellular Ltd	Birla Aditya group
Ultratech Cement Ltd	Birla Aditya group
Birla Power Solutions Ltd	Birla Ashok group
Zenith Birla (India) Ltd	Birla Ashok group
Century Enka Ltd	Birla B.K. group
Century Textiles & Industries Ltd	Birla B.K. group
Jay Shree Tea & Industries Ltd	Birla B.K. group
Kesoram Industries Ltd	Birla B.K. group
Borosil Glass Works Ltd	Borosil group (Kheruka) group
Gujarat Borosil Ltd	Borosil group (Kheruka) group
Chettinad Cement Corpn Ltd	Chettinad group
Chowgule Steamships Ltd	Chowgule group
Cosmo Ferrites Ltd	Cosmo group
Cosmo Films Ltd	Cosmo group
Jindal Drilling & Inds Ltd	D P Jindal group
Maharashtra Seamless Ltd	D P Jindal group
Dalmia Bharat Sugar & Industries Ltd	Dalmia group
Datamatics Global Services Ltd	Datamatics group
Deccan Cements Ltd	DCL group
Deccan Polypacks Ltd	DCL group
Goa Carbon Ltd	Dempo V.S. group
Dhunseri Petrochem & Tea Ltd	Dhanuka S.L./C.K. group
Dharani Finance Ltd	Dharani group
Dharani Sugars & Chemicals Ltd	Dharani group
Elder Health Care Ltd	Elder group
Elder Pharmaceuticals Ltd	Elder group
Elder Projects Ltd	Elder group
Eimco Elecon (India) Ltd	Elecon group
Elecon Engineering Co Ltd	Elecon group
Acclaim Industries Ltd	Elpro group
International Conveyors Ltd	Elpro group
International Conveyors Ltd	Elpro group
Emami Ltd	Emami group
Emami Paper Mills Ltd	Emami group
Empee Distilleries Ltd	Empee group
Empee Sugars & Chemicals Ltd	Empee group
Escorts Ltd	Escorts group

Excel Crop Care Ltd	Excel Industries group
Excel Industries Ltd	Excel Industries group
Punjab Chemicals & Crop Protection Ltd	Excel Industries group
Transpek Industry Ltd	Excel Industries group
Facor Alloys Ltd	FACOR group
Facor Steels Ltd	FACOR group
Ferro Alloys Corporation Ltd	FACOR group
Fedders Lloyd Corpn Ltd	Fedders Lloyd group
Lloyd Electric & Engineering Ltd	Fedders Lloyd group
Finolex Cables Ltd	Finolex (Chhabria P.P.) group
Force Motors Ltd	Firodia group
Kinetic Engineering Ltd	Firodia group
Z F Steering Gear (India) Ltd	Firodia group
Flex Foods Ltd	Flex group
Uflex Ltd	Flex group
Pantaloon Retail (India) Ltd	Future group
Gallantt Ispat Limited	Gallantt group
Gallantt Metal Ltd	Gallantt group
Ganesh Benzoplast Ltd	Ganesh Benzoplast group
Garden Silk Mills Ltd	Garden Vareli group
Surat Textile Mills Ltd	Garden Vareli group
Garware Marine Inds Ltd	Garware group
Garware Offshore Services Ltd	Garware group
Garware Polyester Ltd	Garware group
J K Cement Ltd	Gaur Hari Singhania group
Great Eastern Shipping Co Ltd	GE Shipping group
Futura Polyesters Ltd	Ghia group
Sonata Software Ltd	Ghia group
Gillanders Arbuthnot & Co Ltd	Gillanders Arbuthnot group
Ginni Filaments Ltd	Ginni Filaments group
Glenmark Pharmaceuticals Ltd	Glenmark Pharmaceuticals group
G T L Ltd	Global Tele-Systems group
Geometric Ltd	Godrej group
Godrej Consumer Products Ltd	Godrej group
Godrej Industries Ltd	Godrej group
Godrej Properties Ltd	Godrej group
Andhra Cements Ltd	Goenka G.P. (Duncans) group
Duncans Industries Ltd	Goenka G.P. (Duncans) group
Maharashtra Polybutenes Ltd	Goenka G.P. (Duncans) group
Nrc Ltd	Goenka G.P. (Duncans) group
Star Paper Mills Ltd	Goenka G.P. (Duncans) group

Stone India Ltd	Goenka G.P. (Duncans) group
Oriental Carbon & Chemicals Ltd	Goenka J.P. group
Schrader Duncan Ltd	Goenka J.P. group
G T N Industries Ltd	GTN group
Patspin India Ltd	GTN group
Gujarat Ambuja Exports Ltd	Gujarat Ambuja Proteins group
Acrow India Ltd	Gulabchand Doshi group
Hindustan Construction Co Ltd	Gulabchand Doshi group
Indian Hume Pipe Co Ltd	Gulabchand Doshi group
Ravalgaon Sugar Farm Ltd	Gulabchand Doshi group
Asian Hotels (West) Ltd	Gupta group
G S L Nova Petrochemicals Ltd	Gupta group (Surat)
G V K Power & Infrastructure Ltd	GVK Reddy (Novopan) group
Novopan Industries Ltd	GVK Reddy (Novopan) group
Taj G V K Hotels & Resorts Ltd	GVK Reddy (Novopan) goup
J K Lakshmi Cement Ltd	Hari Shankar Singhania group
J K Sugar Ltd	Hari Shankar Singhania group
J K Tyre & Inds Ltd	Hari Shankar Singhania group
Jk Agri Genetics Ltd	Hari Shankar Singhania group
Jk Paper Ltd	Hari Shankar Singhania group
Umang Dairies Ltd	Hari Shankar Singhania group
Hariyana Ship Breakers Ltd	Hariyana group
Inducto Steel Ltd	Hariyana group
Hero Motocorp Ltd	Hero (Munjals) group
Omax Autos Ltd	Hero (Munjals) group
Himadri Chemicals & Inds Ltd	Himadri group
Indian Metals & Ferro Alloys Ltd	IMFA group
Ankit Metal & Power Ltd	Impex group
Impex Ferro Tech Ltd	Impex group
Indoco Remedies Ltd	Indoco (Suresh Kare) group
Infotech Enterprises Ltd	Infotech Enterprise group
Gujarat Flurochemicals Ltd	Inox group
Inox Leisure Ltd	Inox Ggoup
Hindustan Dorr-Oliver Ltd	IVRCL group
I V R C L Assets & Holdings Ltd	IVRCL group
I V R C L Ltd	IVRCL group
J B Chemicals & Pharmaceuticals Ltd	J B Chemicals group
J B F Industries Ltd	J B F Industries group
J B M Auto Ltd	J B M group
J we K Industries Ltd	J we K Industries group
J J Exporters Ltd	J J Exporters group

Jay Ushin Ltd	J P M group
Jagatjit Industries Ltd	Jagatjit Industries group
Milkfood Ltd	Jagatjit Industries group
Jagran Prakashan Ltd	Jagran group
Jagsonpal Pharmaceuticals Ltd	Jagsonpal group
Jamna Auto Inds Ltd	Jai Springs group
Jain Irrigation Systems Ltd	Jain Pipe group
Indian Toners & Developers Ltd	Jain Shudh group
Pasupati Acrylon Ltd	Jain Shudh group
Rama Vision Ltd	Jain Shudh group
Asian Hotels (North) Ltd	Jatia group
Supreme Holdings & Hospitality (India) Ltd	Jatia group
J D Orgochem Ltd	Jaysynth group
Jaysynth Dyestuff (India) Ltd	Jaysynth group
Jindal Poly Films Ltd	Jindal (Ahmedabad) group
Jindal Worldwide Ltd	Jindal (Ahmedabad) group
Kashyap Tele-Medicines Ltd	Jindal (Ahmedabad) group
Salora International Ltd	Jiwrajka group
Jyoti Ltd (Duplicate Name, Gujarat)	Jyoti group
Kanoria Chemicals & Inds Ltd	Kanoria group
Ludlow Jute & Specialities Ltd	Kanoria group
Jeypore Sugar Co Ltd	KCP group
K C P Ltd	KCP group
Ellora Paper Mills Ltd	Kedia V. group
Khaitan (India) Ltd	Khaitan Fans group
Khaitan Electricals Ltd	Khaitan Fans group
Informed Technologies India Ltd	Khandelwal group
Gujarat Poly-Avx Electronics Ltd	Kilachand group
Kesar Enterprises Ltd	Kilachand group
Kesar Terminals & Infrastructure Ltd	Kilachand group
Polychem Ltd	Kilachand group
Envair Electrodyne Ltd	Kirloskar group
G G Dandekar Machine Works Ltd	Kirloskar grroup
Kirloskar Brothers Ltd	Kirloskar group
Kirloskar Electric Co Ltd	Kirloskar group
Kirloskar Ferrous Inds Ltd	Kirloskar group
Kirloskar Oil Engines Ltd	Kirloskar group
Kirloskar Pneumatic Company Ltd	Kirloskar Group
Kabra Extrusiontechnik Ltd	Kolsite group
Plastiblends India Ltd	Kolsite group
Kothari Fermentation & Biochem Ltd	Kothari M.M (Guwahati) group

Kothari Products Ltd	Kothari Products group
Mavi Industries Ltd	Krishna Vinyls group
Lahoti Overseas Ltd	Lahoti goup
Amal Ltd	Lalbhai group
Atul Ltd	Lalbhai group
Hotel Leelaventure Ltd	Leela Hotel group
Lloyds Metals & Energy Ltd	Lloyd Steel group
B S L Ltd	LNJ Bhilwara group
Cheslind Textiles Ltd	LNJ Bhilwara group
H E G Ltd	LNJ Bhilwara group
R S W M Ltd	LNJ Bhilwara group
Lumax Auto Technologies Ltd	Lumax group
Lumax Automotive Systems Ltd	Lumax group
Lumax Industries Ltd	Lumax group
Indokem Ltd	Mahendra Khatau group
Mahindra & Mahindra Ltd	Mahindra & Mahindra group
Mahindra Composites Ltd	Mahindra & Mahindra group
Mahindra Forgings Ltd	Mahindra & Mahindra group
Mahindra Holidays & Resorts India Ltd	Mahindra & Mahindra group
Mahindra Lifespace Developers Ltd	Mahindra & Mahindra group
Mahindra Ugine Steel Co Ltd	Mahindra & Mahindra group
Swaraj Engines Ltd	Mahindra & Mahindra group
Tech Mahindra Ltd	Mahindra & Mahindra group
Mardia Samyoung Capillary Tubes Co Ltd	Mardia Extrusions group
Marsons Ltd	Marson's goup
Deepak Fertilisers & Petrochemicals Corpn Ltd	Mehta C.K. group
Deepak Nitrite Ltd	Mehta C.K. group
Menon Bearings Ltd	Menon (Kolhapur) group
Menon Pistons Ltd	Menon (Kolhapur) group
Motor & General Finance Ltd	MGF group
Minda Industries Ltd	Minda S.L. group
S B E C Sugar Ltd	Modi Umesh Kumar
Blue Coast Hotels Ltd	Monnet group
Monnet Ispat & Energy Ltd	Monnet group
J S W Energy Ltd	Om Prakash Jindal group
Jindal Saw Ltd	Om Prakash Jindal group
Jindal Stainless Ltd	Om Prakash Jindal group
Jindal Steel & Power Ltd	Om Prakash Jindal group
Jsw Steel Ltd	Om Prakash Jindal group
Mirc Electronics Ltd	Onida group
Pidilite Industries Ltd	Parekhgroup

Vinyl Chemicals India Ltd	Parekh group
Kopran Ltd	Parijat group
Oricon Enterprises Ltd	Parijat group
Nesco Ltd	Patel J.V. Group (New Std. Engg.)
Skyline Millars Ltd	Patel J.V. Group (New Std. Engg.)
Patel Integrated Logistics Ltd	Patel Roadways Ggoup
P C S Technology Ltd	Patni Computers group
Eurotex Industries & Exports Ltd	Patodia Eurotex (PBM Polytex group)
P B M Polytex Ltd	Patodia Eurotex (PBM Polytex group)
House Of Pearl Fashions Ltd	Pearl Pet group
Pearl Engineering Polymers Ltd	Pearl Pet group
Pearl Polymers Ltd	Pearl Pet group
Morarjee Textiles Ltd	Piramal Ajay group
Peninsula Land Ltd	Piramal Ajay group
Piramal Glass Ltd	Piramal Ajay group
V we P Industries Ltd	Piramal Dilip group
Poddar Pigments Ltd	Poddar Bros. (Calcutta) group
Polar Industries Ltd	Polar group
Polar Pharma India Ltd	Polar group
Prakash Industries Ltd	Prakash (Surya Roshni) group
Surya Roshni Ltd	Prakash (Surya Roshni) group
Pritish Nandy Communications Ltd	Pritish Nandy group
Priyadarshini Spinning Mills Ltd	Priyadarshini group
Rain Commodities Ltd	Priyadarshini group
Sagar Cements Ltd	Priyadarshini group
Borax Morarji Ltd	Pudumjee (Jatia) group
Dharamsi Morarji Chemical Co Ltd	Pudumjee (Jatia) group
Pudumjee Industries Ltd	Pudumjee (Jatia) group
Pudumjee Pulp & Paper Mills Ltd	Pudumjee (Jatia) group
Punj Lloyd Ltd	Pudumjee (Jatia) group
Anjani Portland Cement Ltd	Raasi group
Khaitan Chemicals & Fertilizers Ltd	Radico (Gajanan Khaitan) group
Radico Khaitan Ltd	Radico (Gajanan Khaitan) group
Hindustan Composites Ltd	Raghu Mody group (Rasoi group)
J L Morison (India) Ltd	Raghu Mody group (Rasoi group)
Rasoi Ltd	Raghu Mody group (Rasoi group)
A P M Industries Ltd	Raheja Rajan group
Hathway Cable & Datacom Ltd	Raheja Rajan group
Orient Abrasives Ltd	Raheja Rajan group
Perfectpac Ltd	Raheja Rajan group
Prism Cement Ltd	Raheja Rajan group

Advanta India Ltd	Rajju Shroff group
United Phosphorus Ltd	Rajju Shroff group
Madras Cements Ltd	Ramco group (Madras Cements)
Rajapalayam Mills Ltd	Ramco group (Madras Cements)
Ramco Industries Ltd	Ramco group (Madras Cements)
Ramco Systems Ltd	Ramco group (Madras Cements)
Rana Sugars Ltd	Rana group
Standard Industries Ltd	Rasesh Mafatlal roup
Apollo Tyres Ltd	Rathi P.C./R.C. group
Bharat Gears Ltd	Rathi P.C./R.C. group
Rathi Graphic Technologies Ltd	Rathi P.C./R.C. group
Rathi Steel & Power Ltd	Rathi P.C./R.C. group
Anik Industries Ltd	Ruchi group
National Steel & Agro Inds Ltd	Ruchi group
Ruchi Infrastructure Ltd	Ruchi group
Ruchi Soya Inds Ltd	Ruchi group
Ruchi Strips & Alloys Ltd	Ruchi group
Landmarc Leisure Corpn Ltd	S. Kumars group
Shree Ram Urban Infrastructure Ltd	S. Kumars group
Sahara One Media & Entertainment Ltd	Sahara India group
Samtel Color Ltd	Samtel group
Sterling International Enterprises Ltd	Sandesara group
Sandur Manganese & Iron Ores Ltd	Sandur Manganese group
Sanghi Industries Ltd	Sanghi Polyester group
Anil Special Steel Inds Ltd	Satya group
Shalimar Wires Industries Ltd	Satya group
Savita Oil Technologies Ltd	Savita Chemicals group
M P Agro Inds Ltd	Sayaji Hotels group
Sayaji Hotels Ltd	Sayaji Hotels group
Shreyans Industries Ltd	Shreyans group
Benares Hotels Ltd	Tata group
Indian Hotels Co Ltd	Tata group
Oriental Hotels Ltd	Tata group
A B C India Ltd	TCI-Bhoruka group
Gati Ltd	TCI-Bhoruka group
U B Engineering Ltd	UB group
United Breweries (Holdings) Ltd	UB group
United Breweries Ltd	UB group
United Spirits Ltd	UB group
Cadila Healthcare Ltd	Zydus Cadila group
Zydus Wellness Ltd	Zydus Cadila group

Appendix 2

List of Business Groups

Group Name	Number of Firms
Adani group	3
Amrit Banaspati group	2
Amtek group	3
Ansal group	2
Aurobindo group	1
Autopal group	1
Avantha group	1
Bajaj group	7
Bajoria B.P./K.K. group	1
Bangur G.D. group	1
Bangur P.D./B.G. group	2
Bangur Shreekumar group	2
Bharatia group	2
Binani group	1
Birla Aditya group	6
Birla Ashok group	2
Birla B.K. group	4
Borosil Group (Kheruka) group	2
Chettinad group	1
Chowgule group	1
Cosmo group	2
D P Jindal group	2
Dalmia group	1
Datamatics group	1
DCL group	2
Dempo V.S. group	1
Dhanuka S.L./C.K. group	1
Dharani group	2

Elder group	3
Elecon group	2
Elpro group	3
Emami group	2
Empee group	2
Escorts group	1
Excel Industries group	4
FACOR group	3
Fedders Lloyd group	2
Finolex (Chhabria P.P.) group	1
Firodia group	3
Flex group	2
Future group	1
Gallantt group	2
Ganesh Benzoplast group	1
Garden Vareli group	2
Garware group	3
Gaur Hari Singhania group	1
GE Shipping group	1
Ghia group	2
Gillanders Arbuthnot group	1
Ginni Filaments group	1
Glenmark Pharmaceuticals group	1
Global Tele-Systems group	1
Godrej group	4
Goenka G.P. (Duncans) group	6
Goenka J.P. group	2
GTN group	2
Gujarat Ambuja Proteins group	1
Gulabchand Doshi group	4
Gupta group	1
Gupta group (Surat)	1
GVK Reddy (Novopan) group	3
Hari Shankar Singhania group	6
Hariyana group	2
Hero (Munjals) group	2
Himadri group	1
IMFA group	1
Impex group	2
Indoco (Suresh Kare) group	1
Infotech Enterprise group	1

Inox group	2
IVRCL group	3
J B Chemicals group	1
J B F Industries group	1
J B M group	1
J we K Industries group	1
J J Exporters group	1
J P M group	1
Jagatjit Industries group	2
Jagran group	1
Jagsonpal group	1
Jai Springs group	1
Jain Pipe group	1
Jain Shudh group	3
Jatia group	2
Jaysynth group	2
Jindal (Ahmedabad) group	3
Jiwrajka group	1
Jyoti group	1
Kanoria group	2
KCP group	2
Kedia V. group	1
Khaitan Fans group	2
Khandelwal group	1
Kilachand group	4
Kirloskar group	7
Kolsite group	2
Kothari M.M (Guwahati) group	1
Kothari Products group	1
Krishna Vinyls group	1
Lahoti group	1
Lalbhai group	2
Leela Hotel group	1
Lloyd Steel group	1
LNJ Bhilwara group	4
Lumax group	3
Mahendra Khatau group	1
Mahindra & Mahindra group	8
Mardia Extrusions group	1
Marson's group	1
Mehta C.K. group	2

Menon (Kolhapur) group	2
MGF group	1
Minda S.L. group	1
Modi Umesh Kumar	1
Monnet group	2
Om Prakash Jindal group	5
Onida group	1
Parekh group	2
Parijat group	2
Patel J.V. group (New Std. Engg.)	2
Patel Roadways group	1
Patni Computers group	1
Patodia Eurotex (PBM Polytex group)	2
Pearl Pet group	3
Piramal Ajay group	3
Piramal Dilip group	1
Poddar Bros. (Calcutta) group	1
Polar group	2
Prakash (Surya Roshni) group	2
Pritish Nandy group	1
Priyadarshini group	3
Pudumjee (Jatia) group	5
Raasi group	1
Radico (Gajanan Khaitan) group	2
Raghu Mody group (Rasoi group)	3
Raheja Rajan group	5
Rajju Shroff group	2
Ramco group (Madras Cements)	4
Rana group	1
Rasesh Mafatlal group	1
Rathi P.C./R.C. group	4
Ruchi group	5
S. Kumars group	2
Sahara India group	1
Samtel group	1
Sandesara group	1
Sandur Manganese group	1
Sanghi Polyester group	1
Satya group	2
Savita Chemicals group	1
Sayaji Hotels group	2

References

Alderfer, C. P. 1988. 'Understanding and Consulting to Family Business Boards.' *Family Business Review* 1(3): 249–261.

Aldrich, H. 2008.*Organizations and Environments.*Stanford: Stanford University Press.

Amsden, A. H. and T. Hikino. 1994. 'Project Execution Capability, Organizational Know-How and Conglomerate Corporate Growth in Late Industrialization.' *Industrial and Corporate Change* 3(1):111–147.

Anderson, R. C., S. Mansi, and D. M. Reeb. 2003. 'Founding Family Ownership and the Agency Cost of Debt.' *Journal of Financial Economics* 68(2):263–285.

Anderson, R. C. and D. M. Reeb. 2004. 'Board Composition: Balancing Family Influence in S&P 500 firms.' *Administrative Science Quarterly* 49(2): 209–237.

Arrow, K. J. 1971. *Essays in the Theory of Risk-Bearing.* Chicago: Markham Publishing Company.

Athey, M. J. and P. S. Laumas. 1994. 'Internal Funds and Corporate Investment in India.' *Journal of Development Economics* 45(2):287–303.

Athey, M. J. and W. D. Reeser. 2000. 'Asymmetric Information, Industrial Policy, and Corporate Investment in India.' *Oxford Bulletin of Economics and Statistics* 62(2): 267–292.

Bae, K. H., J. K Kang, and J. M. Kim. 2002. 'Tunneling or Value Added? Evidence from Mergers by Korean Business Groups.' *The Journal of Finance* 57(6):2695–2740.

Baek, J. S., J. K. Kang, and I. Lee. 2006. 'Business Groups and Tunneling: Evidence from Private Securities Offerings by Korean Chaebols.' *The Journal of Finance* 61(5): 2415–2449.

Ball, R., S. P. Kothari, and A. Robin. 2000. 'The Effect of International Institutional Factors on Properties of Accounting Earnings.' *Journal of Accounting and Economics* 29(1): 1–51.

Ball, R., A. Robin, and J. S. Wu. 2003. 'Incentives versus Standards: Properties of Accounting Income in Four East Asian Countries.' *Journal of Accounting and Economics* 36(1–3): 235–270.

Barclay, M. and C. G. Holderness. 1991. 'Negotiated Block Trades and Corporate Control.' *The Journal of Finance* 46(3): 861–878.

Barker, J. 1992. *Discovering the Future: The Business of Paradigms.* Lake Elmo, MN: ILI Press.

Barth, M. E., W. H. Beaver, and W. R. Landsman. 1998. 'Relative Valuation Roles of Equity Book Value and Net Income as a Function of Financial Health.' *Journal of Accounting and Economics* 25(1):1–34.

Beasley, M. S. 1996. 'An Empirical Analysis of the Relation Between the Board of Director Composition and Financial Statement Fraud.' *The Accounitng Review* 71(4): 443–465.

Becker, G. S. 1981. *A Treatise on the Family.* Cambridge: Harvard Business Press.

Bédard, J., S. M. Chtourou, and L. Courteau. 2004. 'The Effect of Audit Committee Expertise, Independence, and Activity on Aggressive Earnings Management.' *Auditing* 23(2): 15–37.

Beedles, W. L., P. Dodd, and R. R. Officer. 1988. 'Regularities in Australian Share Returns.' *Australian Journal of Management* 13(1): 1.

Benston, G. J. 1985. 'The Validity of Profits-Structure Studies with Particular Reference to the FTC's Line of Business Data.' *American Economic Review* 75(1): 37–67.

Berger, P. G. and E. Ofek. 1995. 'Diversification's Effect on Firm Value.' *Journal of Financial Economics* 37(1): 39–65.

Berglöf, E. and E. Perotti. 1994. 'The Governance Structure of the Japanese Financial Keiretsu.' *Journal of Financial Economics* 36(2): 259–284.

Bergstrom, T. C. 1995. 'On the Evolution of Altruistic Ethical Rules for Siblings.' *The American Economic Review* 85(1): 58–81.

Berkman, H., R. A. Cole, and L. J. Fu. 2009. 'Expropriation through Loan Guarantees to Related Parties: Evidence from China.' *Journal of Banking and Finance* 33(1): 141–156.

Bertrand, M., P. Mehta, and S. Mullainathan. 2002. 'Ferreting Out Tunneling: An Application to Indian Business Groups.' *Quarterly Journal of Economics* 117(1): 121–148.

Besanko, D., D. Dranove, and M. Shanley. 1996. *Economics of Strategy.* New York: John Wiley & Sons.

Bhagat, S., A. Shleifer, R. W. Vishny, G. Jarrel, and L. Summers. 1990. 'Hostile Takeovers in the 1980s: The Return to Corporate Specializations', Brookings Papers on Economic Activity Microeconomics 1990:1–84.

Bhattacharya, U. and B. Ravikumar. 2001. 'Capital Markets and the Evolution of Family Businesses.' *The Journal of Business* 74(2):187–219.

Bianchi, M., M. Bianco, and L. Enriques. 2001. 'Pyramidal Groups and the Separation Between Ownership and Control in Italy.' In *The Control of Corporate Europe*, edited by F. Barca and M. Becht, 154–187. Oxford: Oxford University Press.

Bittlingmayer, G. and T. W. Hazlett. 2000. 'DOS Kapital: Has Antitrust Action Against Microsoft Created Value in the Computer Industry?' *Journal of Financial Economics* 55(3): 329–359.

Boone, P. and D. Rodionov.2001. 'Rent Seeking in Russia and the CIS', paper prepared for the EBRD Tenth Anniversary Conference, Brunswick USB Warburg, Moscow.

Bose, S. 2005. 'Securities Market Regulations: Lessons from US and Indian Experience.' *The ICRA Bulletin, Money and Finance* 2(20–21).

Brockman, P. and D. Y. Chung. 2003. 'Investor Protection and Firm Liquidity'. *Journal of Finance* 58(2):921–938.

Brown, P., W. Beekes, and P. Verhoeven. 2011.'Corporate Governance, Accounting and Finance: A Review'. *Accounting and Finance* 51(1):96–172.

Buchanan, J. M. 1997. 'The Samaritan's Dilemma.' *International Library of Critical Writings in Economics* 83: 261–278.

Burkart, M., D. Gromb and F. Panunzi. 1997. 'Large Shareholders, Monitoring, and the Value of the Firm'. *Quarterly Journal of Economics* 112(3): 693–728.

Burkart, M., F. Panunzi and A. Shleifer. 2003. 'Family firms.' *Journal of Finance* 58(5): 2167–2201.

Caves, R. E. 1989. 'Mergers, Takeovers, and Economic Efficiency: Foresight vs Hindsight.' *International Journal of Industrial Organization* 7(1): 151–174.

Chakrabarti, R., W. Megginson and P. K. Yadav. 2008. 'Corporate Governance in India.' *Journal of Applied Corporate Finance* 20(1): 59–72.

Chakrabarti, R., K. Subramanian and F. Tung. 2010. 'Independent Directors and Firm Value: Evidence from an Emerging Market'. Available at SSRN 1631710.

Chang, S. J. and U. Choi. 1988. 'Strategy, Structure and Performance of Korean Business Groups: A Transactions Cost Approach'. *The Journal of Industrial Economics* 37(2): 141–158.

Chang, S. J. and J. Hong. 2000. 'Economic Performance of Group-Affiliated Companies in Korea: Intragroup-Resource Sharing and Internal Business Transactions'. *Academy of Management Journal* 43(3): 429–448.

Cheung, Y. L., L. Jing, T. Lu, P.R. Rau, and A. Stouraitis. 2009. 'Tunneling and Propping Up: An Analysis of Related Party Transactions by Chinese Listed Companies.' *Pacific-Basin Finance Journal* 17(3): 372–393.

Cheung, Y. L., P. R. Rau, and Stouraitis, A. 2006. 'Tunneling, Propping, and Expropriation: Evidence from Connected Party Transactions in Hong Kong.' *Journal of Financial Economics* 82(2): 343–386.

Chhibber, P. K. and S. K. Majumdar.1999. 'Foreign Ownership and Profitability: Property Rights, Control, and the Performance of Firms in Indian Industry.' *Journal of Law and Economics* 42(1): 209.

Chua, J. H., J. J. Chrisman, and P. Sharma. 1999. 'Defining the Family Business by Behavior.' *Entrepreneurship: Theory and Practice* 23(4): 19–39.

Claessens, S., S. Djankov, J. Fan, and L. Lang. 1999. 'Expropriation of Minority Shareholders: Evidence from East Asia.' In *Policy Research Paper 2088*. Washington, DC: World Bank.

Claessens, S., S. Djankov, J. P. H. Fan, and L. H. P. Lang. 2002. 'Disentangling the Incentive and Entrenchment Effects of Large Shareholdings.' *The Journal of Finance.* 57(6): 2741–2771.

———.2003. 'When Does Corporate Diversification Matter to Productivity and Performance? Evidence from East Asia.' *Pacific-Basin Finance Journal* 11(3): 365–392.

Claessens, S., S. Djankov, and L. H. P. Lang. 2000. 'The Separation of Ownership and Control in East Asian Corporations.' *Journal of Financial Economics* 58(1–2): 81–112.

Claessens, S., J. P. H. Fan, and L. H. P. Lang. 2006. 'The Benefits and Costs of Group Affiliation: Evidence from East Asia.' *Emerging Markets Review* 7(1):1–26.

Coffee, J. C. Jr. 1991. 'Liquidity versus Control: The Institutional Investor as Corporate Monitor.' *Columbia Law Review* 91(6): 1277–1368.

———. 2002. 'Racing Towards the Top: The impact of Cross-Listing and Stock Market Competition on International Corporate Governance.' *Columbia Law Review* 102(7): 1757–1831.

Cornell, B. and Q. Liu. 2001.'The Parent Company Puzzle: When Is the Whole Worth Less than One of the Parts?' *Journal of Corporate Finance* 7(4): 341–366.

Dalton, D. R., C. M. Daily, A. E. Ellstrand and J. L. Johnson. 1998. 'Meta-Analytic Reviews of Board Composition, Leadership Structure, and Financial Performance.' *Strategic Management Journal* 19(3): 269–290.

Dandekar, V. M. 1992. 'Forty Years after Independence.' In *The Indian Economy: Problems and Prospects*, edited by B. Jalan, 38–91. New Delhi: Viking.

Davidoff, S. M. 2005. 'Fairness Opinions.'*American University Law Review* 55(6): 1557–1625.

Davis, G. F., K. A. Diekmann, and C. H. Tinsley. 1994. 'The Decline and Fall of the Conglomerate Firm in the 1980s: The Deinstitutionalization of an Organizational form.' *American Sociological Review* 59(4): 547–570.

De Long, B. 1991. 'Did J.P. Morgan's Men Add Value? A Historical Perspective on Financial Capitalism.' In *Inside the Business Enterprise: Historical Perspectives on the Use of Information*, edited by P. Temin, 205–250. Chicago: University of Chicago Press.

DeAngelo, L. E. 1981. 'Auditor Size and Audit Quality.' *Journal of Accounting and Economics* 3(3): 183–199.

DeFond, M., M. Hung, and R. Trezevant. 2007. 'Investor Protection and the Information Content of Annual Earnings Announcements: International Evidence.' *Journal of Accounting and Economics* 43(1): 37–67.

Demsetz, H. 1983. 'Structure of Ownership and the Theory of the Firm.' *Journal of Law and Economics* 26(2): 375–390.

Demsetz, H. and K. Lehn. 1985. 'The Structure of Corporate Ownership: Causes and Consequences.' *Journal of Political Economy* 93(6): 1155–1177.

Denis, D. K. and J. J. McConnell. 2003. 'International Corporate Governance.' *Journal of Financial and Quantitative Analysis* 38(1):1–36.

Dewenter, K., W. Novaes, and R. H. Pettway. 2001. 'Visibility versus Complexity in Business Groups: Evidence from Japanese Keiretsu.'*The Journal of Business*74(1): 79–100.

Dewenter, K. L. and P. H. Malatesta. 2001. 'State-Owned and Privately Owned Firms: An Empirical Analysis of Profitability, Leverage, and Labor Intensity.' *The American Economic Review* 91(1): 320–334.

Douma, S., R. George, and R. Kabir. 2006. 'Foreign and Domestic Ownership, Business Groups, and Firm Performance: Evidence From a Large Emerging Market.' *Strategic Management Journal* 27(7): 637–657.

Dutta, S. 1997. *Family Business in India*. New Delhi: Response Books.

Easton, P. D. and T. S. Harris. 1991. 'Earnings as an Explanatory Variable for Returns.' *Journal of Accounting Research* 29(1): 19–36.

Eastwood, R. and R. Kohli. 1999. 'Directed Credit and Investment in Small-Scale Industry in India: Evidence from Firm-Level Data 1965–78.' *Journal of Development Studies* 35(4): 42–63.

Eddleston, K. A. and F. W. Kellermanns. 2007. 'Destructive and Productive Family Relationships: A Stewardship Theory Perspective.' *Journal of Business Venturing* 22(4): 545–565.

Eddleston, K. A., F. W. Kellermanns, and R. Sarathy. 2008. 'Resource Configuration in Family Firms: Linking Resources, Strategic Planning and Technological Opportunities to Performance.' *Journal of Management Studies* 45(1): 26–50.

Ehrhardt, O. and E. Nowak. 2003. 'Private Benefits and Minority Shareholder Expropriation (Or What Exactly Are Private Benefits of Control?)', EFA Annual Conference Paper no. 809.

Eisenberg, T., S. Sundgren, and M. T. Wells. 1998.'Larger Board Size and Decreasing Firm Value in Small Firms.' *Journal of Financial Economics* 48(1): 35–54.

Eisenhardt, K. M. 1989. 'Agency Theory: An Assessment and Review.' *The Academy of Management Review*14(1): 57–74.

Enriques, L. 2015. 'Related Party Transactions: Policy Options and Real-World Challenges (With a Critique of the European Commission Proposal).' *European Business Organization Law Review* 16(1):1–37.

Evans, D. S. 1987. 'The Relationship Between Firm Growth, Size, and Age: Estimates for 100 Manufacturing Industries.'*The Journal of Industrial Economics* 35(4): 567–581.

Faccio, M., L. H. P. Lang, and L. Young. 2001. 'Dividends and Expropriation.'*The American Economic Review* 91(1): 54–78.

Fama, E. F. 1980. 'Agency Problems and the Theory of The Firm.' *Journal of Political Economy* 88(2): 288–307.

Fama, E. F. and M. C. Jensen.1983a. 'Agency Problems and Residual Claims.' *Journal of Law and Economics* 26(2): 327–349.

———. 1983b. 'Separation of Ownership and Control.' *Journal of Law and Economics* 26(2): 301–325.

Fan, J. P. H. and T. J. Wong. 2002. 'Corporate Ownership Structure and the Informativeness of Accounting Earnings in East Asia.' *Journal of Accounting and Economics* 33(3): 401–425.

Farrar, D. E. and R. R. Glauber.1967. 'Multicollinearity in Regression Analysis: The Problem Revisited.' *Review of Economics and Statistics* 49(1): 92.

Fauver, L., J. Houston, and A. Naranjo. 2003. 'Capital Market Development, International Integration, Legal Systems, and the Value of Corporate Diversification: A Cross-Country Analysis.' *Journal of Financial and Quantitative Analysis* 38(1): 135–157.

Francis, J. and K. Schipper. 1999. 'Have Financial Statements Lost Their Relevance?' *Journal of Accounting Research* 37(2):319–352.

Francis, J., K. Schipper, and L. Vincent. 2005. 'Earnings and Dividend Informativeness When Cash Flow Rights Are Separated From Voting Rights.' *Journal of Accounting and Economics* 39(2): 329–360.

Friedman, E., S. Johnson, and T. Mitton. 2003.'Propping and Tunneling.' *Journal of Comparative Economics* 31(4) 732–750.

Gallery, G., N. Gallery, and M. Supranowicz. 2008.'Cash-Based Related Party Transactions in New Economy Firms.' *Accounting Research Journal* 21(2) 147–166.

Ge, W., D. H. Drury, S. Fortin, F. Liu, and D. Tsang. 2010. 'Value Relevance of Disclosed Related Party Transactions.' *Advances in Accounting* 26(1): 134–141.

Gerlach, M. L. 1992.'The Japanese Corporate Network: A Blockmodel Analysis.' *Administrative Science Quarterly* 37(1): 105–139.

Gersick, K. E. 1997. *Generation to Generation: Life Cycles of the Family Business.* Boston: Harvard Business Press.

Ghemawat, P. and T. Khanna. 1998. 'The Nature of Diversified Business Groups: A Research Design and Two Case Studies.' *Journal of Industrial Economics* 46(1): 35–61.

Ghemawat, P. and K. Kothavala. 1998. 'Repositioning of Ranbaxy.' *Case#9–796–181.* Boston: Harvard Business School Publishing.

Gilson, S. 1990. 'Management Turnover and Financial Distress.' *Journal of Financial Economics* 25(2): 241–262.

Gomez-Mejia, L. R., M. Larraza-Kintana, and M. Makri. 2003. 'The Determinants of Executive Compensation in Family-Controlled Public Corporations.' *Academy of Management Journal* 46(2): 226–237.

Gopalan, R., V. Nanda, and A. Seru. 2007. 'Affiliated Firms and Financial Support: Evidence from Indian Business Groups.' *Journal of Financial Economics* 86(3): 759–795.

Graham, J. R., C. R. Harvey, and S. Rajgopal. 2005. 'The Economic Implications of Corporate Financial Reporting.' *Journal of Accounting and Economics.* 40 (1–3): 3–73.

Greenwald, B. C., and J. E. Stiglitz. 1993. 'Financial Market Imperfections and Business Cycles.' *Quarterly Journal of Economics* 108(1): 77–114.

Grossman, S. J., and O. D. Hart. 1980. 'Takeover Bids, the Free-Rider Problem, and the Theory of the Corporation.' *The Bell Journal of Economics* 11(1):42–64.

Guest, P. M. 2009. 'The Impact of Board Size on Firm Performance: Evidence from the UK.' *The European Journal of Finance* 15(4):385–404.

Guillen, M. F. 1997. 'Business Groups in Economic Development.' *Academy of Management Annual Meeting at Boston* 1997(1):170–174.

Guriev, S. and A. Rachinsky. 2005. 'The Role of Oligarchs in Russian Capitalism.' *Journal of Economic Perspectives* 19(1):131–150.

Hart, O. and J. Moore. 1990. 'Property Rights and the Nature of the Firm.' *Journal of Political Economy,* 98(6):1119–1158.

Hazra, A. and M. Micevska. 2004. 'The Problem of Court Congestion: Evidence from Indian Lower Courts.' In*Royal Economic Society Annual Conference*, Royal Economic Society, University of St. Andrews.

Heugens, P. P. M. A. R., M. Van Essen, and J. Van Oosterhout. 2009. 'Meta-Analyzing Ownership Concentration and Firm Performance in Asia: Towards a More Fine-Grained Understanding.' *Asia Pacific Journal of Management* 26(3):481–512.

Holderness, C. G. and D. P. Sheehan. 1988. 'The Role of Majority Shareholders in Publicly Held Corporations: An Exploratory Analysis.' *Journal of Financial Economics* 20:317–346.

Hoshi, T., A. D. Kashyap, and D. Scharfstein. 1991. 'Corporate Structure, Liquidity, and Investment: Evidence from Japanese Industrial Groups.' *Quarterly Journal of Economics* 106(1):33–60.

Hoskisson, R. E. and M. A. Hitt. 1990. 'Antecedents and Performance Outcomes of Diversification: A Review And Critique of Theoretical Perspectives.' *Journal of Management* 16(2):461.

Jensen, G. R., D. P. Solberg, and T. S. Zorn. 1992. 'Simultaneous Determination of Insider Ownership, Debt, and Dividend Policies.' *The Journal of Financial and Quantitative Analysis* 27(2):247–263.

Jensen, M. C. 1986. 'Agency Costs of Free Cash Flow, Corporate Finance, and Takeovers.' *The American Economic Review* 76(2):323–329.

———. 1993. 'The Modern Industrial Revolution, Exit, and the Failure of Internal Control Systems.' *Journal of Finance* 48(3):831–880.

Jensen, M. C. and W. H. Meckling. 1976. 'Theory of the Firm: Managerial Behavior, Agency Costs and Ownership Structure.' *Journal of Financial Economics* 3(4):305–360.

Jian, M. and T. Wong. 2003. 'Earnings Management and Tunneling Through Related Party Transactions: Evidence From Chinese Corporate Groups.' EFA 2003 Annual Conference Paper No. 549.

Jian, M. and T. J. Wong. 2010. 'Propping Through Related Party Transactions.' *Review of Accounting Studies* 15(1):70–105.

Jiang, G., C. Lee, and H. Yue. 2005. 'Tunneling in China: The Surprisingly Pervasive Use of Corporate Loans to Extract Funds from Chinese Listed Companies.' *Johnson School Research Paper Series* No. 31–06.

Joh, S. W. 2003. 'Corporate Governance and Firm Profitability: Evidence from Korea Before the Economic Crisis.' *Journal of Financial Economics* 68(2):287–322.

Johnson, S., R. La Porta, F. Lopez-De-Silanes, and A. Schleifer. 2000. 'Tunneling.' *The American Economic Review* 90(2):22–27.

Jon, D. 1972. 'The Development of Diversified and Conglomerate Firms in the United States, 1920–1970.' *The Business History Review* 46(2):202–219.

Joshi, V. and I. M. D. Little. 1996. *India's Economic Reforms: 1991–2001.* Delhi: Oxford University Press.

Kali, R. and J. Sarkar. 2005. 'Diversification, Propping and Monitoring: Business Groups, Firm Performance and the Indian Economic Transition.' Working Papers 2005–06. Mumbai: Indira Gandhi Institute of Development Research.

———. 2011. 'Diversification and Tunneling: Evidence from Indian Business Groups.' *Journal of Comparative Economics* 39(3):349–367.

Kang, J.K. and R. M. Stulz. 1997. 'Why Is There A Home Bias? An Analysis of Foreign Portfolio Equity Ownership in Japan.' *Journal of Financial Economics* 46(1):3–28.

Kang, N. and N. Nayar. 2004. 'The Evolution of Corporate Bankruptcy Law in India.' *Money and Finance* Oct 03–Mar 04:37–58.

Kaplan, S. N. and D. Reishus. 1990. 'Outside Directorships and Corporate Performance.' *Journal of Financial Economics* 27(2):389–410.

Kedia, B., D. Mukherjee, and S. Lahiri. 2006. 'Indian Business Groups: Evolution and Transformation.' *Asia Pacific Journal of Management* 23(4):559–577.

Keister, L. A. 1998. 'Engineering Growth: Business Group Structure and Firm Performance in China's Transition Economy.' *American Journal of Sociology* 104(2):404–440.

Kets de Vries, M. F. 1996. *Family Business: Human Dilemmas in the Family Firm Text and Cases.* London: International Thomson Business Press.

Khanna, T. 2000. 'Business Groups and Social Welfare in Emerging Markets: Existing Evidence and Unanswered Questions.' *European Economic Review* 44(4–6):748–761.

Khanna, T. and K. Palepu. 1997. 'Why Focused Strategies May Be Wrong for Emerging Markets.' *Harvard Business Review* 75(4):41–51.

———. 1999. 'Emerging Market Business Groups, Foreign Investors, and Corporate Governance.' in National Bureau of Economic Research.

———. 2000a. 'The Future of Business Groups in Emerging Markets: Long-Run Evidence from Chile.' *Academy of Management Journal* 43(3):268–285.

———. 2000b. 'Is Group Affiliation Profitable in Emerging Markets? An Analysis of Diversified Indian Business Groups.' *Journal of Finance* 55(2):867–891.

Khanna, T., K. Palepu and D. M. Wu. 1998. 'The House of Tata, 1995: The Next Generation (A).' In *Case#9–798–037.* Boston: Harvard Business School Publishing.

Khanna, T. and J. W. Rivkin. 2001. 'Estimating the Performance Effects of Business Groups in Emerging Markets.' *Strategic Management Journal* 22(1):45.

Khanna, T. and Y. Yafeh. 2005. 'Business Groups and Risk Sharing Around the World.' *Journal of Business* 78(1):301–340.

———. 2007. 'Business Groups in Emerging Markets: Paragons or Parasites?' *Journal of Economic Literature* 45(2):331–372.

Khanna, V. and S. J. Mathew. 2010. 'Role of Independent Directors in Controlled Firms in India: Preliminary Interview Evidence.' *National Law School of India Review* 22:35.

Khatri, J. and A. Master. 2009. 'Convergence with International Reporting Standards ('IFRS')—Impact on Fundamental Accounting Practices and Regulatory Framework of India.' *Bombay Chartered Accountant Journal* 71–74.

Khosa, A. 2017. 'Independent Directors and Firm Value of Group-Affiliated Firms.' *International Journal of Accounting and Information Management* 25(2):217–236.

Kim, D., D. Kandemir, and S. T. Cavusgil. 2004. 'The Role of Family Conglomerates in Emerging Markets: What Western Companies Should Know.' *Thunderbird International Business Review* 46(1):13–38.

Kohlbeck, M. and B. W. Mayhew. 2010. 'Valuation of Firms That Disclose Related Party Transactions.' *Journal of Accounting and Public Policy* 29(2):115–137.

Kole, S. R. 1997. 'The Complexity of Compensation Contracts.' *Journal of Financial Economics* 43(1):79–104.

Kook, C. P., Y. S. Park, and J. J. Lee. 1997. 'Investment Decision and Cost of Capital of Korean Conglomerate.' *The Korean Journal of Finance* 13:101–130.

Kothari, S. P. and J. L. Zimmerman. 1995. 'Price and Return Models.' *Journal of Accounting and Economics* 20(2):155–192.

Krishnan, G. V. 2003a. 'Audit Quality and the Pricing of Discretionary Accruals.' *Auditing* 22 (1):109.

————. 2003b. 'Does Big 6 Auditor Industry Expertise Constrain Earnings Management?' *Accounting Horizons* 17:1–16.

Kwon, S. H. and M. O'Donnell. 2001. *The Chaebol and Labour in Korea: The Development of Management Strategy in Hyundai*. London: Routledge.

La Porta, R., F. Lopez-de-Silanes, and A. Shleifer. 1999. 'Corporate Ownership Around the World.' *Journal of Finance* 54(2):471–517.

La Porta et al. 2000. 'Investor Protection and Corporate Governance.' *Journal of Financial Economics* 58(1–2):3–27.

————. 1998. 'Law and Finance.' *Journal of Political Economy* 106(6):1113–1155.

La Porta, R., F. Lopez-de-Silanes, and G. Zamarripa. 2003. 'Related Lending.' *Quarterly Journal of Economics* 118(1):231–268.

Lee, K., M. W. Peng, and K. Lee. 2008. 'From Diversification Premium to Diversification Discount During Institutional Transitions.' *Journal of World Business* 43(1):47–65.

Lemmon, M. L. and K. V. Lins. 2003. 'Ownership Structure, Corporate Governance, and Firm Value: Evidence from the East Asian Financial Crisis.' *Journal of Finance* 58(4):1445–1468.

Lensink, R., R. van der Molen, and S. Gangopadhyay. 2003. 'Business Groups, Financing Constraints and Investment: The Case of India.' *Journal of Development Studies* 40(2):93–119.

Leuz, C., D. Nanda, and P. D. Wysocki. 2003. 'Earnings Management and Investor Protection: An International Comparison.' *Journal of Financial Economics* 69(3):505–527.

Lew, M. I. and E. A. Kolodzeii. 1993. 'Compensation in a Family-Owned Business.' *Human Resources Profeesional* 5(3):55–57.

Li, M., K. Ramaswamy, and B. Pecherot Petitt. 2006. 'Business Groups and Market Failures: A Focus on Vertical and Horizontal Strategies.' *Asia Pacific Journal of Management* 23(4):439–452.

Lincoln, J. R., M. L. Gerlach, and C. L. Ahmadjian. 1996. 'Keiretsu Networks and Corporate Performance in Japan.' *American Sociological Review* 61(1):67–88.

Lins, K. V. 2003. 'Equity Ownership and Firm Value in Emerging Markets.' *Journal of Financial and Quantitative Analysis*, 38 No. 1:159–184.

Lins, K. V. and Servaes, H. 2002. 'Is Corporate Diversification Beneficial in Emerging Markets?' *Financial Management* 31(2):5–31.

Liu, Q. and Z. Lu. 2007. 'Corporate Governance and Earnings Management in the Chinese Listed Companies: A Tunneling Perspective.' *Journal of Corporate Finance* 13(5):881–906.

Lo, A.W., R. M. Wong, and M. Firth. 2010. 'Can Corporate Governance Deter Management from Manipulating Earnings? Evidence from Related-Party Sales Transactions in China.' *Journal of Corporate Finance* 16:225–235.

MacDonald, J. M. 1985. 'R&D and the Direction of Diversification.' *Review of Economics and Statistics* 67(4):583–590.

Majumdar, S. K. 2004. 'The Hidden Hand and The License Raj to an Evaluation of the Relationship Between Age and the Growth of Firms in India.' *Journal of Business Venturing* 19(1):107–125.

Mak, Y. T. and Y. Kusnadi. 2005. 'Size Really Matters: Further evidence on the Negative Relationship Between Board Size and Firm Value.' *Pacific-Basin Finance Journal* 13(3):301–318.

Manikutty, S. 2000. 'Family Business Groups in India: A Resource-Based View of the Emerging Trends.' *Family Business Review* 13(4):279–292.

Maury, B. and A. Pajuste. 2005. 'Multiple Large Shareholders and Firm Value.' *Journal of Banking and Finance* 29(7):1813–1834.

McChesney, F. 1997. *Money for Nothing: Politicians, Rent Extraction and Political Extortion.* Cambridge: Harvard University Press.

McConnell, J. J. and H. Servaes. 1990. 'Additional Evidence on Equity Ownership and Corporate Value.' *Journal of Financial Economics* 27(2):595–612.

Megginson, W. L., R. C. Nash, and M. Van Randenborgh. 1994. 'The Financial and Operating Performance of Newly Privatized Firms: An International Empirical Analysis.' *The Journal of Finance* 49(2):403–452.

Mikkelson, W. H. and R. S. Ruback. 1991. 'Targeted Repurchases and Common Stock Returns.' *The RAND Journal of Economics* 22(4):544–561.

Mitton, T. 2002. 'A Cross-Firm Analysis of The Impact of Corporate Governance on the East Asian Financial Crisis.' *Journal of Financial Economics* 64(2):215–241.

Mohan, R. 1992. 'Industrial Policy and Controls.' In *The Indian Economy: Problems and Prospects,* edited by B. Jalan. New Delhi: Viking.

Montgomery, C. A. and S. Hariharan. 1991. 'Diversified Expansion by Large Established Firms.' *Journal of Economic Behavior & Organization* 15(1):71–89.

Morck, R. 1996. 'On the Economics of Concentrated Ownership.' *Canadian Bus. Law J* 26:63–85.

Morck, R., A. Shleifer, and R. W. Vishny. 1988. 'Management Ownership and Market Valuation: An Empirical Analysis.' *Journal of Financial Economics* 20: 293–315.

Morck, R., D. Wolfenzon, and B. Yeung. 2004. 'Corporate Governance, Economic Entrenchment and Growth.' National Bureau of Economic Research.

Mulbert, P. 1997. 'Banks' Equity Holdings in Non-financial Firms and Corporate Governance: The Case of German Universal Banks.' Available at SSRN 11352.

Myers, S. C., and N. S. Majluf. 1984. 'Corporate Financing and Investment Decisions When Firms Have Information That Investors Do Not Have.' *Journal of Financial Economics* 13(2):187–221.

Nelson, J. F., and P. A. Frishkoff. 1991. 'Boards of Directors in Family-Owned Business.' *Akron Bus. and Econom. Rev.* 23(8):88–96.

Nolan, P. 2002. 'China and the Global Business Revolution.' *Cambridge Journal of Economics* 26(1):119–137.

OECD. 2012. *Related Party Transactions and Minority Shareholder Rights.* OECD Publishing. Available at http://dx.doi.org/10.1787/9789264168008-e.

———. 2014. *Related Party Transactions: Managing New Requirements Under Companies Act, 2013 and SEBI Guidelines.* OECD Publishing.

Ohlson, J. A. 1995. 'Earnings, Book Values, and Dividends in Equity Valuation.' *Contemporary Accounting Research*, 11(2):661–687.

Pan, L. 1999. *The Encyclopedia of the Chinese Overseas*. Cambridge: Harvard University Press.

Pathan, S. and R. Faff. 2013. 'Does Board Structure in Banks Really Affect Their Performance?' *Journal of Banking and Finance* 37(5):1573–1589.

Patton, A. and J. C. Baker. 1987. 'Why Won't Directors Rock the Boat?' *Harvard Business Review* 65(6):10–18.

Pearce, J. A. and S. A. Zahra. 1992. 'Board Composition From a Strategic Contingency Perspective .' *Journal of Management Studies* 29(4):411–438.

Peng, M. W. 2001. 'How Entrepreneurs Create Wealth in Transition Economies.' *Academy of Management Executive* 15(1):95–108.

Peng, M. W. and Y. Jiang. 2010. 'Institutions Behind Family Ownership and Control in Large Firms.' *Journal of Management Studies* 47(2):253–273.

Peng, W. Q., K. C. J. Wei, and Z. Yang. 2011. 'Tunneling or Propping: Evidence From Connected Transactions in China.' *Journal of Corporate Finance* 17(2):306–325.

Perez-Gonzalez, F. 2006. 'Inherited Control and Firm Performance.' *American Economic Review* 96(5):1559–1588.

Perotti, E. C. and S. Gelfer. 2001. 'Red Barons or Robber Barons? Governance and Investment in Russian Financial–Industrial Groups.' *European Economic Review* 45(9):1601–1617.

Pound, J. 1988. 'Proxy Contests and the Efficiency of Shareholder Oversight.' *Journal of Financial Economics*, 20:237–265.

Prowse, S. D. 1990. 'Institutional Investment Patterns and Corporate Financial Behavior in the United States and Japan.' *Journal of Financial Economics* 27(1):43–66.

Rajan, R., H. Servaes, and L. Zingales. 2000. 'The Cost of Diversity: The Diversification Discount and Inefficient Investment.' *The Journal of Finance* 55(1):35–80.

Rajan, R. G. and L. Zingales. 1998. 'Power in a Theory of the Firm.' *Quarterly Journal of Economics* 113(2):387–432.

Ramanujam, V. and P. Varadarajan. 1989. 'Research on Corporate Diversification: A Synthesis.' *Strategic Management Journal* 10(6):523–551.

Ramaswamy, K., L. Mingfang, and R. Veliyath. 2002. 'Variations in Ownership Behavior and Propensity to Diversify: A Study of the Indian Corporate Context.' *Strategic Management Journal* 23(4):345.

Rediker, K. J. and A. Seth. 1995. 'Boards of Directors and Substitution Effects of Alternative Governance Mechanisms.' *Strategic Management Journal* 16(2):85–99.

Rozeff, M. S. 1982. 'Growth, Beta and Agency Costs as Determinants of Dividend Payout Ratios.' *Journal of Financial Research* 5(3):249.

Rubenson, G. C. and A. K. Gupta. 1996. 'The Initial Succession: A Contingency Model of Founder Tenure.' *Entrepreneurship Theory and Practice* 21:21–36.

Sarkar, J. and S. Sarkar 2000. 'Large Shareholder Activism in Corporate Governance in Developing Countries: Evidence from India.' *International Review of Finance* 1(3):161.

———. 2009. 'Multiple Board Appointments and Firm Performance in Emerging Economies: Evidence from India.' *Pacific-Basin Finance Journal* 17(2):271–293.

Scharfstein, D. S. and J. C. Stein. 2000. 'The Dark Side of Internal Capital Markets: Divisional Rent-Seeking and Inefficient Investment.' *Journal of Finance* 55(6):2537–2564.

Schulze, W. S., M. H. Lubatkin, and R. N. Dino. 2003. 'Toward a Theory of Agency and Altruism in Family Firms.' *Journal of Business Venturing* 18(4):473–490.

Schulze, W. S., M. H. Lubatkin, R. N. Dino, and A. K. Buchholtz. 2001. 'Agency Relationships in Family Firms: Theory and Evidence.' *Organization Science* 12(2):99–116.

Schwartz, A. 1992. *A Nation in Waiting: Indonesia in the 1990s.* Sydney: Allen & Unwin.

Selarka, E. 2005. 'Ownership Concentration and Firm Value: A Study from the Indian Corporate Sector.' *Emerging Markets Finance and Trade* 41(6):83–108.

Shin, H. H. and Y. S. Park. 1999. 'Financing Constraints and Internal Capital Markets: Evidence from Korean "chaebols".' *Journal of Corporate Finance* 5(2):169–191.

Shin, H. H. and R. M. Stulz. 1998. 'Are Internal Capital Markets Efficient?' *Quarterly Journal of Economics* 113(2):531–552.

Shleifer, A. and R. W. Vishny. 1986. 'Large Shareholders and Corporate Control.' *Journal of Political Economy* 94(3):461–488.

———. 1997. 'A Survey of Corporate Governance.' *Journal of Finance* 52(2):737–783.

Shumilov, A. and N. Volchkova. 2004. 'Russian Business Groups: Substitutes for Missing Institutions?' Working Papers, w0050. Moscow: Center for Economic and Financial Research.

Singer, J. and C. Doronho. 1992. 'Strategic Management Planning for the Successful Family Business.' *Family Business Review* 4(3):39–51.

Spence, M. and R. Zeckhauser. 1971. 'Insurance, Information, and Individual Action.' *The American Economic Review* 61(2):380–387.

SSB (Shanghai Statistical Bureau). 2000. *China Statistical Yearbook.* Beijing: China Statistical Press.

Srinivasan, P. 2013. 'An Analysis of Related-Party Transactions in India.' IIM Bangalore Research Paper No. 402. Available at: https://ssrn.com/abstract=2352791 or http://dx.doi.org.ezproxy.lib.monash.edu.au/10.2139/ssrn.2352791.

Stein, J. C. 1997. 'Internal Capital Markets and the Competition for Corporate Resources.' *Journal of Finance* 52(1):111–133.

———. 2003. 'Chapter 2 Agency, Information and Corporate Investment.' In *Handbook of the Economics of Finance*, edited by G. M. Constantinides, M. Harris, and R. M. Stulz, 111–165. Elsevier.

Strachan, H. W. 1976. *Family and Other Business Groups in Economic Development: The Case of Nicaragua.* New York: Praeger.

Stulz, R. 1988. 'Management Control of Voting Rights.' *Journal of Financial Economics* 20:25–59.

TOI. 2014. 'AAP Government Orders CAG Audit of Three Private Power Distribution Companies.' 1 January.

Tripathi, D. 2004. *Oxford Encyclopedia of Indian Business.* Oxford: Oxford University Press.

Vachani, S. 1997. 'Economic Liberalization's Effect on Sources of Competitive Advantage of Different Groups of Companies: The Case of India.' *International Business Review* 6(2):165–184.

Villalonga, B. and R. Amit. 2006. 'How Do Family Ownership, Control and Management Affect Firm Value?' *Journal of Financial Economics* 80(2):385–417.

Wang, D. 2006. 'Founding Family Ownership and Earnings Quality.' *Journal of Accounting Research* 44(3):619–656.

Ward, J. L. 2011. *Keeping the Family Business Healthy: How to Plan for Continuing Growth, Profitability, and Family Leadership.* New York: Macmillan.

Watts, R. 1974. *Accounting Objectives.* Rochester: University of Rochester, Graduate School of Management.

Westphal, J. D. 1998. 'Board Games: How CEOs Adapt to Increases in Structural Board Independence from Management.' *Administrative Science Quarterly* 43(3):511–537.

White, L. J. 1974. 'Industrial Concentration and Economic Power in Pakistan.' Princeton: Princeton University Press.

Williamson, O. E. 1975. *Markets and Hierarchies: Analysis and Antitrust Implications.* New York: Free Press.

Wolfenzon, D. 1999. 'A Theory of Pyramidal Ownership.' Cambridge: Harvard University Press.

Wong, R., J. B. Kim, and A. Lo. 2013. 'Are Related-Party Sales Value-Adding or Value-Destroying? Evidence from China.' European Accounting Association Annual Congress, Paris, France.

Wright, M., I. Filatotchev, R. E. Hoskisson, and M. W. Peng. 2005. 'Strategy Research in Emerging Economies: Challenging the Conventional Wisdom.' *Journal of Management Studies* 42(1):1–33.

Yafeh, Y. 2003. 'An International Perspective of Corporate Groups and Their Prospects.' In *Structural impediments to growth in Japan,* edited by M. Blomström, J. Corbett, F. Hayashi, and A. Kashyap, 259–284. Chicago: University of Chicago Press.

Yiu, D., G. D. Bruton, and L. Yuan. 2005. 'Understanding Business Group Performance in an Emerging Economy: Acquiring Resources and Capabilities in Order to Prosper.' *Journal of Management Studies* 42(1):183–206.

Young, M. N., M. W. Peng, D. Ahlstrom, G. D. Bruton, and Y. Jiang. 2008. 'Corporate Governance in Emerging Economies: A Review of the Principal–Principal Perspective.' *Journal of Management Studies* 45(1):196–220.

Index